THE CALL
TO THE FAR SHORE

"*The Call to the Far Shore* is well written, deeply personal, level-headed, thoughtful, and fueled by compelling stories—the author's own and those of others. Nancy MacMillan proves to be a most knowledgeable and compassionate guide on the journey we all eventually will make to the other side."

LAWRENCE SCANLAN,
AUTHOR OF *A YEAR OF LIVING GENEROUSLY*

"You must read this book, and you must make sure that those you love read it, because it offers profound spiritual wisdom and practical, empathic guidance for navigating the inevitabilities of death. Beautifully written, this is as essential a resource for helping the dying as *Spiritual Midwifery* was for assisting birth. Sure to be a classic."

PERDITA FINN, AUTHOR OF *TAKE BACK THE MAGIC*
AND *THE WAY OF THE ROSE*

"Nancy walks us through the deeply sacred journey of her mother's death, capturing the essence of home funerals while inspiring the reader to imagine caring for the dead in a slow and loving way. Her stories are artfully woven together while poignantly painting a picture of the incredible healing and feeling of completeness when grace prevails. I highly recommend this book for both those unfamiliar and those experienced with death; it is a loving guide to assist all who want to connect with the rituals that can be created at this portal."

JERRIGRACE LYONS, FOUNDER OF FINAL PASSAGES: INSTITUTE OF
CONSCIOUS DYING, HOME FUNERAL & GREEN BURIAL EDUCATION
AND AUTHOR OF *CREATING HOME FUNERALS*

"This book brings a great lesson and healing to the world. One can feel the impact of what it will bring to so many people who are suffering because of disconnection from life itself, hence a fear of dying. When we realize that we are one and that we are connected deeply through the breath we take in, life is inevitable and death is the transformation of it. Nancy describes this phenomenon very beautifully in this inspiring book."

"*The Call to the Far Shore* invites us to share Nancy's experiences and the hard-won insights about the transformative aspects we can have around death and dying. If you choose to walk with her on the journey we all take, you will find fresh perspectives and resources that can strengthen you in your own encounters with the richness and restrictions of this mortal coil. You can begin to experience the wisdom of the deep embrace life holds us in as we struggle with fear, pain, and loss. She navigates and interweaves the physical challenges with the emotional and spiritual dimensions as one who has gone through the fire herself and found the light and warmth that is generated as the old, stiff wood is consumed."

"What a weight in gold the pages of this book *The Call to the Far Shore* offer us! In this new gospel of the natural response to death, we witnesses of MacMillan's soul experiences are invited to walk beside her as she shows us the mansions of grace to be experienced in following her call to us to be present and awake in the mysteries of life, death, and transition. This book must be available to all who walk the earth and will depart from it."

"I enjoyed this reflection on life and dying. It is an interesting mix of narrative and contemplation. I have worked in geriatric medicine and palliative care for thirty years and got new perspectives on aging and death from the book."

THE CALL
TO THE
FAR SHORE

Carrying Our Loved Ones
through Dying, Death, and Beyond

A Sacred Planet Book

NANCY MACMILLAN

Destiny Books
Rochester, Vermont

Destiny Books
One Park Street
Rochester, Vermont 05767
www.DestinyBooks.com

Destiny Books is a division of Inner Traditions International

Sacred Planet Books are curated by Richard Grossinger, Inner Traditions editorial board member and cofounder and former publisher of North Atlantic Books. The Sacred Planet collection, published under the umbrella of the Inner Traditions family of imprints, includes works on the themes of consciousness, cosmology, alternative medicine, dreams, climate, permaculture, alchemy, shamanic studies, oracles, astrology, crystals, hyperobjects, locutions, and subtle bodies.

Cataloging-in-Publication Data for this title is available from the Library of Congress

ISBN 979-8-88850-109-2 (print)
ISBN 979-8-88850-110-8 (ebook)

Printed and bound in the United States by Lake Book Manufacturing, LLC

10 9 8 7 6 5 4 3 2 1

Text design and layout by VirginiaScott Bowman
This book was typeset in Garamond Premier Pro, Gill Sans, and Legacy Sans with Begum used as the display typeface

To send correspondence to the author of this book, mail a first-class letter to the author c/o Inner Traditions • Bear & Company, One Park Street, Rochester, VT 05767, and we will forward the communication, or contact the author directly at **NancyMacMillan.com**.

Lean in Dear Ancestors and Beloveds
Of Past, Present, and Future.
Lean in Dear Wisdom Keepers, and All Beings,
Of Earth and Sky, of Fire and Water.

—⁓—

These words are dedicated to you.

—⁓—

May They Quench Your Thirst, and
Bring Nourishment to the Fields of Presence,
Helping to Transmute Fear and Awaken Love
In Our Hearts and World.

Contents

Foreword

Robert Sardello

The Call to the Far Shore brings understanding of the dying process and stories of a devotional way of being present with a dying beloved. *Devotion* in this context means something more than being devoted to a dear one. Nancy MacMillan's relationship with her dying mother and with many others exemplifies being *within* devotion, radiating it and feeling it within the heart. Devotion becomes a way of being and does not end. One's life transforms through this powerful act of devotion—helping the dying person to do death better—which is extraordinary, so extraordinary that I wish the phrase *doing death better*, which appears in the book, had been in its title.

Nancy describes the way of devotion by recounting her actual experiences of carefully attending her mother and others. She writes of these experiences with direct immediacy rather than at a cognitive distance. We find the deeper value of this book in how she transmits her growing wisdom through poetic writing shaped by rhythm, form, and cadence, constituting a rare and most valuable contribution that goes beyond intellect while remaining deeply thoughtful.

Suffering always brings with it an awakening and a deepening of the inner life. One definition of the word *suffer* is "to allow." Often, suffering is not chosen, but we can choose to allow ourselves to enter the suffering—ours and others—and to undergo significant change as we do so. We can also choose to stay at a distance and observe what is happening rather than entering it.

In this writing, we are given the gift of listening in as Nancy tells the intimate story of her mother's dying process, as well as many other stories of dying people she has attended, and takes us into the interior of her many decisions, which she had to make with spontaneity and immediacy. We find how the dying can be approached directly and carefully, taking all the time we need to do so with true feeling and skill while avoiding sliding into practiced responses. In fact, true tending means staying away from providing the person who is dying with information that we may think we know about dying.

Through developing inner stillness, we can learn to listen deeply to the one who is dying. It is a kind of initiation, and in the stories of this book, we find that stillness is not automatically present but must be developed. A new kind of work arises with caring for the dying—a kind of "antiprofession"—as the work requires putting aside any professional knowledge and being spontaneous rather than seeming to know what to say and do. Answers emerge from the stillness.

Noticing and deep listening to one who is dying is a spiritual act, a spiritual practice. The many stories in this writing awaken the capacities of being within the silence, which is an inner region, close to the heart. Being present there always marks being within spiritual experience rather than just becoming quiet around the dying because we are afraid, which can be another way of avoiding being fully present. This difference comes through radically in the writing. No advice or techniques are given; one might say that they are taken away, just as in dying everything is taken away. The work is to be within the "taken away."

The key to being within the taken away can be summed up as allowing whatever is happening to unfold—no matter what! Nancy writes the book this way too. Each paragraph enters the unknowing. If we read and inwardly feel this nonknowing knowing, we, too, can begin an initiatory movement into death—our own and others.

You will, as you read, find yourself entering an entirely different sense of death: death is not the end of life; it is the beginning of life. Such an understanding cannot arrive by study nor by thinking, nor by being aloof from the one dying. In caring for the dying, you lose yourself and find yourself anew, as if you never truly knew yourself as you thought you did. Life emerges from the unknown, minute by minute, and the real shock is that you and the one dying are in this emerging *together*.

Tending to the dying of a beloved also involves tending to the survivors. How to tell the survivors of their beloved's death forms a wonderfully helpful section of this book. Once again, the person who must tell the survivors of the death of their loved one does best by eliminating any attempts to predetermine the moment by having a prepared way of doing so. When this nonknowing manner presents itself, those who are near to the beloved who is dying also find themselves anew.

Given these surprises, imagine what an unusual person it takes to enter the work, daily, of caring for the dying. Here, we can also understand the way Nancy describes how tending her dying mother formed her being into "coming into being"—that is, in tending the dying as described in this book, we also discover life as reflected in our living, and life as what is arising from the future rather than practiced knowing, which comes from the past.

As I list and reflect on some of these moments of being with the dying, I am attempting, through reading the stories closely, to get a sense of tangibly feeling the presence of the spirit of those dying and who have died. It is not possible to feel spirit presence with our usual consciousness. This book introduces us into nonknowing but with full feeling, not "having" feelings but the creative inner heart-feeling arising and unfolding. Nancy does a wondrous job of avoiding "humanizing" the death processes and instead, rightly, notices spirit revealing itself within what she does without ever abandoning human responses and reactions.

While there are now people trained as spiritual coordinators who work with the dying, this title seems unfortunate, as it risks keeping the whole process on a level that may become a mundane professional activity, coordinating an ending that we must all undergo, organizing the most profound, spontaneous moment of life. None of us knows when we will die. The remarkable time of approaching dying can be guided through tender care—that of attending someone by entering the unknown with them. Then, dying and death can be felt as what it truly is: a transformation rather than an end.

Over time, dying has become increasingly medicalized and more and more is seen as simply a natural process when it is perhaps the deepest of all spiritual processes, given as a gift to human beings. This book by Nancy has the strong possibility of recovering the true nature of dying and how to be with it, retrieving it as a spiritual experience.

Nancy covers each aspect of dying within a devotional way of being, including, besides what I have mentioned so far, encountering—in inner and meaningful ways—fear and pain, the emotional pain experienced by the dying, which the medical profession often handles by giving the dying person medications, sometimes radical medications such as morphine. Such medication reinforces a passive entry into the most important moment of life, a moment that cries out for consciousness rather than its extinction, resulting in entering a new life in oblivion. The most difficult question becomes that of alleviating pain without obliterating consciousness, allowing the dying person to choose to enter suffering. This can be done with accompanying medications if they are administered with a true understanding of the dying process as spoken of within these pages.

Because this culture does not encourage long-term preparation for dying, the preparation must occur quickly when the process is in its ultimate moment. Nancy's book helps us understand the importance of introducing the theme of death and dying while a person may be ill but not yet near the end of their life. Working with death only at the time of dying shortens the opportunity we are given of living our lives with an ever-present awareness of and preparation for the next state. A cultural revision is needed to encourage us to know and feel death as a part of life, the part that opens the door of Life. Perhaps a more significant meaning of this book, one emerging from the immediacy of the stories, is its implication that this revision, this awakening of consciousness and awareness of spiritual presence, is needed.

The inner presence of dying all the time while living creates the needed conscious awareness to change our culture. Stories like those told in this book are central to forming a full consciousness—a change from living day-to-day in civilization to a much larger, much more comprehensive view of life. The word *culture* is related to *agriculture*, suggesting the need to turn over and create anew through the collective soul of a people. The presence of death in life creates depth awareness, something intangible but incredibly real and effective. This book asks not just individuals but civilization to cultivate this awareness, which could also change the materialistic focus of present civilization.

Nancy's stories of the last days of her mother quite naturally open to a consideration of how to live with a beloved who, though not ill, is nearing the end of their life, as well as how to be with someone who is dying. She tells deep and meaningful stories of caring for her mother during earlier times too, including the decisions around her mother going to a retirement home and then into long-term care. As these kinds of decisions often happen without much inner consideration, her reflections of how to house our aging relatives bring consciousness to what has become just another practical decision within an unconscious civilization.

As Nancy enters the deeper ways of caring for the dying that *are* more culturally conscious, she enters the realm of wholeness, with almost endless aspects that require consideration, such as the multigenerational dimension, which deepens the healing intent of the book as a whole. Multigenerational remembrances and stories become a significant way to broaden and deepen the ebbing of life. Older people engage in remembrance continually and also sporadically. Nancy presents more formed intergenerational memories, which add another significant aspect to caring for the dying.

The book is a finely woven tapestry of stories, so please take this introduction as no more than a cursory look at the whole, one intended to indicate the fineness of the fabric that Nancy has woven. The fabric does not unwind in the way I may be presenting in this overview; Nancy has written the book with a sense of wholeness rather than following a linear progression. For example, her own brushes with death form a significant portion of the whole fabric. The wholeness of the book suggests the possibility that death can become an ongoing and pervasive dimension within the stories of our lives.

Death, in this kind of fullness of imagination, is not about the end but the presence of continual endings, as death and dying exist everywhere within the stories of the living. Going beyond personal stories, the mythic dimension of death and dying is considered in a chapter on the story of Inanna, as is the mythic dimension of our own stories of death in life—how our ancestors approached death, as they typically were much more present to the fullness of their heritage.

Even more, the presence of the deceased beloved continues when we dream of them while we sleep and experience images of them. Their imaginal presence occurs in the innumerable ways in which the beloved shows up during the day, seeming from out of nowhere. Their presence is also felt when we notice how our own bodies have changed through tending their death. We now can begin to live in the ongoing presence of inner Silence, a region rather than an act of being quiet. Nancy does not categorize or name these experiences with the deceased but instead approaches them through stories—that is, through imagination that is true.

Our beloveds also include animals, such as pets, who have become part of our daily lives. Their deaths can throw us into immediate grieving, which is strong though somewhat different than grieving the death of a beloved person. When a beloved animal dies, our soul is deeply touched. Considering the death of animals is not a departure from the primary theme of the book; rather, the theme deepens our imagination into living within the consideration of *all* death, fructifying any individual contact of death we may experience.

More than half of the book concerns these themes. Then, Nancy enters a very different dimension of death—the religious dimension, where concerns of soul and of spirit (and the difference between them) show up. First, she directly addresses the difference between soul and spirit. At the death of a beloved, we more strongly experience these two dimensions, often seemingly mixed together.

Soul can be so intimate and so close in our living that we tend to miss the dimension of soul itself, which is also, in part, beyond us—in the archetypal dimensions of being. Dimensions of ourselves are always being influenced by the deep dimensions of form from the deep impersonal past that create the way we express ourselves. Our beloveds who have died reveal themselves as soul presences, which helps us in knowing ourselves just as archetypal stories do. For example, in dreams and in many aspects of our behavior, we find that we are tending the soul of one who has died by taking on one of the characteristics of the beloved. Daily memories of one who has died also belong to the soul dimension of the deceased.

With spirit, dimensions of ourselves also participate in the realms of ongoing creation: with awe, we become aware of this aspect of our continually being created. In this dimension are both elemental and angelic beings as well as the presences of those who have died, who perhaps have become our guides. And spirit determines how we are in the world—perhaps a get-up-and-go spirit or an inner calm, contemplative spirit. Our spirit changes with our ongoing relationship with one who has died, a subtle but very true happening.

To experience soul and spirit requires study and practice, cultivating dimensions that many people are not aware of. Instead, religion has encompassed these soul and spirit dimensions, and for many people, it provides a way to imagine where their deceased beloved now resides and to deal with the incredibly deep sorrow of losing a beloved. Creeds thus affect and change the immediate experience of death and, for many, have *replaced* it, so that people experience those who have died according to their religious beliefs. Now, though, more people are taking their soul and spirit dimensions into their own hands through contemplation and meditation. This book is a great help in this cultural awakening process.

I hope that this overview inspires you to now dive into the ocean-like depth of this writing. *The Call to the Far Shore* is one of those rare books that is both an inspirational work of art and a narrative that moves beyond the intellect alone. To read this book is to invite radical change, both personal change and changes in the lives of those around you, for these stories will increase the depth of your being, which cannot be held within: it radiates into the world.

ROBERT SARDELLO, PH.D., is cofounder (with Cheryl Sanders-Sardello, Ph.D) of the School of Spiritual Psychology. At the University of Dallas, he served as chair of the Department of Psychology and as graduate dean. He worked as a Jungian therapist for more than four decades, is cofounder and faculty member of the Dallas Institute of Humanities and Culture, and is the author of eleven books and eight monographs, including *Facing the World with Soul* (2003); *Silence: The Mystery of Wholeness* (2008); *Love and the Soul: Creating a Future for Earth* (2008); *Heartfulness* (2015); and a forthcoming book on love and the era of the heart to be published with Inner Traditions. An independent scholar, teacher, and consultant, he continues his exploration of phenomenological, soul-based spiritual psychology through the Heartful-Soul Network.

A few weeks prior to Mum's death, in my wilderness hideaway, I lit a fire of smoking sage and cedar, and the green and blue Earth around me seemed to open. The gray clouds started moving, coalescing into a perfect circle of blue overhead. The silence, a presence as palpable as touch, spoke the word grace. Grace. In the quiet of the moments that followed, I somehow felt that whatever I asked for would be heard by a greater dimensionality. I said out loud: "May this grace be directed to my mother. That she may have a complete death, without fear and suffering." I then added, "And may it not break or crush my own body in the process."

PREFACE

Reimagining Death

*We're all storytellers, really. That's what we do. That is
our power as human beings. Not to tell people how to think
and feel and therefore know—but through our stories allow
them to discover questions within themselves.*

RICHARD WAGAMESE, *EMBERS:
ONE OJIBWAY'S MEDITATIONS*

Last night, I dreamt I was going on a journey, taking a flight somewhere. So was my sister, but to a different destination. There were
coffins behind us, waiting to board the plane as well. We had almost
forgotten about them—*as if we could go away and not carry our dead
with us.* Somehow, this has become my work: caring for, tending to,
and now carrying the dead—in my dreams, in my contemplations, in
my profession as a psychotherapist, in my daily conversation, and in my
very body as I undertake this writing.

The following thoughts and musings, research, and study took
shape in the years subsequent to the death of my mother, Marion Ruth
MacMillan. They offer a glimpse of a mother and daughter together
navigating the dying–death journey amid the collective denial, hush,
miseducation, and fear of death that underlies—and haunts—much of
Western life today. This story spun off into others and borrowed from
others, as the writing compelled me to ask: How did I get here? How
did I become drawn to this work? In answer, the threads of my own

1

biography kept entering in, and I realized something obvious. I was doing what we are all called to do after loss and major events: *making meaning through making story*, using the metaphors and images that offer themselves—digesting, distilling, and becoming transformed by them. All while the world echoed back in its own parallel language of synchronicity. Shifting between the present and the past tense—and between storytelling and reflection—my writing takes a serpentine path bridging memoir, imagination, and contemplation.

In my experience, there are a few basic questions that we all carry about death: How do I live with my fear of it? Have I done enough? Am I prepared? Will I be in pain? What happens after I die? What is the meaning of it all, anyway? By living into these questions, I found that subjects such as life cycles, consciousness, grief, ancestors, and our living Earth came into sharper focus. And, to my surprise, I discovered that beauty—yes, *beauty*—can coexist along with death.

To approach death with fuller consciousness might sound morose or daunting, something to hide from rather than to meet. But in practice it is a *transformative* act, radical even. And the surprise is that most of us will find death not as frightening as we've been taught but rather gentle. Ultimately, the more attention we give anything, the more abundantly life is revealed, and with it the potential to transform and restore meaning to our place and purpose in the universe.

The Call to the Far Shore weaves around three themes:

1. Being with dying more fully and more consciously *before* we die.
2. Tending our loved ones *at the time* of death and immediately after in a way that honors their bodies and spirits.
3. Continuing the connection with our loved ones *after* death and by doing so awakening to the realm of our ancestors.

Whether out of fear, ignorance, or greed, society's mandate over the past decades has increasingly turned to conquering and controlling death, forgetful of the ancient wisdom of the rhythms and cycles of life. More and more people, however, are having personal experiences and insights that enable them to see that death is not a fearful, empty void but rather part of the miraculous wholeness of life. Sustaining these insights and integrating them into our life can bring up a different kind of fear. For those with an inner willingness to engage with such varied fears, to look around corners and be challenged, this book will resonate and unlock more of the vast innate knowing we all share.

We humans go through a lot. I have been privileged in my professional work to be inspired by so many people, who out of the ashes of their own suffering and turmoil have shown me what true resilience looks like. The stories herein have been woven to illustrate these encounters around real events. They are not case studies, and to honor privacy, names and all identifying details have been changed, while some accounts are composites of several situations.

My own story is just one among many that attempt to enter into the mystery that meets us all at the edge of life. Our dying, our death, and that of our loved ones: each is unique, each filled with character, tragedy, humor, miracles, and misses. I must note, however, that navigating the natural death of an elderly parent, though grievous, is less fraught than most other death experiences. My mother had a long life, dying at the age of ninety-six. This was just a few months before COVID-19 began, so I was spared the cruel challenges that were to come for those accompanying the elderly and dying. Still, my hope is that this account serves to awaken a reimagining of the profound realm of our endings— as well as the attendant becomings—following the winding path from ancient times to the abiding far shore.

1

Mum's Breathing Has Changed

Traveler, there is no path. The path is made by walking.

ANTONIO MACHADO,
FROM "TRAVELER, THERE IS NO PATH"

It's 5 a.m. and the phone is ringing. It's one of the nurses, Alexa, saying that Mum's breathing has changed. Long spells of apnea are occurring. She says that though it's not likely urgent, I may want to come in, "just in case." I get ready, dragging my feet. The day feels like it is going to be a long, hard one. Michael, my husband, is up too, and we drive together to the long-term-care home.

Journal Entry: October 30, 2019

At bedside, I say quietly, "You are looking so frail, Mum. How many last whispers of you in this body are left?" You acknowledge my presence from a far-off place. Amid nursing staff coming in and out, we sit together in a jagged way with your jagged breathing. Was it just a few days ago that you said, almost lyrically,

I accept whatever happens.
I accept whatever happens.
I accept everything that happens,
and I will carry on.

Mum, I can't tell you what a staggering thing this was to hear you say. In these many months of seeing a deeper side of you emerge—the result of.the long haul of aging and dying and old self stripped away—I have come to see you as a sage, someone to look up to and listen to. You opened wide the door for death, no longer resisting the pull, no longer feeling the pain of separation, becoming the elder I longed for.

Alexa comes in to say that because of Mum's rapid breathing she may be in discomfort, and she would like to give her something to make her more comfortable. I am surprised because what I see is my mum dying. I have become minutely attentive to possible signs of pain, and I don't see them. I can't know for sure if she is "uncomfortable," nor do I know what this really means. Does it mean she is suffering? I do not see my mum suffering. I see her dying.

Mum is hard to rouse but not completely unconscious. Her breathing is now softer and irregular but not with mouth wide open and eyes glazed over as I have come to expect from my work in hospitals tending the dying. Yesterday, I asked one of the staff, "How much longer?" The response took me by surprise, "Well, this is new for us—I mean, she's not on any pain medication so things look different. She's not like the rest of them, so it's harder to tell and harder to know what to do." It's true, many doctors and nurses do not *have a lot of experience being with unmedicated dying. Similarly, a midwife told me there is less and less experience in being with unmedicated birthing.*

I remember Mum's recent words, I accept everything that happens. *So I stall the medication, saying, "Let's see how things unfold for the next few hours and reevaluate."*

It's a tall order, supporting the spiritual, soul, and physical needs of the dying and dead, especially when you think of the myriad of ways our death time can take. We are all indebted to the pioneers in death and dying studies, such as Elisabeth Kübler-Ross, who in the late 1960s opened the way to talk about death and be present with people who were dying, instead of what had become the norm in the West of virtually shunning them. Her efforts and those of others catapulted the topic of death and dying into the limelight and were part of the movement to create hospices and palliative care options.

We are now in an era where *prolonged dying* is the norm. In the past, we didn't get a heads-up on, say, a cancer diagnosis, years in advance, and then try to beat it with more and more treatments. In earlier times, we'd find out we were dying by our symptoms, and death would follow much sooner. Or death would be a sudden occurrence due to the many ways accident and misadventure could claim us. We are inexperienced in how to die this new dying way. Ironically, now with more time than ever before to prepare for it, we seem less prepared. Not to mention the confusion and conflict that arises in being a dying person in a medical system that was never intended to let us die but is rather hell-bent on saving us. Ask anyone about where they'd like to die, and the answer invariably is, "At home, with loved ones." Yet the ICU is where most of us will die.

The tension we now hold is that between prolonging living or prolonging dying. A friend, an ICU nurse for thirty years who sees death daily, says wearily to me, "We can do death so much better. We still have the attitude that death is a medical failure." I nod, realizing the many ways my own life has become centered on this goal of doing death better, not the least of which is the profession I ended up in.

2

Scenes from Frontline Health Care

Suffering, the Buddha said, if it does not diminish love, will transport you to the farther shore.

HUSTON SMITH, *TALES OF WONDER*

Anyone who has experienced the passing of someone close knows that death is a portal to love.

CHARLES EISENSTEIN, "THE CORONATION"

In my work in an acute care hospital, I was with a lot of people in the last stages of dying and at the time immediately following death—supporting the very ill and their families, providing advocacy, and being with the fierce emotional winds, the grasping for meaning and the shedding of old selves, that come with the terrain of dying. We used to be called multifaith chaplains; now the more apt, though admittedly more ambiguous term *registered spiritual care practitioner* is most often used. We are required to undergo intensive training and certification, and most of us are registered psychotherapists. Belonging to an organized religion is not an expectation, nor is it for a patient in requesting a visit or for a referral to be made. In fact, during my first encounters with an individual or family, especially in the midst of a crisis, I sensitively try to ascertain whether the person is religious (what kind and whether

7

devoted or lapsed), spiritual (nature-based, pagan, angels, eclectic, unsure), humanist (kindness, fairness, realism, philosophical), or committed atheist. This knowledge helps me lean into the language most familiar to them to meet their psyche and soul needs, crucial to offering sensitive care at pivotal times.

When a person says, "I'm not religious," it often means, "I want to relate to you authentically, not through a prescriptive lens of religious language." When people do want to be met through their religious beliefs, they may be struggling to reconcile their faith with their situation: Why would God do this to me? Am I being punished? Is it cruel or a sin to take my husband off life support? My task is to be present to where a person is in their theology and listen to their hard questions of God. Easy answers are not wanted and not needed. Sometimes, it's possible to support people in evolving their images of God, helping them let go of limiting notions that don't serve them anymore—especially around an image of a distant God who punishes. Most of all, patients surprise me with a great pluralism and a healthy resistance to labeling.

For a patient with a life-threatening diagnosis, having someone to speak with is important medicine. Yet few are comfortable in this role! Just about everyone dances around the central concerns of a dying person. I remember being asked to mentor a resident doctor, Brent, on the art of listening. He was soon graduating with a specialty in palliative care, but his supervisor felt he had some ground to cover on bedside etiquette. Brent accompanied me on my rounds one day, and at last I asked him to take over the conversation with a female patient who had recently been told her prognosis was worsening and that she should "get her affairs in order." After introductions, I left them alone. Brent came and found me about forty-five minutes later, his eyes on fire. He was thrilled at what had transpired: freed from his doctor agenda, he had realized his role was to empathetically listen to her struggles, fears, and concerns. He witnessed that through her being able to speak without restraint she turned a corner, in the end reassuring him that "she knows what she has to do now." Brent said in astonishment, "Just *listening* was the hardest thing I've ever done and totally exhausting. I don't know how you do this all day!" That was certainly validating to hear—yes, focused listening requires inner stillness involving our whole being. We are then in a relational field with the other person where so much more is present than the words being spoken.

While for me listening is relatively easy, what's harder is something else. Going into the family room of the ER, intensive care unit, or cardiac unit, after someone has died—the room often filled with the accident victim's family or the unsuccessful surgery patient's family—being present as the worst news is delivered, and *not knowing what to do.*

Our first instinct as human beings is to "make things better." When nothing we do will change the radical outcome that has just happened, the impulse to *fix* or *rescue* must be held in check. Eventually, I learned that this adrenaline-fueled impulse is counterproductive: *doing* is not called for at this moment but *being with* is. Even then, I thought it my job to know how to *do this well*, to offer the right words, to find the right degree of involvement without becoming enmeshed. But inwardly I usually felt uncomfortable, stiff, reduced to platitudes, and *in the way.*

I remember one night when I was on call in my early training. The pager went off at 4 a.m. It was the cardiac unit calling for support. Chad, a young man of thirty-four, a family doctor himself, was suddenly dead from a cardiac arrest. His wife, Helen, wanted to talk to me. I arrived to a hushed room crowded with family members and friends. Helen, clearly in shock, holding herself stoically together, took me aside. Her one burning question: "Should I bring my four-year-old daughter in to see her father's body?"

I spoke with her about their child, Katie, and heard of her easy-going nature and adoration of her daddy. I told her that children are less afraid of what they can see than what their imaginations may fill in, that her daughter's presence here would make her part of a pivotal marker in their life as a family, and that, whenever possible, it's a gift to let children be familiar with death. I said, "Children need simple, direct truthfulness. But," I went on, "the most important question is: How comfortable are you? Your daughter will take her cues from you and the others around." Helen went home to get Katie.

A little while later, Katie was holding tight to her stuffed dog on the bed next to Chad's body, the mood in the room shifting. Grandparents were holding her and lovingly talking to her about why her dad looked asleep and that it was more than sleep: he had left his body, he had died.

Although children will express distress, confusion, and need by regressing in their behavior—maybe bed-wetting, thumb-sucking, withdrawing, clinging, or worrying that they or their other parent will also die—the consistent, warm response of close caregivers makes all the difference. Tears, trembling, and shaking are ways our bodies naturally come out of shock. Allowing this to unfold and be validated with reassuring words and gentle touch, while resisting the urge to talk someone out of their feelings, is the best thing we can offer. Children best express themselves through play and art, and when this is combined with consistent routine and boundaries, then a safe container is made to help a child rework their experience. It helps when we know children grieve in spurts and that innately they have the instinct to transform it as they mature, over time.

Other than the conversation affirming that it was good to include four-year-old Katie in this charged moment, I did very little. I stayed in the background, a quiet presence. Sometimes, it's hard to know when to leave and *how* to leave a room and a family amid such a magnitude of loss. At last, I told them that I would be in the family room down the corridor if anyone wanted to speak with me privately. After a period of time, Helen came to find me. She, who had seemed so intact and not wanting to let anyone get too close, said, "Thank you, you were just so helpful to us all," and broke down crying. In my head, I had been fighting the thoughts of being an intruder, a voyeur, an imposter, but with this last interaction I was left wondering about the greater truth that can lie in a receptive, quiet presence.

Another hard part of the work of a spiritual care practitioner: morgue viewings.

Being around dead bodies is unfamiliar to most of us. People shiver at the thought. "How can you possibly be around dead people every day?" people would exclaim to me. Over time, I have lost much of this aversion. But not entirely. There is always a trembling at the doorway when meeting someone recently dead, for there is so much that is still present, yet unfathomable, and it's hard to keep any sense of "usualness." Hospital staff will go out of their way to keep a person who has just died in their bed until family can arrive; however, there may be patients waiting for a bed in hallways or crowded ward rooms, or family members may be hours away. When this happens, the body is taken to the morgue where visitations can be arranged before the funeral transportation arrives.

I recall countless times escorting families down the long corridor to the morgue visiting room. The body may have been in the freezer room for hours or days. The pathology staff will have covered the body of the person in a shroud, arranged the body on a stretcher, and wheeled it through a steel door connected to the viewing room. I go in and do my own arranging, little touches to make the space as hospitable as possible. The viewing room is small and peach colored, with dim lighting, a few paintings on the walls, two chairs, and a small table with tissues. It's not terrible, but it is always cold, and the lighting never quite right. I introduce myself to the newly dead person, gently touch their body, and let them know their family or friend is coming to see them. If they look uncomfortable, I may find a pillow for their head. Under the shroud, they are in a plastic body bag, and I may zip this farther down and make it easier for the family to touch the body. Especially the hands. I try very hard to allow a hand to be available for touching, for holding. Then I go and get the family.

This time it is a mother and father who have just found out that their son is dead from drowning. A late-night party at a friend's cottage, too much to drink, a tipped canoe, a poor swimmer. Ali is twenty-two, a student in a high-pressure program. He was in the water a long while before his body—bloated, now frozen and stiff—was found. Difficult, difficult. The death of a child is the deepest grief of all. I try to prepare the family, spending time outside the visiting room, explaining carefully, gently, what to expect when they go through the door. I explain what the room looks like: Go down a few stairs and then a slight turn and you are in a room and the lights are low. Your son is lying on a gurney covered with a blanket. His face is bruised on his left side.

Slowing things down is what I'm doing, preparing them, pacing things so that more and more can be absorbed, remembered. Trauma clutching them, they need to keep moving; my clarity and calmness is a cane to get them through the door.

Survivors of traumatic loss have the complex task of not just mourning the loss of their loved one but also processing the traumatic circumstances of their death. On the other side of the door, with this family and most families, there is a rush of feeling. A crippling collapse into the new reality. That is what looking at the dead loved one does. It shows us what death looks like. Shows us that our living, breathing, funny, joyful, sad, troubled, mischievous, full-of-life dear one is not to be found in the body before us. We may find them elsewhere, in another way, but not yet.

When my work in the morgue and with the family is done, I go back to my office and decompress. I usually have a lot of stored-up adrenaline and feel buzzy and the need to talk to a colleague—someone who well knows this terrain. It is not something I can take home and talk about. I remember a day when a colleague said to me, "I've had the hardest day," and went on to tell me of the many crises she had been involved in. I then told her of my day that included accompanying a family of an ICU patient through withdrawal of life support, a medical assistance in dying (MAID) case* that had become complicated, and two morgue viewings with large families. She said, "You win." We both laughed heartily, black humor letting our bodies breathe out and bring us back to earth.

The work was not always this intense. A lot of the time, I would be at the bedside visiting with patients who were lonely and needed some company, some reassurance, or someone to pray with. This was especially so on the geriatric unit where the elderly or frail were placed, often for one or two years, as they awaited a bed in a long-term-care facility. If one is not used to seeing a lot of very old people in a room together who need care for most of their needs, it is like witnessing dying of a different sort, the long and prolonged kind, and it can be distressing. It certainly was for me when I first began this work. My instinct was to back away. As I got braver, I began to uncover the secret life behind the frail bodies and eccentricities of the very old. This hidden life could surface with the smallest of my attentions.

Dorothy, a woman in her nineties with dementia, held her glass of ginger ale up to the light and stared at it for a long time. When I took a seat next to her, she included me in the marvel: luminescent, sparkling bubbles rising over and over again! Her eyes in wonder at this miracle before her. Looking into her glass with new eyes, I, too, had a moment of utter surprise. This forged our friendship in delight: we would laugh

_____

*In 2016, Canada legalized euthanasia, called medical assistance in dying (MAID), which allows eligible individuals to receive assistance from a medical practitioner to end their life.

in a conspiratorial way whenever we saw each other. However, sometimes Dorothy would be agitated. This is often the case with the very old (and young) when there is sensory overload. I would then bring Dorothy to a quiet place and sit beside her. Mindful voice, slow movement, heart presence, eye contact. After all, a calming presence is usually the best offering we can give anybody, whether very old or not! As hard as it was to perceive some days, I found much beneath the surface of a person struggling with diminishing memory and identity. This prepared me well for being with my mum in her last years.

It is eighty-nine-year-old Hannah who I sit with on another day. In the weeks I have been visiting her, I have seen her face change, the lines on her forehead, cheeks, and around her mouth and eyes softening and her skin becoming translucent. I'd seen it before—dying seems to make our faces younger, even beautiful at times. Now, however, in the last stages, her hands are cold, and her feet have a purplish tinge, called mottling. She is nonresponsive, with breathing sometimes fast and shallow and other times heavier and slower. Her mouth is wide open, making her appear as if she is gasping for air. Hannah has already stopped breathing several times for intervals of thirty seconds to two minutes. This kind of apnea at the end of life is called Cheyne-Stokes respiration, and many times I have thought the person before me has died, only for them to take another deep gasp and resume where they left off. In this way, I could feel the push and pull, and the in and out that our bodies rhythmically do as we die.

Being aware of these changes is important, for as they become more pronounced so does the dying person's sensitivity to stimuli. For example, music and sound that may have been soothing a few days ago will now cause irritation. Touch as well. Vision can become overactive, so there can be a tendency to withdraw and push sights or people away. These are protective ways of toning down the senses, enabling the person to focus on their inner journey. I certainly don't know everything about dying, but I've learned that paying attention to these changes, and the oscillations back and forth, opens up the panorama of what active and natural dying is like.

Hannah's daughter, Eloise, has been traveling all day to get to her mother's side. Having visited just a month ago to celebrate her birthday, Eloise is in shock that so much could have changed in such a short time. She, like most people, has little experience of what active dying looks like. The breath of a dying person in the last stages can sound like panting or gasping; it is an automatic reflex, and sometimes saliva or phlegm gets stuck in the back of the throat and there is a gurgling noise from not being able to clear it. This is sometimes referred to as the "death rattle." But for those who are experienced in these matters, it really indicates that the person is so deeply unconscious that they cannot feel even this sensitive reflex at the back of the throat.[1] Hannah's breathing sounds raspy and rattly, and she has been receiving Dilaudid (hydromorphone) as a routine pain protocol. For her anxious daughter, Eloise, who frequently rings the call bell for a nurse to do something, I can offer reassurance: "Your mum is doing what she needs to be doing right now. Though her breathing sounds alarming, she's not short of breath or choking. She's not moaning or agitated, so it doesn't look like she's suffering. She is letting go gradually. This is what dying looks like." Eloise sits back, sighs deeply, her hands unclutching the bedrail.

In her book *With the End in Mind: Dying, Death, and Wisdom in an Age of Denial*, palliative care physician Dr. Kathryn Mannix helps us understand that death is often way gentler than Hollywood would have us believe. As she comments in a 2020 CBC interview, "That's what makes me confident in saying that usually, ordinary dying with symptoms, with symptoms well-palliated, is okay. You know, none of us is going to be in a hurry to go. It's not going to be your best day, but you have had way worse days in terms of uncomfortable experiences than that last day is likely to be."[2] It's hard work to die, but as Mannix

writes, "Watching death is like watching birth. . . . Mainly, both processes can proceed safely without intervention, as any wise midwife
knows."[3] It really helps if family, friends, and caregivers know this in
order to reduce anxiety and fear in this unfamiliar terrain.

I am now telling myself this very thing as I sit with my mum's dying.

3

Maybe Even Joyous

For to the degree that we have been conscious in our life,
we shall be conscious in our death.

SRI AUROBINDO, FROM SATPREM, *SRI AUROBINDO*
OR THE ADVENTURE OF CONSCIOUSNESS

Science has nothing to say about consciousness, so it focuses
on the brain instead, and assumes that's the same as
consciousness. That's why science believes that when you're
dead, you're dead.

RAM DASS

The focus at the end of life should be on care and comfort, and medication is often part of the picture. But in my work, and now with my mother, I'm seeing that there is a point where there are trade-offs. Trade-offs between dying with pain, or discomfort, and dying with awareness. My question that morning—Would the drugs interfere with awareness?—felt pivotal. I asked this in turn to the charge nurse, nurse practitioner, and nurse coordinator on my mother's floor. They each said yes, pain medication would affect Mum's consciousness, but that from their perspective and in keeping with their protocols, it was called for. They were all very kind and concerned, trying to reason with me. This was so hard—to take a different stance. No family member wants to be seen by health professionals as rigid, neglectful, and difficult. I was no exception.

Fortunately, the spiritual care coordinator, Kate, was also a part of the discussion. She brought us all together in a conference room to talk. (It was not lost on me that most of my time that morning was taken up in talking to various nurses, both singly and together, and *not* at my mother's bedside.) It was a sincere and careful conversation. I could see the concern in the faces of those around me and also their willingness to be open and collaborative. Although I was feeling vulnerable in expressing my beliefs, I knew I needed to cut to the core issue. So I said, "I am not afraid of my mum dying. I don't want to hasten it, nor do I want to prolong it. I don't want my mother to suffer. Right now, I am not seeing evidence that she is suffering. I put a lot of value on her dying with as much consciousness as possible. I believe that doing so helps her cross into death more easily because she will be aware that she is no longer in a body. She will be less muddled and confused and clearer about what's happening. *Maybe* even joyous."

At this point, Kate spoke up, linking dying and birthing. "I remember when I gave birth, I wanted it to be as natural as possible. I didn't want my awareness dimmed even though I was in a lot of pain. I would not trade that experience of giving birth consciously for anything."

Those of us gathered around that small round table soon reached agreement that no medication would be given until it became more evident that it was needed. And most amazingly, the clinical nurse co-coordinator said, "Nancy, you are teaching us a lot. Thank you. How would you feel about coming back and speaking to us more about all this in the future?" I left feeling that the world was becoming an easier place to be in, though no less surprising.

I know firsthand how big pain can hijack nerve centers, blocking awareness of anything outside itself. I'm sure we all do. What few people know, however, is that when death is imminent, it seems that our own natural endorphins are released, reducing stress and providing pain relief. Palliative care physicians have also noticed that if pain has not been an issue for a person earlier, it may not become one, perhaps again likely due to endorphins. Thankfully, few people now die with uncontrollable pain. Palliative care has come a long way, with physicians striving for a delicate balance between a patient's pain level and their desired level of consciousness (or, we could say, being awake or aware). It is a refined skill. The carefully managed fine-tuning and titrating of drugs tailored for an individual's symptoms can do wonders to address this, and in many cases patients themselves can administer their own pain relief as needed. But finding the best balance can be tricky. And I do wonder if our collective *fear* of pain leads to increased anxiety and the use of more medication than may be really necessary. As one patient on the palliative care unit put it, "I want to play with the pain medication as much as I can, so, you know, I'm not asleep at the wheel! It's a little scary, but why wouldn't I want to be aware at that last moment?"

There are many ways to work with fear, pain, and suffering that allow for more consciousness to be present if this is someone's desired goal. A registered spiritual care practitioner, employed by many hospitals and hospices, is a great resource at this juncture. We can all learn and grow from practicing body-centered mindfulness, there being endless approaches to choose from. However, the reality is that most people don't want to meet their own dying time, the sober reckoning of a life coming to completion, so this is a hard sell. Passivity is the norm, as others have recognized, and it's what we've been taught. Those coming from a spiritual or religious perspective are not exempt from blind spots on the interplay between life and death. This existential ducking, or clinging to rigid ideas, may in fact be the root of our suffering—to want to die without having to do the dying. And if we are unmoored and unconscious leading up to death, why wouldn't we be afterward?

Pain is not always physical; emotional pain is often the more challenging part of dying. Adding more drugs to the mix may appear to be the fix, but it's not always. Anxieties and inner struggling are natural, making it all the more important for there to be meaningful connection to others, be it family, friends, staff, or trained volunteers—those who can offer a sensitive loving presence, enabling the person to chart their own course on how things should unfold while not denying that death is in the room This brings grounding and true pain relief for an ill or dying person.

Walking back to my mum's room, I encounter a woman dressed in flowing, colorful garments dragging a small suitcase behind her. She starts walking with me and then realizes who I am, saying she is so happy to meet me as she is on her way to give Mum a massage. I'm incredulous. *My mum getting a massage?* That would be well out of her comfort zone, and besides, she is dying! I thank Bahira but say that it's not appropriate now; she goes into my mum's room nonetheless. Before I can say anything more, the nurse practitioner approaches and asks if she can talk with me. So back I go for *more* discussions. I'm surprised, as she is asking about *home funerals* and even *green burials* and is very interested in learning more about them. It is now known that I intend to bring my mother's body home after she dies and tend her there before cremation. I then ask if Mum can stay in her room undisturbed after she dies for a period of time before being transported. I want to give her time to adjust, given that she is in a transition state, before all the lifting, transporting, and preparation of her body. Everyone is supportive of this and open to considering that death is a process that fully unfolds over several days.

Other questions have arisen over the past days and are voiced again this morning. They are good ones—ones that I have been mindful of since the beginning. "Is your mum on board with what you have

planned? Does she share your convictions and hopes about dying consciously and without medication? How does she feel about her body
being taken to your home after death and washed and prepared by you?
How is your sister with this?" Some are easy to answer, but I still feel a
little on the defensive.

My biggest assurance is that I have a recording of Mum and me
talking about dying that clearly conveys her sentiments. The previous May, I was visiting her on a Sunday afternoon. I brought up the
subject of dying and the planning that we had talked about before.
At this point in her life, Mum craved this kind of conversation, the
kind that went beyond endless small talk. She couldn't converse readily about the past or a future but speaking of something meaningful
(and maybe the *most* meaningful and relevant topic for the very old is
about their dying) broke through the muddle of Mum's mind, calling
to her soul. I continue speaking, and with her eyes lighting up, Mum
leans forward, wanting to hear and understand it all again, lucidity
gripping her. But I'm wondering how to convey this side of Mum that
few get to hear, especially to my older sister, Carolyn, who lives five
hours away and sees Mum only every few months. I take out my cell
phone and press record.

ME: *Mum, we just had a conversation about dying and planning for death, and
I'm thinking it would be good to record this so that Carolyn can hear it too.
So, to go over it again for the recording, I was saying that we would like to
bring you home after you die and care for your body there.*

MUM: *Are you talking to me?*

ME: *Yep. I'm recording us on my phone. What did you feel when I said that
we would like to care for you at home after you died?*

MUM: *How did I feel? [Mum is leaning forward, looking right into the
camera.] Completely honored. And thinking what a wonderful family I*

have that would want their mother with them. [Hazy brown eyes filling
with tears.] And, I repeat, I feel completely honored.

ME: *[My voice trembling.] We'll be able to gather around you and talk and*
sing . . .

MUM: *The only thing is, I won't be around for it.*

ME: *Maybe you continue even after your body's let go. I'm sure your spirit*
will be very present with us.

MUM: *Well, that sounds good. If there is something going on about me, I*
want to be there to know about it! [Her eyes crinkling now, a mischie-
vousness lilting her voice.]

ME: *Mum, do you feel more ready to die?*

MUM: *I am more ready, but I don't want to go just yet. I do want to see them*
all again. Mum and Dad, Aunt Elizabeth, Uncle John, Aunt Carrie . . .
I really believe I will. Though I wouldn't say that out loud or people
would think I'm stupid and full of crap. But I am looking forward to my
afterlife. You see, I'm not all without religious feeling. When my mother
died, I was only eighteen, and I couldn't properly mourn her. And I think
that meant . . .

There is an interruption at the door. Mum loses her train of thought
and is upset that she cannot find it again. I am too. I keep trying to
prompt her to return to where she left off. It seems important to her to
remember, but she becomes frustrated and cannot go back. I would have
so loved hearing this self-revelation, of not having been able to mourn
her mother—an insight that has probably never seen the light of day,
and now never will.

MUM: *We were talking about a funeral, weren't we? Tell me more. I want a*
small one.

I tell her about the funeral home that we have been in contact with. We discuss who should be in attendance and so on.

MUM: *It's funny you doing all this without me. But it's OK. I'm so proud. Make sure you tell Carolyn.*

And that is how I could later show Carolyn, my family, and my community death care group a ninety-six-year-old woman cogently expressing her heartfelt feelings of being cared for at home after death. I still weep when I think of her words, the light and wonder in her eyes. So, yes, I could relay confidently both Mum's consent and also my sister's after she was shown the video. Regarding the medication question, I could only say that Mum avoided medication whenever possible. She passed this inclination on to me, and so in this way I was following her lead. No, I could not say that Mum shared the same ponderings about how consciousness continues after death—she came from a different generation where such language and concern were held differently. But I could relay Mum's awareness of life beyond the grave in her continual talk of her own mother's abiding presence. I was happy to have this chance to talk about what is truly important, on this cusp of life and death, and to feel an openness and acceptance among the nursing staff. It was a vulnerable, challenging, and humbling time for us all.

Now, remembering I left a massage therapist with my mother, I quickly go back to her room. I enter to the sound of tinkling bells, the scent of rose and frankincense and sandalwood, and Bahira finishing an exquisite luxurious massage. My mother is glistening with sweet oil, her countenance peaceful and deep. Bahira looks at me, and the depth of love in her eyes takes me to eternity. What had I just walked into? How did this wonderful human being arrive in this room with my mother just at this moment? I later found out that Bahira was a personal care worker at the long-term-care home who was also trained in palliative care massage therapy. Several times a week, she went to residents who were actively dying and provided massage. That many peacefully died soon after had become something of note. The home was seeking to employ her more in this capacity, and I see this as an exciting adjunct to palliative care support.

As Bahira was finishing up, the nurse practitioner came in and checked my mum's respiration. Two hours ago, they had said that it might be another twenty-four hours before Mum died. Now, they said her dying was imminent, maybe within the next few hours. The massage had helped her turn a corner, and she was shifting peacefully into the final stage of letting go. I felt elated! Not the response they may be used to getting at such news, but for me it was exactly what I was hoping for. She was at the doorway and had gotten there with a little help and a lot of grace.

It was noon. I had been on since 5 a.m. I needed to eat something nourishing and thought I would quickly go home and get back before anything happened. My spouse, Michael, was with Mum at this point and said he would stay. My daughter, Elena, had arrived an hour earlier, and she and I returned home for a short break. I had a bowl of carrot soup, then thought it would be nice to have a cup of tea. Another voice inside of me was saying, *Tea? Really? Why are you dragging your feet?* Indeed, why was I slowing things down now that the time was right at hand? I wonder about this even now. I have counseled many people in the hospital who wanted to be there for their loved one's last breath, and as closely as they kept vigil, it would sometimes happen that a chance occurrence had them out of the room at that moment. I felt confident in helping relieve them of their disappointment and guilt by saying, "Sometimes, it's easier for a dying person to take that last step of letting go when there is a little space between them and those who care for them the most."

A little space. For that last breath.

As I'm pouring tea, a glint of light bounces off the teapot. Looking out the window, I say to Elena, "The sun just came out." Then the phone rings. Elena and I exchange bleak looks, and I pick it up. It's Michael.

"Your mum has died."

I shouldn't have been surprised, yet I was. The permanence of those words was a cold dagger. I could barely respond. Dropping the phone, my instincts had me running into our backyard. Rolling wails moved through me. Gutted, like the grieved can only know. Overtaken, by the ancient power of keening that pierces through a heart broke open, defying both reason and dignity. Bowed over on the ground, this current ripping through me like lightning. And then, just as suddenly, it was over. It was time to call my sister and to get to my mum's side.

Michael greeted me at the doorway to her room. He was in awe and surprised at having been the one to be with her for her last breath. He described it as among the most gentle and uplifting experiences of his life—witnessing and sensing the surge of energy as her spirit released her body, joyous in the accomplishment. He then left me alone with Mum.

Breaking down at the magnitude of this moment, I felt myself return to being a little girl wanting to curl up into my mother's arms. *No mummy no*, I felt myself saying, as I literally crawled into bed with her. A minute later, another voice, louder—*Let your mother have this moment to herself. She's working hard right now and doesn't need your emotions crowding this subtle time. Give her some loving space.*

Straightening myself, I backed a little away. I told her that she had died. I said, "You are now on the other side, and we will still be close. I am so proud of you and so grateful for all the ways that helped make your peaceful dying happen. You did it, Mum. Your way and completely!" My tears were all of sorrow and joy and relief.

Details and planning would now take over, and it would be a mix of tensions between feeling and doing for the next three days. I had, in theory, been preparing for this moment to care for my mother at home for a long time.

4

The Long Decline and the Hard Conversation

Caring for people makes you better. Period.

JANN ARDEN, *FEEDING MY MOTHER:*
COMFORT AND LAUGHTER IN THE KITCHEN AS
MY MOM LIVES WITH MEMORY LOSS

Just because you can doesn't mean you should.

COMMON SAYING

Mum had spent the last two years of her life in the long-term-care home and before that spent four years in a seniors' retirement home. These moves, and the ones leading up to them, took an increasing toll on her fragile mind.

Mum had moved (I'm counting on my fingers) ten times since my dad died in 1995. Perhaps living in the same house with him for twenty-five years had pinned her down, and afterward she became unleashed, on the lookout for new experiences. She would become so dissatisfied with wherever she was living that a move was necessitated every few years or so. My brother-in-law, Braden, would recount this repeated packing, hauling, and unpacking in many a humorous anecdote. Most of the moves were positive, but the last ones not so much, as she moved in quick succession from a condo to a retirement home and finally to a long-term-care home. I still berate myself, realizing in retrospect that, despite my good intentions, I should have encouraged her to move sooner to facilities that provided more care.

Before moving to the condo, Mum lived in a mobile home community. She had jumped at the chance to move closer to friends in her shuffleboard club, two years earlier, from her tiny, and rather dark, seniors' apartment building. She was eighty-five years old at the time and doing the opposite of downsizing. I got excited by her radical reach for more life and helped her gut and refurbish her new home. She loved it. She felt young again: she had a little flower garden, and friends would frequently drop by. I had to recalibrate to this new image of her. This was wonderful for several years, but then something changed.

It began with her getting annoyed at her neighbors. Then it was because she had a falling out with her longtime friend Joyce, who, at the age of eighty, met a "gentleman," whom she subsequently married. All Mum could talk about on *every* phone call was her disbelief that Joyce could want to be with *that man* and that she herself had been summarily dropped. Normal stuff, but it colored everything, and Mum could not seem to get over it. Brooding and dissatisfaction increasingly ruled her day, until she declared that she was unhappy and needed to "get out of here," restless to find yet another place. Something smaller this time. As it turned out, there was a for-sale sign up outside the condo building behind my home. I knew I would be glad to have her close by and be able to drive less. The next day, we went through the place, and Mum loved it, asking, "When can I move in?"

The move became arduous, however. A winter storm on moving day meant everything was hours behind schedule, and then the moving truck was in an accident. It was not until late at night that it arrived. I couldn't leave her alone as she appeared dazed and lost, confusion rearing its head in a way that I hadn't seen before. She had suddenly lost her familiar routine, the comforting habit of knowing where she was and where her things were. It took *months* to recover from this and find enough confidence to go out on her own once again. Even then, however, the long walk along the condo hallways to the parking lot proved difficult. And there was no one to talk with.

She thought she would make new friends—I *so* wanted her to make some friends—but for an eighty-nine-year-old woman in a busy condo, where even a seventy-five-year-old neighbor seems young, there are no obvious friends. In such places, there used to be coffee groups or card game nights, but they were few to nonexistent.

I have fond memories of Mum coming over to our house on a Sunday afternoon, sinking into the big leather armchair, while we would put on music from the 1940s. With Vera Lynn singing "The White Cliffs of Dover" or "We'll Meet Again," my mum would be transported to a place I couldn't go. Sometimes, these memories seemed to cut to the heart, and she would become teary, so we would switch to some orchestral music. Artie Shaw's clarinet would then woo my mother onto the dance floor of her youth, and she would peacefully drift off. But this pleasant routine eventually became complicated. Taking her home after dinner became anguishing. She would become disarrayed: "Where are my shoes? Where is my purse?" Then, "I can't find my keys! They were here a minute ago." Sometimes, she'd completely fall apart, crying, "I don't want to go!" Transitions, sundowning; we could never quite get it right. What I called orneriness (or worse) was really her being depleted and not knowing what home she was going to. "I want to go to my real home," she'd cry or yell. To her great credit, and my relief, she never, or only in a joking manner, suggested moving in with us. She somehow knew that would not be a good idea.

For ten years, I had been phoning or visiting Mum every day, but after the move to the neighboring condo, the calls intensified. I would often dash over to her place (bringing my dog, who was eager to eat the cat food that could be found in all the corners), just to check in and do some cleaning. I was distressed to see how complacent Mum had become about basic washing up, alarmed to see dirty dishes put back in the cupboard, the coffee filter never replaced, crumbs everywhere. Macular degeneration was increasingly taking a toll, so I knew eyesight played a role, but to this extent? Mum would get frustrated with me, exclaiming, "What are you doing? I'll take care of that *later*. Just sit down."

Still driving, living independently, and with good mobility, Mum certainly conveyed the image of a healthy old woman; however, bouts of neediness and low mood would overtake her, along with worry over her worsening vision. She hadn't been in her new condo a year before the telltale signs of depression were there. I felt guilty. Why hadn't I noticed that it was her inability to cope with *everything* that was at play—not something moving elsewhere would rectify? I guess I was in denial myself.

Thinking back, yes, she wanted me to stop fussing about and just sit down and tell her newsy things that would help her feel connected. *Normal.* But it was easier for me just to dash around, letting my adrenaline take over rather than relaxing into simply being with her. Then, when I tried to leave, there would be the inevitable, "But you only just got here!" to jar my nerves.

My training taught me the therapeutic importance of being a nonanxious presence. The clinical term used is *coregulation*—the ebb and flow of being with another that sends signals of safety and invites connection—but I couldn't always be that calm and centered presence for my mother. Though I got better with it over time, I still feel pangs of regret that I didn't offer her more of this then. She really needed my healthier nervous system to bolster hers. The trouble was, my *own* was often in disarray. Maybe, if I had just sat down, made that cup of tea, we could have helped each other. I let my deeper attention go, not wanting to see what was in front of me. Until the day I found cat food in her coffee cup and her teabag in the cat's dish.

A few months before her ninetieth birthday, I was able to navigate her into accepting the new possibilities that a seniors' retirement home could offer—where, thankfully, she would not need a car, where there was lots of support, and lots of old people. She approached this next move with glee. And it was a good place for her, again at first. This next little apartment was cozy, there was a friendly buzz about the place, and you could be assured of being smiled at and greeted as you walked the hallways. But it was not good in other ways. Mum was an introvert, used to being alone, eating a hotdog or a bowl of canned soup for lunch in front of *The Young and the Restless*. Eating at a formally set table, with strangers, three times daily was daunting and distinctly uncomfortable. "I'm not going down there all the time!" she protested. "I'm used to doing things my own way, and if I want to stay in my old clothes and have a piece of toast with peanut butter, that's what I'm doing." Despite what could be interpreted as maintaining her independence, for Mum, it was nevertheless a gradual slide into the dreaded decline of dementia, though I could still delude myself about it.

I would get frustrated with her relentlessly complaining about having nothing to do while at the same time refusing to join in the many activities being offered. I'd say, "Mum, there's music down in the lobby. The group is pretty good." Or "I see that there are games in the dining room. Why don't you check it out?" But unless I coaxed and went with her, she'd remain in her big blue comfy chair, nodding off or ruminating, idleness driving her stir-crazy, until the urge to move and do something, *anything*, would mean she'd move objects from one place to another, and then not be able to find them again. Or she'd painstakingly fold tissues, then hide them in random places like a squirrel burying its nuts. It made me aware of my own need for work with my hands. The menial but purposeful daily tasks that I take for granted, that provide subtle satisfaction, orienting my body and mind, over and over. Physical work has become something to try to avoid in our society; until suddenly, there's not enough of it, and its value becomes paramount to bring ballast to our minds.

Even after four years, most of the friendly residents at the retirement home would remain strangers. For even they were younger than my mother, more with it. What a strain it must have become for Mum to try and appear together when she could not see people's faces clearly or remember them. During this time, I initiated the paperwork for long-term care—both dreading it and surrendering to the inevitability. However, with a two-year wait list, it felt like *anything* could happen in the meantime, including dying, but with such good health, from what?

One day, I decided to ask why she was always trying to scratch her back. She told me to take a look; there was something irritating her. When I peeked under her shirt, I was aghast. There was a suppurating, open wound there. She could only say that she'd felt something there for a while and that it was annoying. I should say so. The skin all around the wound was red and inflamed. A visit to the doctor followed. It was recommended that she get a biopsy, as it likely was cancerous. I asked about the biopsy process and the treatment options if it was cancerous. I felt that any route into the medical world at this point would entail interventions that would each have their own impacts, especially on Mum's mind. With these concerns, further investigation was put on hold. In the meantime, I began going to see Mum daily, bathing her back, anointing the area with herbal preparations, and protecting it with gauze and bandages. It was such a tender time. Having to be so physically intimate with her, talking soothingly to her, making jokes. My restlessness eased as a feeling of quiet devotion took over. After a few weeks of this, the inflammation cleared; another week and the wound began closing over. By the end of the month, there was only a small mark left. We were all astonished. It wasn't lost on me that another level of healing had been touched on as well.

In relaying this incident to a friend of mine, I witnessed her shoulders sag as she spoke of missing her own mother, who died when she was twenty-two. Linda said, "I know this is such hard work for you, Nancy, but even so, I have to tell you I would give anything to be able to tend my mother in her old age. And it won't last forever." And so I was reminded of my privilege in still having a mother and in having important caring work to do.

A colleague once suggested that I imagine Mum's brain as an onion, with the layers of onion representing functions processed by the brain. Higher-order, executive functioning resides in the outer layers, and it goes first, together with visual short-term memory. As dementia or Alzheimer's disease progress, typically deeper levels of knowing how to do something peel away, until core brain functions (like remembering how to dress, how to walk, and how to swallow) dim. Sometimes, Mum wouldn't know what to wear, so she would just end up wearing what she had on the day before, *again and again*. She'd forget to wash herself. Wearing food-stained clothes and developing an odor did not endear her to other residents, who began distancing themselves, whispering.

But Mum was determined to show her capability and independence, even when it was clear that she was no longer taking her medication properly. We went to her new family doctor for a drug reconciliation, that is, to look at all her medications (some of which she had been on "forever"). It was essential to avoid duplications, to monitor drug interactions, reflecting her geriatric stage of life. Mum's new drug regime was whittled down to one pill for her heart and one capsule of vitamin D.

Her new doctor was a godsend. When Mum's family doctor of forty years retired, she was first enrolled in a group practice clinic. Although she was assigned a doctor, he often was not there, and someone else would see her. Over the course of a few years, her blood pressure medication was changed several times, depending upon who she had seen. Or a pill would be added. She would have some reactions but couldn't really make herself understood at the next appointment or, I had to wonder, wasn't given the time to be taken seriously.

Older people outlast their familiar family doctors, through retirement and attrition, at a time when familiarity is most needed. They then have to begin again, often with a much younger, less-experienced doctor. Eventually, I asked my own family doctor, Liz, about accepting my mother as a patient. I was so grateful that she agreed, knowing she knew the importance of developing a relationship with an elderly patient. Liz had experience in geriatric medicine, a field that is lamentably underserviced. She said that geriatricians are few and far between and that medical schools provide minimal training. She went on, "There is much we can do in medicine, but the key question in geriatric care is what we *should* do."

After completing the necessary paperwork to change doctors, it felt like a new start, and the first step was the topic of advance care planning (ACP). ACP is the process of reflecting on values and wishes, one that helps others know what kind of health and personal care you would want if you were unable to speak for yourself. Most of us resist talking about our own death or that of our loved ones, and ACP encourages us to have hard, in-depth conversations in forthright, concrete terms about death and dying. Even the most obliging of us come up against a block of inertia that impedes our efforts or willingness to write things down and to make sure our close family members clearly know our wishes. One only needs a short time working in a hospital to know how central this planning is and the difficult conundrums that arise when no family conversation has occurred.

A set of questions has been developed to facilitate what is now called an advance care directive. Liz was very familiar with these and began gently trying to help Mum understand the point of all this. Still, it was a good thing I was with her, providing assurance, rephrasing, and translating. Mum's recent experience of the suspicious skin wound on her back reminded us that there are consequences to each choice we make as we age, and simpler is sometimes safer. Some of the questions Liz asked were: What do you value most? What concerns or worries do you have about your health or how it will change in the future? What might you trade for the chance of gaining more of what you value or what's important to you? If you were at the end of life, what would make this time meaningful? This type of questioning set the groundwork for the more complex questions that came next, ones relating to resuscitation, life support, and withdrawal of life support. Basically, would you want to be kept alive at all costs? This is one of the more agonizing, conflict-mired decisions for family members to make in the absence of prior input from the person.

Mum seemed vague and perplexed by most of these questions, but she got the gist and had no problem stating bluntly at the end, "I figure when my time is up, just let me go." Liz went further, needing to clarify what this really meant, carefully asking that if she was already very ill, would she want life-prolonging antibiotics. Mum said with a shudder, "Not if it kept me lying around in a hospital bed forever, no!" The unfamiliarity and busyness of the hospital, I also knew, would undo her.

There is a difference between offering a medical treatment that will be curative and palliative treatment that will relieve symptoms. When cure is no longer a likely outcome of the treatment, then symptom management, without the goal of extending life, will likely become the preferable approach. But this is a decision that needs to be made between a well-informed patient and a doctor. And too many times it is not addressed, especially in older people.

Mum was exhausted by the end of this long intake appointment. And so was I. Liz, however, had been able to determine that Mum was not hoping to live at whatever cost and that she was accepting of her death and preferred to be allowed to die a natural death. Being in her nineties, this could come in a variety of ways, and palliative symptom management would be the approach used to offer comfort and pain relief without heroic attempts to keep her alive. It was while determining this that Liz reviewed Mum's medications and eliminated the drugs that were no longer curative and that could be taxing her liver unnecessarily. By a certain age, or stage of illness, this careful drug whittling is important to do. The more prescriptions being taken the greater risk for error or drug interactions, and it just gets harder to down them all.

It was an important meeting on many levels because now we also had a do not resuscitate (DNR) order, which could be placed on her refrigerator at home. This would give paramedics the direction to *not* perform or use resuscitation practices, like chest compressions or defibrillation shocks or breathing machines, in the event of responding to an emergency call for my mother outside the hospital. What many people don't realize, however, is that at least in Ontario, a doctor *cannot* take an order from a piece of paper. The DNR order is *not* enough once you get taken to an emergency room at a hospital. Once there, medical professionals are *required* to provide life-saving treatments, even if that means doing aggressive chest compressions, which will break all of Granny's ribs, unless the patient or their substitute decision-maker says not to. There is a movement afoot to replace the term *do not resuscitate* with the more accurate *allow natural death*, removing the stigma that comes with the former for both families and medical professionals.

In this regard, I remember being paged to the hospital emergency room when an elderly man was brought in because fluid from pneumonia was filling his lungs. He had bone cancer and was on a lot of medication to control the pain and even more medication to manage the side effects. The response in an emergency room setting is to give antibiotics and other life-saving treatments unless the patient or legal substitute decision-maker directly and clearly states *not* to do this. The old adage "Pneumonia is an old person's friend" clearly applies in this situation. When the team presented to Sam and his family the options of letting him die a relatively easy, natural death from pneumonia or intervening with life-saving drugs that would prolong the arduous, dying journey with cancer, the choice, though fraught, became agonizingly clear. Sam, weary through and through, had had enough; he just wanted "nature to take its course." The family reluctantly had to agree. Sam went back to his retirement home and, with loved ones around, died in his sleep four days later.

Advance care planning goes much further than clarifying medical wishes. Preparing for one's own dying brings into view the less tangible, unique, personal things that bring meaning to body, soul, and spirit. Jane Duncan Rogers, in her book *Before I Go: The Essential Guide to Creating a Good End of Life Plan*, is an excellent resource for considering the many components, above and beyond the very important legal will, that contribute to death being met with consciousness and responsibility. Again, communication is key. Having this end of life plan written out and easily located in a "death file" is enormously important for family and friends who will not have to guess what we want—or worse, have differing opinions that lead to conflict. This lesson about miscommunication came home to me recently in a big way.

My friend Joan, living in a seniors' residence, suffered a debilitating stroke and lay in the hospital for two weeks before being placed in palliative care. Her sons were by her bedside and, caught up in the needs of the moment, didn't seek out any of her dear friends, who knew her in a different way than her children did. They would have known what would have given her great comfort in her last days. As it turns out, through a great act of serendipity, I found out that Joan was in the palliative care unit, and as her daughter-in-law held up the phone, I was able to speak to her. Amazingly, Joan, who had been unconscious throughout the day, stirred, turning to hear my voice. I was able to convey my love and the love and gratitude of her many friends and colleagues, as well as recite some of her favorite verses and prayers. Her daughter-in-law then spoke about how important this seemed to be for Joan, who visibly relaxed and became peaceful. I then contacted a small group of her close friends, suggesting we each light a candle at 8 p.m., in honor of Joan, and offer our love and warmth to her. We were all feeling a dismal kind of regret at not having known her grave condition, and this small ritual gave us something meaningful to do to honor this old friend. During the night I dreamt of Joan, her breath being drawn into the starry sky. First thing in the morning I received the call that she had died.

Mum's crisis moment came during the heat wave in the summer of 2018. She was living in her retirement home, the rooms were stifling hot, and Mum hated the loud air-conditioning noise: "I can't think straight with that blasted thing on!" One morning, a personal care worker went in to check on her only to find Mum slumped in her armchair, barely conscious from heatstroke. The thermostat read 103 degrees. She had turned the heat on instead of the air conditioner.

Maybe the heatstroke was reported because shortly afterward the phone call came—a room was available. We were lucky: it had only taken eighteen months, but it was way overdue for Mum. She received this news with delight. "Oh goody, that's the best news. I've had it with this place. I can't believe my luck."

I'm teary remembering this. Many of us know the extreme stress of helping an elderly parent through big changes in life, and of all these transitions, the move to long-term care seems unrivaled. Older people often fight tooth and nail as they fear the loss of all that is familiar as well as their identity. But Mum was full of girlish optimism that this *next* new place would be more to her liking. "I know where

I'm going. I think it's time I just take it easy and let others help me."

It was such a relief to get Mum more nursing support, and she so wanted to like her new semiprivate room. But her bewilderment took over. Again, unable to rely on habitual memory of where things were and devoid of familiar routines, Mum languished; it took a toll on her already fragile mind. It was utterly heartbreaking. More than that, I felt like I was abandoning her, and the instinct to just bring her home wracked my body. Her roommate, separated by half a wall and a curtain, was younger and had the TV on very loud all the time. She also had her family there a lot. This overstimulation further taxed Mum's mind. One night, I got a call from her very kind nurse, Kim. Mum was confused and inconsolable. Kim put her on the phone, but talking with her only confused her further because she didn't remember who I was. Worse, *she didn't remember that she had a daughter!* And Mum was furious that she had lived her life without anyone telling her this! I cried for a long time that night. Nothing I could do could help. The next day Mum seemed better, having little recall of the previous night's distress. I certainly remembered, though. I went seeking a private room for Mum in the hope that this would help. And it did. But my heart needed continual reassurance.

I thought back to my three years working at a long-term-care facility. For each new resident, there was often a pattern of breaking down ("I want to go home . . . Why am I here? . . . I don't know these people"), and then a period of gradual adjusting ("OK, I'll let you help me shower, get dressed"), followed by a kind of acceptance. To varying degrees I have reassured and guided family members through this difficult transition with their loved ones many times. Now I was the one seeking reassurance. Mum did eventually accept her new "home." But I do wonder if I didn't delay each of her transitions too long. We all want to live as independently as possible until the last moment; however, what our loved ones may miss in this delay is the ability to adjust well to a new environment with new people.

I took her out as much as I could, and these outings at first refreshed and reoriented her for short periods of time. On her ninety-fifth birthday, going for a drive, we ended up at our local farmers' market. With her walker in hand, we managed to slowly maneuver the market stalls and vendors. Mum was in fine form, greeting people and making jokes. Sitting at a picnic table, listening to the fiddlers playing, we drank lemonade and took in the bounty and goodness of an autumn day. Nearby, a gray-haired woman was selling handwoven shawls, made with handspun and hand-dyed wool from her own sheep. I got it into my mind to buy a shawl for Mum. *What a great birthday present* I thought! Though very pricey, I felt the shawl would become an heirloom. "I'll wear it after Mum does and my daughter after me," I dreamily thought. Never mind that Mum hated to be coddled or made to feel like an old lady needing a shawl. She only wore polyester pants with an elastic waist and a loose shirt or her favorite pink sweatshirt with cats on it. I elaborately presented Mum with this gift later in the day, making a big deal of it. She, of course, didn't remember the woman weaver. "Isn't that nice," she politely exclaimed. Then told me to put it "over there." It sat "over there" until I brought it home months later, where it sits in a cupboard now, until I feel sufficiently like an old lady myself, I guess.

Television was the next obstacle. She had stopped watching TV for the most part, saying she wasn't interested in any of the programs. She really couldn't understand them anymore. And, more than that, she couldn't figure out how to make the damn thing work. No matter how simple we made using the remote, she would end up pushing a wrong button, and the whole thing would get bungled up. I was the last person to be able to help with this, not having had a TV of my own for years. So we simply said it wasn't working anymore, and that seemed to satisfy her. Until the man living across the hall would wander over and tinker with it, and it would suddenly come to life. Then, we would have raging circular conversations about whether the television worked or not and who kept breaking it and when was the repairman coming—and then, when it was working, "Why is that blasted thing going all the time? I can't hear myself think!"

The care-worn nursing staff liked the residents having their TVs or radios on. It made them feel less burdened that the residents were being entertained and were doing something "normal." But if the resident, like my mum, couldn't hear well, see it, or turn it down or off by themselves, then to me it felt like they were being overwhelmed by inescapable noise and flashing lights, heightening the general anxiety and irritability that was always in the air.

I did have my sister to call and complain to, regularly. Carolyn is two and a half years older than I am, and she lives a good five hours away in southwestern Ontario. She called Mum every morning, and they would talk; she and Braden came to visit Mum every two months for three days at a time. When they came, it was like I was on holiday. I'd have a day or two when I didn't have to check in with Mum, when I could do something different or not do something different, but at least not have a corner of my mind constantly preoccupied with my ailing mother. So I would be grateful, but I always wanted more, especially as things got increasingly difficult with Mum.

Carolyn had stronger boundaries than I did. She was a little tougher, at least on the outside, and stood her ground about how often she could make the trip. I understood some of her reasons, but as time went on, with both Mum and I faltering in our own ways, my anger toward her was something I really struggled with. I have since heard how often this is the case: siblings trying to manage the care of needy, aging parents and the lurking rivalries this can stir up. The sibling on the ground gets overloaded; the sibling farther away gets guilty or side-lined. To my sister's credit, she didn't say, "Well, you took it on, Goody

Two-shoes. There are other ways you could do things. Don't blame me!" Which, honestly, she could have. As for me, I didn't see any other way to do things, but was I kidding myself? I was starting to feel helpless, a victim to the demands of caring for Mum. Anger was the result, but I struggled with it, trying to resist it, arguing with myself instead. "I can't change the way Carolyn is or what she feels capable of." Then I would say, "I can manage by trying to do less"—but I continued to feel crippled by the weight and the strain of always being on call, plus carrying the pressures of many other responsibilities.

Yes, my sister and I had differences, but it took being stretched to my limit to finally understand that our childhood experiences differed too. One day, driving alone with her and trying carefully to go deeper into why she just doesn't "come and stay for a while with Mum," I'm told why. She says she *can't*. She cannot spend much time *alone* with Mum, and then tells me something I never knew. Something pivotal, a bitter, late-night argument that cut to the core in her teenage years, causing a lasting wound. Hearing about the burden my sister has carried all these years shifts things; compassion displaces the anger. The burden I find *myself* carrying, as the primary caregiver for my mother, I then decide to try to carry more graciously.

5

It's a Multigenerational Story

The Truth must dazzle gradually,
Or every man be blind—

EMILY DICKINSON, FROM "TELL ALL THE
TRUTH BUT TELL IT SLANT—(1263)"

There are no great answers, you could say, but only great
questions made greater when their answerers are nobly
defeated by the awe and mystery of the way things are.

STEPHEN JENKINSON, *DIE WISE:*
A MANIFESTO FOR SANITY AND SOUL

Gathering stories and telling them is an ancient practice. We would do well to remember the healing storytelling provides. We all do a version of a life review as we come to the end of our lives. How fortunate if someone can help us find the great arc of our life, helping us clarify and resolve things, while our inner truths, lessons learned, values, wishes, and blessings become illuminated, a treasure to be passed on. Keep in mind that factual accuracy is not the goal; memories mellow, and for-getting or re-membering differently is part of healing and integration.

This needn't wait until the last chapter of our life, but it does serve as tremendous preparation for death, helping us carry more self-acceptance and consciousness as we die into a new reality.*

I stumbled upon this art of making a living legacy when my paternal grandmother was nearing the end of her days, and I wanted to have a lasting remembrance. Born in 1891, Nanna was a big part of my childhood, living as she did in the upstairs apartment of our house. I remember her cookies and the warm refuge she provided from tensions swirling down below. A funny, tenacious, and stubborn woman, she broke her hip doing the highland fling, her Scots tartan wrapped around her waist, when she was eighty-five. She went on to recover, spending her last years living in a nursing home. Always jovial and with lots of visitors, she seemed to weather the storm of living in an institutional setting (although my aunt Jean may recollect differently). I seem to remember a family story about her having to be carried out in her rocking chair!

It was a warm May day in 1988 that I went to see her, a bunch of lilacs in one hand and a tape recorder in the other. I asked all sorts of questions about her childhood and growing up. It was mostly laughing as I recall: a wonderful keepsake to have of her, especially given that she died a year to the day later, age ninety-eight. Now, thanks to my sister Carolyn's archival skills, I have it before me. Astonishingly, back when I was twenty-nine, I was asking the same questions as I do today: Are you afraid of dying? What happens and where do we go? Now, I'm feeling her presence well up inside me, and she is right *here*, so I guess that's my answer.

_____

*The current name given to this in palliative care circles is "Dignity Therapy," a psychotherapeutic tool of Canadian psychiatrist Harvey Chochinov that is designed to alleviate existential distress in terminally ill patients.

A Recorded Conversation with Nanna (Excerpts)

NANCY: *What's for lunch today?*

NANNA: *Oh, Sugar, you never know until you get there. Sometimes you can eat it and sometimes you can't.*

NANCY: *What's your favorite food right now?*

NANNA: *Well, I like sandwiches. You can eat them, but when you get a whole lot of stuff, a spoonful of this and you get bacon fried up too hard, it breaks in your teeth and then it makes my mouth sore. I must tell you a little joke—you know Heather's little boys were here the other day, and I gave them a cookie apiece and one of them asked me, "How old are you, Aunt Jane?" "Oh," I said, "I'm an old, old lady." "Well," he says, "you may be old, but you sure got nice teeth." [Laughter.]*

NANCY: *There you go.*

NANNA: *He said that! . . . Holy Moses, I thought, what an expression for a kid . . . Well, I just had to fall back in my chair. [Laughs.] We used to make our own fun, didn't we?*

NANCY: *Yes, we had a lot of fun.*

NANNA: *Oh dear, dear. Gone are the days. All my brothers are gone; my sisters are all gone. My father and husband, Dunc. You know, they all spoke Gaelic, every one of them . . . You know what they call chickens? Cearc. And a cow is* makkaroosh *and a horse is—oh I forget what they call a horse.*

NANCY: *And what were you called? What was your name in Gaelic?*

NANNA: *Sine. That was my name.*

MICHAEL: *That was for Jane?*

NANNA: *Yes, don't forget to tell your mother that.*

NANCY: *I like that name. Jane's my middle name.*

NANNA: *Oh, it is? Oh well, then you can tell her that Sine is [Gaelic] for Jane. Oh, they'd be talking that in the house . . .*

NANCY: *Your birthday's coming up.*

NANNA: *Oh yes.*

NANCY: *How old are you going to be?*

NANNA: *Makes no difference. I'm an old lady but I got nice teeth! [Laughter.]*

NANCY: *Yes!*

NANNA: *I only wish I had a nice place. I could feed you a little bit, wait on you a little bit.*

NANCY: *You've done enough of that.*

NANNA: *I had enough of that, but I'd love to do more. You're my girl. Just look at you, goin' goin' all the time.*

NANCY: *Nanna, what do you think happens when you die?*

NANNA: *What's goin' to happen? To me?*

NANCY: *To all of us.*

NANNA: *Oh gee. Well, nobody's come back to tell us. So, we're taught to be good. I've tried to be good. That's the way I've tried to be, and maybe I think I'm bad sometimes, telling jokes and craziness. No? Do you think I'm bad?*

NANCY: *No. [Laughter.]*

NANNA: *I think we're bad. [Laughter.]*

NANCY: *Are you afraid of dying?*

NANNA: *Oh, I don't know. I'm just sittin' here, wishing everybody good. That's all I can do. . . . Will you come again, dear?*

NANCY: *Yes, I'll come again. You've got good stories.*

NANNA: *It's not bad when it's somebody of your own. That's why I like it. It's you, you know. It's us, that's it.*

Even though our conversation was mundane, this early experience of interviewing my grandmother remained with me, coming out again many years later when I worked as a multifaith chaplain in a long-term-care home. I began interviewing some of the residents and putting their responses into written stories, reading them back to them and their families later. The impact of this ceaselessly surprised me. For the elderly to be given warm attention, to be asked meaningful questions, to be really listened to, and then have their words written and mirrored back provides an essential sort of respect, the honor of *being seen*. And for the families, there were often new revelations that led to deeper conversations and moments of hilarity.

When my mum turned eighty-seven, I felt it was time to gather in her story. I decided to interview her with the idea of writing up a short life narrative composed of her own memories and words. It became known as "Threads of Marion's Life Tapestry." Later, I was able to rely heavily on this interview for her eulogy. Here are some excerpts:

> *Marion says that in her obituary she expects her children may refer to her as a feisty, independent woman who was well loved by her children. "And tell people I'm someone who hasn't been afraid to try new things." She proved this in her later years when she enjoyed traveling to far-off places like Ireland, Rome, and Crete, as well as across Canada with her family. This same adventurous spirit led her to take violin lessons when she was seventy-nine, get in a go-cart a year later, and at the age of eighty-five register for therapeutic horse-riding lessons.*

Marion spends quality time sitting in her "retirement" chair, wrapped in her crocheted blanket, reading the newspapers in the early morning. "I'm comfortable in being alone, but I love it when the kids come over."

Marion, in reflecting about her past, said, "The death of my mother when I was young is the biggest loss I've ever had." She went on, saying, "But after that, I lost my father too. He remarried, and my new stepmother drove a wedge between us all. It was devastating." Then she added, "Good thing I had the air force. They were the best years. It got me out on my own. And boy, did I get the looks walking down the streets of Goderich in my uniform! And at the dance hall, I never was at a loss for dance partners!" When asked about other things she was proud of, she spoke of her twenty years as a secretary at the local animal hospital and her years of independence after Dad died. But Marion insisted that the most important thing she has done is have two daughters: "That is all that really matters."

At eighty-seven, she doesn't feel old, but feels that life has gone so fast, realizing that "it might end, and sooner than I want it to!" She wonders, "Why am I still here?" Then adds, "For months now I've been reviewing my life. I don't know what's getting into me." We spoke of dying and life after death. She believes she will see her loved ones again. This is very comforting to her, as is her cat, Suki, one of her present joys. "He is the light of my life. No matter where I sit, he finds me. I am happy the way I am."

This was fun to do together. The best thing was her response, a week later, after I read her story back to her. "That's not me! Where did you get all that from?" She found the story impressive and very true but found it hard to perceive herself as the person in it. "I don't feel like I have done anything in my life, but when you read about it, I guess I have."

This tapestry work became the bedrock for our subsequent years of conversations about death and dying. Mum was OK with this, as long as we kept death at a distance—kind of hypothetical, kind of humorous—and so long as the conversation didn't go on *too* long. As time went on, Mum got used to hearing the words *dying, death, funeral, afterlife*, and *dead loved ones*, enabling us to go deeper. I would always bring up Dad, who had died years earlier. What Mum made of these forays into acknowledging the presence of the dead was always delightful. She would get drawn into the mystery and magical possibilities of where Dad could be *now*. I was always so happy with her openness and optimism at these times. But she would make sure we didn't get *too* real with these imaginings by saying, "Oh, don't be so stupid."

In her last year, to stay out of the whirlpool of negative thinking Mum was prone to, I would take extra care to have something compelling to speak about—even if this topic was dying and death. And as Mum's memory deteriorated, repeating this same theme was always fresh for her. I remember once asking, "Mum, do you ever think about dying? She replied, "No, I'm not going anywhere. At least not now, and I hope not for a long time." Then, with some indignity, her voice rising, "There is nothing wrong with me!" I backpedaled, not wanting to imply anything, "Yeah, that's true. But it's OK to talk about it—really OK, at any age."

When Mum was focused and being taken seriously, her lucidity was striking. Leaning forward, she would whisper her thoughts to me as if they were secrets: "Well, I've always thought that I'd see my mother again. I've never told anyone this; they'd think I'm stupid. But since she died I always had that thought—I'm going to see Mum again."

Journal Entry

Mum, during the last months before you died, we had so many surprising conversations, though details strangely elude me. Perhaps it's because I'm sad and feeling weighty, resistant to looking back. It's my mum's lifetime of sadness I am bearing, only really seeing it now. I'm feeling it bodily, centering around my breasts. Interesting, as I have only one breast now. I'm writing through this foggy sadness. Don't know what really to make of it, do with it. I'm fighting the impulse to flee and distract myself. But somehow knowing what is mine, and not mine, is growing in importance. OK, I want to go back to my mother's words . . . but as I do, resistance rises, and I'm paddling away from that shore, not wanting to get caught in a vortex that could spin me back to remembering so much. Paddling out of my depths. Sometimes, I feel that way when I look at some of our pictures and remember the different facets of who she was, personality-wise, and the cruel barbs, masked as jokes, that could undo me, crumple me into a nervous wreck. "I was only joking" was a refrain often heard afterward.

Though details of our talks may elude me, the tears that now come to my eyes are from remembering how often we would have the same conversation, one that would end up with her talking about her mum, my maternal grandmother, Etta Richardson Lanaway. She died of cancer when my mother was a young eighteen. The hole of sadness that she carried afterward did not mend; it merely got buried over time. And eventually passed over to me. A miasma of sadness with no overt cause, yet it runs deep within the pulsing of blood and cell, imprinting my core. Also imprinted are the stories of Grandmother's goodness and love such as the following, one that I heard over and over again. It reveals a kindred spirit. How I would have loved knowing her.

Mum's Words from
"Threads of Marion's Life Tapestry"

Mother did good deeds all the time. It was second nature to her. She was always helping the underdog and always very pleasantly. She would be so proud of you. In fact, today is her birthday! She was born in 1898, so she would be 112 years old. I lost a lot of clothes to the neighbors who needed them. I remember having to go buy two dozen eggs all the time from a family down the street who had chickens, just to help the woman out. In the thirties, we didn't have a problem. My father had a good job as a mail clerk on the trains, but there were lots of men who lost their jobs, and they would come around begging. They would come to the back door very politely and ask for food. My mother would always cook them a meal. One time, a guy came with such a shabby coat, and she gave him my dad's big coat. But inside the inner pocket was his license for his job on the train. It would have been a terrible thing if it had been lost, but the man brought it right back when he found it. Our house was marked as a good one.

In mind-boggling ways, biology tells me I know Grandmother Etta intimately, indeed. The egg that, when fertilized, became me was already in my grandmother's womb in the fetus of my mother! Child, mother, grandmother all nestled together at the same time. Baby girls are born with about two million eggs in their ovaries. So, a pregnant woman is carrying not only her own baby but, if that baby is a girl, then also the beginnings of her grandchild. I'm reminded of those stacking Russian matryoshka dolls nested one inside the other. Is this cellular memory why I feel so close to my unborn grandchild even now?

Another thread from this past runs through me as well. And that is the lineage of cancer showing up. Grandmother died at age fifty-two of bowel cancer. And Mum had a big scare with bowel cancer showing up in her early forties. I remember her going to the hospital when my sister and I were very young. She must have been so afraid history was repeating itself, especially with small children at home. How lucky she was to have surgery and be totally cleared. Then it was my turn. Age forty-one. Diagnosed with breast cancer, children five and eight years old.

6

The Deepest Dive

The fear of death follows from the fear of life.

MARK TWAIN

Anyone who takes the sure road is surely dead.

CARL JUNG, *MEMORIES, DREAMS, REFLECTIONS*

When faced with danger, run toward the roar of the lion.

AFRICAN PROVERB

Close encounters with death have punctuated my life. A scary reaction to a medication for nausea, at age fourteen, saw me rushed to the hospital with a severe central nervous system collapse, one that was hard for the doctors to get under control. Later, at age seventeen, fresh from an exuberant, fun-filled season as a summer student naval reservist, I entered my last year of high school, eager to finally be a first-stringer on the senior basketball team. At the first practice, however, I nearly collapsed on the gym floor. The coach rushed over to me and exclaimed, "Nancy, you look *awful*! Go home."

At home, I couldn't get off the couch. I was stricken with a ravaging headache, mouth sores, and a fever. And my eyesight was failing. So I was taken once more to the emergency room. This time, I spent two weeks in the hospital with an indecipherable illness while every test imaginable was done on me. I was blind—the big E on the eye chart a hazy squiggle. I had crippling joint pain, and a rash covered my entire body. Teams of doctors and students surrounded my bed, talking over me, giving my condition long, unpronounceable names, and wagering bets on my recovery. (Well, not exactly, but in my vulnerable state, that's how it felt.)

So this was big. All of a sudden, I found myself facing down some pretty formidable dragons I'd never suspected existed. I might be crippled. I might *stay* blind. I might die. And I really wanted to *look* at this, as closely as I could muster. And hide from my mother, who, understandably, couldn't look at this. From my tenth-floor room overlooking Lake Ontario, as the sun went down, I listened to Hagood Hardy's song on the radio, his moving, wistful instrumental "Homecoming." It became my theme song for a melancholic deepening into life. I never felt so alone, but the aloneness was also a fullness, a seminal moment. An otherworldly comfort filled me; young as I was, I felt complete. (I've experienced this numinous quality with children I've encountered who've had cancer.) But at the thought of not being able to play basketball that season, I came crashing down from that cloud.

For some reason, playing basketball became the gauge for me to measure my reality against and release my pain through. I would vacillate between sublime acceptance and inconsolable sorrow, rolling around and crying in self-pity. I negotiated with God: *please, not blind.* I would even go the distance to settling for being unable to walk, but God, not blind. Kill me first. That was my boundary, my edge, at age seventeen.

Having just written this, I decide to listen to the "Homecoming" song. I easily find it on YouTube and, with some trepidation, begin to listen. I'm immediately transported to that hospital room and see my younger self struggling with these big forces. A kind of initiation, as I see it now. A boundary crossing, a coming home to a deeper level or dimension of myself and of life. In this reverie, words are spoken into my ear: *when your soul was born.*

I did not go blind, did not become physically disabled. The threatening diagnosis—inflammatory ankylosing spondylitis—did not manifest, the dragons withheld their fire, and life returned, albeit more strangely and haltingly, with random symptoms that would plague me over the years. I had changed, grown older than my years, more serious, more contemplative, more wondering. Yet I covered over this side of me because what I yearned for the most was to return to innocence, to youthful fun and adventure.

I had assumed we all have such stories, these unexpected, pivotal meetings with death, but years ago, when I mentioned my close calls at a school staff meeting, everyone turned to look at me. What I had come to regard as "normal" didn't seem so to them. They knew about my experience with cancer—but other encounters? "Well," I said, "two years before my diagnosis, I was in a car accident." I told the story of driving with three young children in the backseat when I was suddenly broadsided by a car running a red light at the corner of Division Street and Unity Road. I took the full impact on the driver's side, the door collapsing into me, a millimeter shy of my body.

I now travel in my mind back to that scene: Shaken, in shock, I can't move. There is a vacant wind in my brain, white noise; I'm out of my body. I can hear crying in the backseat but cannot respond; the children are far away. There is a peculiar freedom in those moments, nothing hinging me to anything. The crying children are not part of the story, not my responsibility. This is about me, and all my focus needs to be right here, in this otherworldly place of absolute stillness. The driver of the other vehicle runs up to my car, hears the children crying, and sobs, "Oh my God, there are children!" I remain motionless. Everyone asking me questions—my muteness bothering them. I don't want to return.

Reliving this now, going back to the scene, slowing the moments down, freeze-framing the moment and my thoughts at the time of impact, I start sobbing. Then shivering, shaking, as my body unwinds the memory stored deep within muscle tissues. I allow this to happen, exaggerate it, and release, release, release, letting my body become animal, fleeing in my imagination from the perceived threat, running free. I can feel the power of my legs, my arms, the wind in my face, crossing a finish line with safety at hand. Then the sun comes out, warmth spreading through my whole body, while what I saw and heard in the disembodied stillness from the actual accident scene comes back to me. I see a protective shield slamming down between me and the imploding car door. And then the quiet words form in my heart, *You are never alone*. I slowly smile, and then laugh out loud, realizing that "death" is wrapped, in each encounter, in a numinous thread.

How did I come, just now, to let my body's animal instinct take over? Shortly after the accident, I fortuitously came across the book *Waking the Tiger* by psychologist Peter Levine. He describes his own experience with trauma and that of others, observing that animals regulate and restore themselves after a trauma by automatically shaking all over. Funny how we use the phrase *shake it off* as a way to dismiss our emotional reactions, but taken literally it means allowing an organic unwinding of tissue and frozen patterns of constriction. Our body remembers even when our minds may not. I'm drawn to this somatic body-centered practice that brings animal instinct, biology, and neuroscience together.

Back to the staff meeting: After giving an abbreviated version of this car accident, I decide to just roll with the theme, speaking about how the previous winter I had again come up to an abyss. It was a snowy Friday in February, and I was on my way to a workshop in Toronto. I'd heard the dire warnings of heavy blowing snow coming but didn't heed them, thinking I would get there before it really hit. I really wanted to go, get away from the demands of being a wife and mother. An hour into the drive, however, there were whiteout conditions, the 401 becoming black ice. I wanted to turn around, but there was no turning back now; every time I put my foot on the brake, the back tires fishtailed. All the cars—ahead of me, behind me—all netted together in this dangerous, dicey situation. If one of us slipped out of control, the chain reaction would be unstoppable. How long could we hold out? Gripping steering wheels, peering through icy windshields, trying to find an exit, all of us as one. Then, the inevitable. The car in front is braking, slowing down, causing me to do likewise; my vehicle's back end starts swerving, and in a slow dance I am swinging around, around in a dizzy circle, until I'm now facing the traffic speeding *toward* me. It's a huge transport truck; it cannot stop. Time freezes. In slow motion, I see the look of horror on the driver's face, and then for a moment our eyes lock . . . until, a few inches from my car, the truck stops. I lean over the wheel of the car and sob.

Was I not getting something? These are pretty strong omens. To be honest, it was pretty obvious that at one level it was about the marital stress I was experiencing and the choices I was facing—first crashing at the intersection of "Division" and "Unity," and then spinning dramatically around to look danger in the eyes. Later, in the hotel room I found off the next exit (the last room left in town), I phoned Michael, shaking uncontrollably as I told him of my close call. Speaking with him felt like I was leaning against the trunk of a tree, so comforting. Taking all this to heart, I subsequently went deeper into the challenges my husband and I faced, and yes, things "turned around." But, at another level, facing my mortality in this graphically head-on way forged yet another link in an uneasy, ongoing, ever unfolding relationship with death.

The deepest dive, however, was yet before me.

"Great danger!" I'm being told, in my Zen koan dream. *"Get back to your house and prepare!" I am running down the hill to my house. Closing*

the shutters, locking them, drawing the curtains upstairs and down, and then bolting the doors, all of them. Now, prepared for impending danger, I'm going to the front door, opening it wide—meeting what is to come. The scene switches to a mound of earth, my own graveside.

Then, a month before the cancer diagnosis, another dream: *I'm on a ship, and for some reason I must jump off. With both fear and resolve, I leap. Down, down I go, disappearing beneath the ocean waves: so far down, and for so long, that the people on board eventually give up, thinking that I will never surface. Just as they turn away, a few air bubbles reach the top, and I awake, heart pounding.* The dream is so vivid. I keep going back to both these dreams—to discover their meaning, to count those air bubbles, to wonder about that graveside.

Tumultuous times, like having cancer, bring forth a necessary heroism for most people; it's a time when meaning is wrenched and titrated out to get through each day. For me, moments of grace arrive unexpectedly, and something new emerged in the process—insights, gratitude, and a greater acceptance of life *and* death. Perhaps that's why I keep being drawn into speaking in more detail about my own encounter with cancer. It was not my intention, and besides, it was over twenty years ago. However, as I deepen into particular moments, more details surface, and an essence begins to take shape that links tending our dead with tending our own inevitable death and perhaps even that of our planet.

Cancer, increasingly prolific, does seem to be a collective kind of illness. My anthroposophical physician in Toronto, Dr. McAlister, gently said to me at the outset, "You're not sick because of doing something wrong, or because you haven't forgiven your mother, or some such thing. You are going through this because cancer is a force in the world, a hardening force, that needs to be met. It has a low archway, and all of us will have to go under and through it." His thoughtful manner touched me, as he added, "Thank you, Nancy. You have taken this on not just for yourself but for the world. How you go through this will help others do so." I didn't know fully what he meant by this, but his words eased my soul and brought meaning to the undertaking. I now wonder about the nature of other forms of collective illness, like COVID, impacting as it does both our bodies and psyche and that of the world. Fear is synonymous with both cancer and COVID and is its own form of contagion.

Fear of death is a rampant force in the world, obscuring understanding of what really matters. It lies just beneath the surface, governing our society and our every breath, reducing the ability to make good decisions. In my work as a psychotherapist, this fear comes up with most of my clients, regardless of what they have come seeking help for. Fear masquerades as any number of maladies and emotional disturbances, which, if investigated, usually have us bumping up against the dread of not being in control. Not being in control of how things work out, of who we think we are, and of our prized competency. Gently becoming aware of this fear can enable us to let go a little more, then a little more, into new waters. Softening our grip, we meet other layers of ourselves that are usually bypassed. So much fear comes from our ego-self being threatened. Meeting this fear, even partway, can open us to the deepest encounters with ourselves and each other, enabling us to look at even our own dying with less resistance. I now remember something else Dr. McAlister said: "You are in a game of Russian roulette, with a gun to your head. Not all of us have this chance to be so heightened in our awareness of the biggest questions of life."

May 1999: A few days after my startling diagnosis, I am in the hospital, shivering in a thin, yellow gown, having X-rays, ultrasounds, body scans, and more blood tests. The radiologist comes into the darkened room, holding my chest X-ray. He is somber as he lights up the pictures of my lungs, pointing to shadowy spots. "This isn't good news." He pauses, and then says, "I'm sorry to have to tell you, but this is evidence of the cancer having spread. We can aspirate some of the liquid to make you more comfortable." Fervently, he goes on, "And there are things that can be done. If you were my wife, you'd be on the operating room table in a week."

I'm mute, so he keeps talking. "The most important thing right now is hope."

I shake my head. "Hope?" I repeat, not believing I'm hearing right. I have *no* idea what that word is supposed to mean. I realize how often I have used the word without really knowing what I was saying. Right now the word feels like a ticket to la-la land. Hope, I'm realizing, must be earned by the hard labor of facing what is in front of us, grieving, lamenting, and brailing our way to a moment when we can hold both the bare-faced reality and the open door to another possibility or view.

I still have to have a body scan to see if there is further spread to my bones. I'm in a daze, a frightened, shocked, shivering deer in the head-lights of a massive truck. Fortunately, a nurse notices this and assigns someone to accompany me, perhaps fearing that I might fall over or lose my way. I'd come to the hospital alone, for tests, totally unaware of the rigors I'd be going through. Now, I always encourage people to make sure they are accompanied to difficult appointments.

Afterward, in the waiting room, I try phoning home to Michael, who has just finished his teaching semester. I call and call for him, blinded by tears and fear. There is no answer. I don't know how I'll drive all the way home. I feel shatteringly alone. But the kids need to be picked up from school, and that gives me enough orientation to gather my strength.

In the schoolyard, filled with children playing, a friendly busyness embraces me. Then I see Michael coming up to me, his face etched with deep concern. "I just got your message," he says as he hugs me, "and came right here to meet you." He went on to tell me that he'd been cleaning and vacuuming all day and didn't hear the phone.

That evening, after Casey and Elena are in bed, I dare to look up the prognosis for my situation. Five months to two years survival rate. I read the words. I take a shower. *Five months.* I collapse on the shower floor. Lying awake in bed, haunted by the mesmerizing croak of bull-frogs, my only relief, strange as it might sound, was in thinking of other women undergoing much worse things in far-flung places of the world: imprisonment, torture, abuse, enslavement. I guess this is what trying to find perspective means. It helped me exit my constricted self-absorption and paralyzing fear for moments at a time.

For the next week, I wouldn't answer any calls from the hospital. I could *not* integrate any more news; I just wanted it all to go away— and be left alone. It could not be true that I would die so young with so much mothering and life yet ahead of me. Complicating things was that in five days my mother was leaving on a much-anticipated trip to England for several weeks. It was an awful conundrum: whether to tell her about this drastic turn of events and risk her canceling the trip, or not tell her, hiding it, while risking that something might go terribly wrong if I got on that operating table. Seeing her so gleeful in anticipation of vacationing with her friend, I felt I just could not lay this on her. I have to admit I was also protecting myself from her worrying and anxious questioning. So I pretended to be fine when she dropped by: she, sitting at the kitchen table having tea; me, doing busy work—chopping vegetables, stirring soup, picking up toys—anything to keep to a level of chitchat that was excruciating for me and to avoid meeting her eyes. Several friends strongly believed I *had* to tell her, so I was also awash in guilt.

Eventually, a phone message got through that said I needed to have a repeat chest X-ray the next day, followed by an appointment with the surgeon. The only way that I got to this next appointment was cling-ing to a book that had just been mailed to me, *Freeing the Soul from Fear,* by Robert Sardello. I had recently attended a seminar with Robert, and he sent this unpublished manuscript because he knew what I was suddenly dealing with. The book felt written for me. The passages and practices focused and assured me that I could meet and engage fear without becoming totally lost.

The day after the X-ray, and accompanied by Michael and a close friend, I arrived for my clinic appointment. The small, shabby room was full when I got there, mostly nervous-looking women, legs tapping, pretending to be reading fashion magazines. My eyes locked with one younger woman with red hair, both of us too young to be here. I couldn't cope with staying in there and asked Michael to come get me when I was close to being called. I paced outside on the street, back and forth, deep breaths. I kept up a steady mantra, saying the word *heart* over and over, in and out, the rhythm steadying me. Nevertheless, it still felt like I was waiting for the firing squad.

Finally, I marched up the long steps into the small, dim office of Dr. Henson. Entering the room, I let an imaginative self, my alter ego, take charge. *She* could sit and hear and respond to what the doctor had to say about me, and *she* would tell me herself what was being said, in a way that I could take in. She was smart and competent, and she would not shatter, like I may have. (I don't necessarily recommend this practice; it sounds a lot like a fragmenting personality or dissociation, but thankfully it seemed to help in the moment.) Within a few short minutes, however, my world turned over. Again. Dr. Henson said, almost casually, "Well, good news. The shadow on your lungs is no longer there."

As I cried in relief, Dr. Henson seemed surprised, then angry, realizing how the radiologist had made some assumptions based on what he saw and considered it *his* call to then disclose his findings to me right then and there. I only vaguely remember the rest of the conversation. It had something to do with staging and multiple tumor sites and poor margins and the need for a full mastectomy, lymph node removal, radiation treatments, and chemotherapy. But I was *glowing*. Again, perspective!

During the hard times that ensued, I admit there were moments when drifting into the light, being released from the struggles, the pain, indignities, and escalating uncertainties seemed like an easier path than that of surviving. I wasn't afraid of death; I was more afraid of the complicated dying time, the treatment regimen, and especially the agonizing goodbyes to my children. And perhaps—without an eight-year-old son eager for me to play basketball and a five-year-old daughter who still sat on my lap and clung to my long braid of hair—I may have indulged this fantasy.

Children kept me focused on the daily needs of some kind of balanced family life, but I couldn't keep pretending that everything was OK. I didn't want them to sense something wrong without it being acknowledged, for that's a lonely, scary place for children who can think it's something about them. We need to have real conversations with them, or they will make up stories about what is happening to help them understand. Needing to keep in mind their ages, it was important to find some words to let them know and be prepared for changes in our lives. I remember the hard moment of saying the word *cancer* out loud to them. All of us were plunked on my son's bed, telling stories. I decided to tell the one that was happening to me. I made light of it, of course, desperately not wanting to scare them, though it was probably evident I was choking back tears. I said I would be going to doctor appointments quite a lot for a while to take care of a lump in my body. It was called cancer, and that meant it needed to be taken off because it wasn't good for me. And when it was gone, I'd be fine. It was kind of a nonevent, and I couldn't tell how, or if, it impacted them.

It would be two years later, however, after treatment was over, and life had become more predictable, that at bedtime Elena clung to me saying, "Mummy, I love you so much. If you were lost I would be crying." The next night, she went on to say, "What would I do without a mother to take care of me? I would die . . . If you go to heaven, I want to go, too." Then, another time, she said, "If I go to heaven with you, can I take my blankie?" Clearly, something had gone underground, as our most dreaded thoughts tend to do, and had broken through the surface when it was safe to do so, and she was old enough to speak of it.

I guess the heavy-duty things in my life are likewise breaking through into fuller awareness. Giving expression in this way, as my daughter discovered early on, is a way toward greater consciousness. Squeezing meaning out of our stories is also good for living healthily, something I've taken an interest in since my late twenties when, intrigued by science and natural therapies, I went back to Kingston's Queen's University. Doing premedical studies, I planned to apply to naturopathic college or perhaps medical school. After finishing the prerequisite courses, however, I got diverted. With marriage on the horizon and baby hormones flirting with my brain, the thought of another four years of serious schooling, away from Kingston and with more debt, sounded daunting. So I sidetracked and began studying nutrition, especially the value of eating whole foods; I even started my own natural foods cooking business for a while, at a time when it was still a hard sell. Exploring, researching, and testing the multitude of natural therapies that were becoming increasingly available also became part of my life. So later, when facing a crisis of cancer, I was motivated and prepared to look for help from that direction. I knew I needed conventional medicine; I also knew that more was needed.

In the first weeks of realizing what was ahead of me, a friend of a friend told me her story of having breast cancer. She had seen an herbalist healer in Toronto, and a miracle seemingly ensued. Her tumor had shrunk after just a few of his treatments. She was thrilled and seemed to be in good health without undergoing further medical treatment. I allowed myself to get excited about this, prone to courting miracles, you might say.

Michael got me to the office of this healer who asked me questions and examined me. He announced that the lump he was feeling was a calcification, not a malignancy. He proceeded to massage, vigorously, the tumor site. This went on for a while. He was sure that this application of healing energy would shrink it. Then he gave me a bottle of his own brand of herbal capsules. When I got home, I found I could not read the ingredients on the bottle, so faded was the type. *Hmmm . . .*

I wanted to feel the reassurance that he was offering me, wanted to find some of that "hope" the radiologist had told me I needed. But I was worried. I hadn't really connected with this person, or he with me. A too-good-to-be-true kind of feeling took hold. I also soon learned that massaging a tumor site is contraindicated and started worrying about cancer cells being released. I checked the lump every day, believing it had gotten smaller. But it hadn't. It was then that I realized how vulnerable I had become to extremes. One extreme: what hard-core medicine offered, the fighting arsenal of poisons, burning and cutting, all confidently aimed at improving "survival outcomes," without considering the consequences for subtler body realms and the need for deeper healing. The other extreme: wishful treatments, grand promises with little scrutiny or accountability. In a very short and indeed overwhelming time, as if strapped to a roller coaster, I had plunged into opposite ends of a continuum stretching from fear and denial to fantasy. Reassessment time: I threw out the sketchy pills, got serious about doing my own research, and began challenging my doctors, trying to find that sweet middle place for making my own informed decisions.

"I want to schedule your surgery, and it should be as soon as possible," declared my surgeon. I asked, "How long can I have and still be considered in the soon-as-possible category?" He looked surprised, with arched eyebrow, declaring, "Most women want it done *immediately*!" I told him I wanted time to arrange childcare for my kids, but really, more than anything, I wanted time to *absorb* this next step, to prepare both body and soul for having my right breast removed and to be in the best possible shape for surgery. He said, "I'll give you a month. That takes us to July 9, no longer."

Eating well, swimming, gardening, talking to my body about what was in store, and trying to calm my nerves filled the time. Then, swallowing my vulnerability, I called together some close women friends for a circle of support. After meditating together, each woman offered a blessing for me. I felt held and seen. I went on to visualize the surgery itself—the knife, the cutting, and offering up my breast as an offering, dying to this part of my body consciously. I'm not sure what this catalyzed, but by the time July 9 arrived, I felt I had done my part in meeting this moment. I was ready.

My memories are of being in a skimpy gown waiting in a little cubicle, preternaturally cold, watching the hands of the clock turning hour by hour, until at last, at 5:20 p.m., I'm called. My hard-won buoyancy had been ground down. But then I saw my surgeon walking by. He was eating the Indian samosa I had brought him, and he gave me a thumbs-up. (His secretary had told me in an aside that the doctor had a habit of filling his pockets with candy to help him through his long days. I was afraid of having a hungry, sugar-high surgeon operating on me, so I had a nurse slip him the treats I had brought!)

"It's over, it's over, it's over," I keep mumbling as I come out of the anesthetic. Nurses hover in a blur around me, taking vitals, making reassuring sounds. But nauseated and dizzy, I'm not in great shape. Late in the evening, my doctor makes a surprise visit (it seems like he has warmed to me since the samosa). In his attempt to be relational and transparent, he is telling me, "I took a good sampling of your lymph nodes, but it looks like you have either another tumor or a suspicious-looking node." Seeing my crumpling face, he hastens to add, "But don't worry." *Right*. I am groggy and unwell; this news sends me tumbling. That entire long night in the recovery unit, I was plagued by the worst nightmares of my life.

Several weeks later, peeling off the last of the bandages, I stand in front of the bathroom mirror and take a deep breath. A bright red slash is crossing the right side of my chest from armpit to heart, with ribs prominent under taunt skin. Hmmm . . . OK, my new body. Instead of recoiling, I have a moment where I feel taller and rather battle-weary proud.

The next day, I find out that the lymph nodes are clear, and there is not another tumor after all.

Next on the radar was radiation treatment, which was to start six weeks after surgery. Unexpectedly, I found out about a residential, anthroposophical medical retreat for cancer patients in Ann Arbor, Michigan, that fit exactly into this time. Michael encouraged me to go, and a friend insisted on helping with expenses, but making the long trek there on my own was a big deal. Feeling worn thin and vulnerable, I was very emotional leaving the kids for three weeks. But it also felt so timely, a stop-off point, a place to pause and gather myself. The medical doctors on staff had additional training in finely honed complementary modalities based on years of research in Europe. But more than that, anthroposophical medicine held a picture of the *whole* human being. It was understood that for *long-lasting* healing to occur, body, soul, and spirit must all be tended. So I went, relishing being served local biodynamic food and receiving a welcome level of nursing care that I didn't know existed. Along with mistletoe treatments (a plant-based medicine that stimulates the immune system), hydrotherapy, rhythmical massage, warm compresses, art and drama therapy, and eurythmy (a harmonious movement therapy akin to tai chi), I spent time alone in contemplation. It was so strange to be away from my role as wife and mother and also hard to be on the receiving end of so much care and warm attention. But among the most important lessons I needed to learn for transformation to occur was exactly this: how to become good at *receiving* help and how to soften, allowing love into my very cellular being.

I got to test this out immediately upon getting home from Ann Arbor. A lump on my *left* breast now. Inconclusive biopsy, so back to surgery for a lumpectomy. My relentless research told me that bilateral tumors were not a good sign at all. Would this wretchedness ever end?

I dream: *Plunging into deep water, taken down rapids, I get sucked under the swirling water once, twice, and yet again. This third time I'm spit out and thrown upon the shore. A shining necklace materializes and is put around my neck.* Breathless upon waking, I remember that three is the magic number of completion. I dare to think that now, with three times precariously tilting to worst-case cancer scenarios, maybe this will be my last plunge.

The pathology report comes back clear.

From the beginning, I was averse to radiation treatment, considering it the very antithesis to life-generating forces. I had been exposed to radiation treatment at age fifteen, when it was used, quite casually, to heal scar tissue on my earlobes after having my ears pierced. Possibly this early exposure might even have helped precipitate my current cancer. Nonetheless, I had a tumor close to my chest wall, and I was told that although I had a full mastectomy the risk of metastatic spread to my ribs was at least 50 percent if I did not undergo radiation. I liked that the odds were so bad and that I really had no choice; otherwise, I would have spent too much time waffling over yet another big decision.

I began my first treatment on Michaelmas Day, September 29. I considered this auspicious, given the mythological account of Archangel Michael, borne upon his white steed, courageously slaying the dragon of destructive underworldly forces. Wielding his bright sword of discrimination, Michael is said to clear the way for transformation, personal and cultural. And such is its nature, timeless mythic reality keeps on happening, over and over, in new guises. Yes, he was going to be important along this trip.

But entering the cancer clinic, taking a seat among the other patients, flattened my courage. Once immobilized on the table with my flat and newly tattooed chest exposed, the high-powered beams of precision laser scattered my attention, as did the unsettling whirring sounds and the penetrating, subatomic heat in that ice-cold room: a modern, high-tech dragon's den, indeed. I was limp and defeated afterward. How could I possibly reconcile myself to *accept* a treatment that was killing *all* cells in its pathway? Day after day, I felt more exhausted, more depressed, unable to resolve this new contradiction, unable to find an inner image that could unite my mind and body to hold this paradox. Something needed to change.

Eventually, writhing around in this crucible, I drew inspiration from the work of Rudolf Steiner (more on him later), specifically his perspective on how one can generate and bring a warm, vital interest to *every* aspect of life—even to the very concrete world of machines and technology—and, in so doing, find a relationship with it, rather than be at its mercy. So I began giving my attention to what was immediately before me each day. Instead of remaining withdrawn and annoyed by the radiation technicians, I looked them in the eye and beckoned them to see me as a person, not simply a code on their charts. I took particular interest in the glistening white metal machinery, noting the angles, admiring the buttons, the craftsmanship, even speaking aloud to the rotating arm that would soon swing above me.

Doing this purposely, several days in a row, while lying on the treatment table, I was suddenly overcome by an inner knowing that was large enough to hold the momentous paradox of destroying life to preserve life: Source, God, Creator was bigger than both the forces of radiation and death and could contain and use this and *all* forces for healing. Surrendering not to fear but to love changed everything.

I made friends with the other patients and staff. I relaxed, even joked. The side effects diminished, and when the final treatment day came (on all Saint's Day, no less), I felt I had slain a few dragons of my own. Maybe even befriended one or two.

But down the road there was, of course, more to come. I wrote the following after receiving an intense intravenous mistletoe (Iscador) treatment.

Journal Entry

Yesterday, lying in bed, a fever raging. Restlessness, then thrashing about, covers off, covers on . . . not being able to bear it, breaking down, crying, but too much effort . . . I am beyond myself, moorings gone, and it's as if I am wrestling with Death itself. Exhausted, I feel a letting go of the heroic journey, the mountain too high and the climber too tired. Collapsing inwardly, all that is left to do is admit failure. "I give up," I whisper into the air. At some point, I'm aware that I am staring at the wall, and what I'm seeing there, in a dreamlike way, is the portrait photograph that Mum has of her mum. The one that has hung on her bedroom wall forever, my grandmother, young, her bodice of white lace, the background misty. Oh, the comfort soaking into me from this mirage! She is with me, the grandma I never knew, who died from cancer, another diver into the depths. A presence fills me, holds and gently rocks me. The atmosphere lightens. The fever is still high, but there is a felt knowing that I am not alone. It was as if she is telling me that whatever arises when facing the terrain of illness and dying you just meet it. Stuff comes up. Whether it is fear, fury, self-pity, or whatever, embrace it, surround it with love, no matter what. This wisdom allowed me to tumble into defeat, to cry in its wake, yet discover that the ground still held. Grandma Etta's picture now hangs on what has become my ancestor wall, right at the top.

Next on the horizon was the decision whether or not to do chemotherapy. My senior oncologist, Dr. Ginsberg, said that a decade ago it would be fifty-fifty as to whether chemotherapy would be recommended in my situation, given the odds of it really helping. However, he went on to say, "Today, chemotherapy is being offered to women even with first-stage cancer. So, protocol would advise you to do so." I jumped on the possibility that this route wasn't a foregone conclusion. I am acutely sensitive to medication of any sort and dreaded the impact that chemo would have on my body. Acknowledging that this kind of systemic treatment is necessary in specific cases, I quizzed him for more information about how essential it seemed for *my* situation. I got back into research mode. My friend and neighbor, Barb, was a family doctor. She helped me find medical journals and studies that could tell me more about chemotherapy's efficacy on estrogen-positive cancers. I learned that in China and in other non-Western countries, those with fewer ties to the pharmaceutical industry, experts reasoned that chemotherapy worked in premenopausal women due to it shutting down the ovaries and medically inducing menopause. Estrogen down, the tumor shrinks. So, instead of using costly chemo drugs, a woman's ovaries were removed, leading to the *same* end goal: early menopause and low estrogen.

I was excited to learn this and showed Dr. Ginsberg the reference to a twenty-year meta-analysis trialing this approach that would soon be publishing its results. He was quite interested. "The trouble is," he noted, "it goes against the standard of care that governs what we can recommend for cancer treatment." He was pensive, however, and decided to take it up with a noted gynecologist colleague in Toronto, one who knew a lot about these clinical trials. He even arranged a phone consultation for us in his office. "The results look promising," she said, "and the indications are that surgical removal of the ovaries is at least as helpful as chemotherapy. However, it can't be recommended under our guidelines." I then put this question to her: "I understand there are guidelines. But would you at least say that if I wanted to *choose* this approach, of having my ovaries removed, that it could be considered a reasonable decision?" She promptly answered, "Yes, I would say that it would be reasonable. Besides, you cannot make a wrong decision when there isn't clearly a right one."

Feeling assured that I was not making a rash or uninformed choice in refusing chemotherapy, I went ahead with the ovarian suppression route. Choosing a year of monthly injections to first see how I tolerated it (*huge* needle penetrating layers of muscle in my buttock, ouch), followed later with laparoscopic surgery, I entered into sudden and severe menopause. Not a small bump on the road, at age forty-one, because it meant sleepless nights of hot flashes, along with the concern of developing osteoporosis, and the possible side effects of the five-year use of the oral chemo drug tamoxifen. But I assured myself that these concerns would have likely come with the chemotherapy route as well. Dr. Ginsberg was quietly pleased to be part of this emerging option, wondering if it could become more common for women going forward. He qualified this by saying, "But I will congratulate you only when in four years you are still alive [the benchmark to know if chemo is helpful]. Then I'll know you made the right choice."

It was an unexpected yet welcome irony that in the middle of the place I wished most *not* to be, the oncology department, I found one of my greatest champions and allies. My oncologist trusted my instincts. He even enjoyed how I turned the tables on him from day one: at my first appointment, I waited until I met him in person, and he saw me with my street clothes on, and we had discussed *my* questions, before changing into the yellow hospital gown that identified me as *patient*. He would tell the other doctors and residents about me, inviting them in to our appointments, telling them I was breaking new ground and they could learn from me. We had fun. As it turns out, I was among Dr. Ginsberg's last patients before he retired.

And as fate would have it, I saw this respected father-figure doctor seventeen years later, when he was visiting a friend of his, a patient with whom I was now working in the very hospital that he had worked in for so many years. He was delighted to see me again and to know that I had survived well past the four-year benchmark. Remembering my case, though, he told me that the protocols had *not* changed, even in the face of growing studies.

During those tricky months of treatment decision-making, a friend took me aside and asked a probing question: "I've heard it said that those people who go on to live a long life after cancer have something that is *calling* them to live for. I've heard you talk about wanting to be alive for your children, but what do *you* want to be alive for?" He placed a considerable challenge before me: finding an inner answer that would meet the seriousness of the question. I couldn't answer him directly. I did not have a worthy goal in mind that felt substantial or true, nor did I feel the drive it would take even if I had. Over the past three months, I had used up a lot of my reserves, three times facing the likelihood that the cancer had spread. Each time waiting for test results that were possibly ominous. That is one thing I *didn't* get good at: waiting for test results. I could well appreciate the Afghan proverb, "Waiting is more difficult than death."

7

A Different Kind of Medicine

The Mythopoetic Story of Inanna

> *There is in every wound a bud and in every injury a*
> *precious jewel.*
>
> HILDEGARD OF BINGEN

> *If we're in fear, we are not in a place of love. When we're*
> *in a place of love, we cannot be in a place of fear.*
>
> ELISABETH KÜBLER-ROSS AND DAVID KESSLER,
> *LIFE LESSONS: TWO EXPERTS ON DEATH AND DYING*
> *TEACH ABOUT THE MYSTERIES OF LIFE AND LIVING*

In the midst of navigating all of this, I have another dream: *I am play-*
ing a game of chess on a giant board. My opponent is the devil, the stakes
high. I wake in panic: I will never win at this game by cleverness alone. I
must find another way. I have no idea what "another way" might mean,
but I wait and eventually experience it in an unexpected way—through
mythology and story.

In the early days of becoming a mother, when hours and hours could
go by in my pastel, flowered easychair nursing a baby, I exercised my
mind and soul by learning stories—mostly fairy and folk tales, stories
that were clever but above all wise. I would later recite them by heart
at our local storytelling circle or onstage at festivals and various events.

I loved the playful art of the storyteller, bringing to life the archetypal wisdom of our psyche, for children and adults alike. A few years later, while spending more long hours recovering from surgery or treatments, I was to experience firsthand the powerfully *transformative* and healing power of story when learning by heart "The Descent of Inanna," as retold by Jalaja Bonheim.[1] This ancient Sumerian myth revolves around the goddess Inanna, Queen of Heaven, who, while "pressing her head against the damp soil, listened into the earth" and felt a deep call to pay a visit to Ereshkigal, her sister below. We learn that Ereshkigal, Queen of the Underworld, is both creator *and* devourer, and that Inanna, being either naive or courageous, thinks, "Surely she will not harm me, her own sister." So down, down she goes, like someone leaping off a ship into the depths.

This story captivated me, in a visceral way, and I wanted to learn it and share it. The descent narrative is a common one in literature: the journey to the underworld and back, into the unconscious and back, is always an element in the hero's or heroine's journey. I kept reading and rereading it.

Descending, Inanna is met by guards who demand that at each gate she take off yet another of her garments, jewels or amulets that are her power, protection, and pride. At each turn she says, "What is this?" and, to herself, "What made me think I was special?" As she descends, she is stripped of more and more externals, until she is naked, and alone. Only then will her sister of the underworld see her. Ereshkigal, we discover, is definitely not in a good mood and is enraged that Inanna should dare come into her realm uninvited; she also recognizes that Inanna is ripe for initiation into the mysteries of death. Hiding her dark face of compassion, Ereshkigal brazenly proclaims, "She shall enter . . . but not as she has planned it. Not as sister shall she know me, but as the great teacher of death." Crossing the seventh and last gate, total weakness overcomes Inanna. Ereshkigal then sounds a tone, "a low vibration more ancient than earth herself," that sucks the last breath from Inanna. Her surrendered body is hung on a meat hook on the wall.

I love how there is no ambiguity, no mincing of words. The body, emptied of spirit, hangs on a meat hook. The coarseness of the image impales me in its sorry bleakness. Inanna has met her end, her call to descend to her sister now seen as death calling her. *What made me think I was special?* Indeed, Inanna. I find myself reflecting upon this more personally than ever. Perhaps it's only when we let go into the drastic realization that there's no escape and resolve to face what *is* that larger forces can come into play.

But, of course, the story is not over.

Inanna has a friend, a very good friend, Ninshubur, who has been entrusted to hold the silvery thread of life connecting Inanna to the upperworld. Three days and three nights go by, and the friend begins to worry. Anxiously, Ninshubur calls to the gods for help. But the gods are busy and dismissive, declaring that Inanna was foolish, that she knew the risks of what she was doing. Now she has to pay the price. Only one god, Enki, the god of plant and water wisdom—natural domains—feels compassion for Inanna: "O my daughter . . . Oh, queen, you foolish one what have you done!" Pacing in his shrine, he wonders what he can do while he also senses that Ereshkigal has come to be in great need as well.

It's important to me that Enki has compassion for *both* sisters. Admittedly, this is an interpretation I am winnowing out for the telling. Because by this time in the story, it's obvious that Inanna and Ereshkigal are polarities, opposites that seek to know each other. Inanna is the younger sister yearning for the dark wisdom of her older sister, instinctively seeking wholeness, even if the price is death. Ereshkigal, who will only see her sister once stripped of her outer adornments, has her own onerous task: birthing new life out of the churning of earth forces below.

From the dirt beneath his fingernails, Enki fashions two small, winged creatures, breathing them to life. Laughing, he throws them up in the air while instructing them to fly down into the great below, into the womb of Earth itself, where they will find Ereshkigal. He tells the winged ones to listen carefully to the cries of Ereshkigal and bring healing words to her, "for she is great with child, yet alone. Great with child, yet alone." Enki knows that the little creatures' presence will bring compassion and ease Ereshkigal's pain, making her happy and wanting to reward. Enki tells the little ones to then "ask for the corpse of Inanna." Handing one of the little flying creatures a crumb and another a drop of water, he goes on to say, "Feed it with the bread. Wash it with the water. She will arise. She will arise. Go now."

Down and down the winged creatures fly, until they hear great cries coming from the very bottom of the underworld. Ereshkigal is crouched, clutching her big belly, crying with the suffering of the universe, for she indeed is in labor, giving birth to Earth itself. "Oh, oh, my inside!" she moans. And the little winged ones moan along with her, "Oh, oh, your inside!" "Oh, oh, my outside," Ereshkigal cries. And the little winged ones cry along with her, "Oh, oh, your outside!" Then, "Oh, oh, my pain in unbearable." And with each cry the winged ones cry along with her, enveloping the queen in Enki's ancient compassion: "Oh, yes, queen, indeed, your pain is truly unbearable."

Finally, Ereshkigal's rocking and moaning ceases. She feels a kernel of sweetness enter her and opens her eyes to the creatures who have brought her companionship, who have eased her suffering. "You, little ones, who are you? Whatever you desire, I shall give you." The winged ones then ask for the body of Inanna, and the guards bring out the decaying corpse.

The little winged ones encircle the corpse and place upon the mouth the bread of life, then wash the whole body with the waters of life. Then they, too, wait. Until—is that a stirring? Is that a breath taken, a heart beating? Like leavened bread, like water at high tide, Inanna rises. Inanna rises from within Earth. Having met the underworld, having been initiated into death's realm, and having reemerged, Inanna now takes her place in the land of the living. She is crowned Queen of Heaven *and* Earth. Her people are filled with amazement and joy, and the land blossoms in abundance.

This is a precursor to the Greek myth of Persephone and an obvious precursor to another well-known story of resurrection from the dead. "The Descent of Inanna" ends thus: "Since that time, it is Inanna whom we can turn to when we journey through the dark unknown, and whom we call upon as our trusted guide through life and death, through time and through eternity." The fact that the iconography of Inanna (who is also known as Ishtar) shows up more than any other deity on the ancient gravestones of that era is a testament to the influence of this goddess and myth.

This ancient story was longer and more complex than any other I had tried to learn. And more possessive of me. *Why* did I feel so compelled to tell it, then as now? Repeating it over and over again, so that I committed the tone, gestures, and nuances of the images and words to heart and mind, became a daunting task that ultimately overcame me. I just couldn't get to the end and hold it all of a piece. At long last giving up the likelihood that I was *ever* going to be able to faithfully recount it, I had a surprising realization. I had been learning the story so that I could tell others, but what I came to see was that it was *myself* who needed this story. I couldn't get to the end of it all and remember it all because I was continually overwhelmed by being thrust into the underworld, falling into the arms of death, yet never quite reaching the turning point.

Breathing into this place, over and over, something began to shift, so that in the end, it was *my own* resurrection I experienced, my own eventual uprising from the depths. I wasn't looking at life; I was in it. The light now *within* my body, scarred as it might be, wrapped with less heaven, more Earth, gently tethered to the ground—a homecoming. It was a breakthrough, psychologically, but also somehow more than that, beyond emotion into a realm of wholeness that true art brings forth. Colliding with this powerful archetype of descent and rebirth carved out a pathway I could trust, and a returning joy enveloped me. It is said that myths keep on happening, in the *now*, which makes them essentially timeless as they continually reverberate across time with a *truth that is truer*. Is this why we've not entirely forgotten them—or them, us? Are these ancestors of another sort? This, then, was a different kind of medicine indeed, a time-tested one, and another way of listening for what was still calling.

For some time, I had been turning over the question, *What is calling me into a life to live for?* discerning, as much as I could, my own living from that of living for my children and husband. After experiencing a sense of resurrection through the story of Inanna, I remember the day, walking our dog, Cedar, up the long laneway from our house in the country, when I felt a sudden jolt in my solar plexus. A spark, a fire, deep inside me, burning out all the dampness and murkiness, allowing me to taste a bodily excitement and a reaching out to life once more, in all its unknowables, as a force coming from within but also as something beckoning. Thinking back, it was like the quickening of a baby in utero. Something had shifted, and I answered *yes*.

Turning to face the outer world again and inspired by the quote taped to my wall for years, "The gods only go with you if you put yourself in their path," I returned to work at Mulberry Waldorf School. Many avenues opened up, and as time went on, I felt the old urgings to take on more and more, but I could only go so far until the pathway would turn and point back to my needing to take care of the self I had begun to know. I had to accept that *this* was part of my calling, though I railed against it, part of me always wanting to *do* more. I knew I had to surrender and still must do so. In this back-and-forth way, continually wrestling with the belief that busy is better, that the grass is greener somewhere else, I gradually found more of myself *right here*. Then, another dream: *Your work is of the far shore, across the threshold.* This is the closest answer to the question of what I'm being called to do in this life. How precisely enigmatic.

In the years that followed, I would explore the ancient Greek axiom, "If you die before you die, you won't die when you die." I did so rather bluntly by undertaking a series of meditative practices to meet the death specter head on. Many traditions encourage this kind of contemplation. The idea is to bodily imagine our corporeal dissolution, consciously going beyond our senses, our mind, the elemental components of our being, to experience our individual awareness merging with vast awareness and the luminescent clarity of our boundless, deathless self.

I initially did this on my own, sitting by a tranquil lake where it felt safe and comfortable. I can't say it was easy but also not as hard as it might sound. Following the directions, I visualized myself stepping off a firm shore and allowing the river of dissolution to take me where attachments and emotions loosened their hold and the flow of surrender had its way. I did this on several occasions. I certainly did not reach the luminescent clarity of a spiritual adept, but even so, I remember feeling a peace and an at-oneness in a realm that included living and dying as a unity. Harder was coming back—not unlike it can be for those who experience near-death experiences, returning to their bodies after being clinically dead. But once back, the immensity of my love and gratitude for Earth and humanity overflowed. Of course, one cannot stay in this numinous space for too long. The stresses and struggles of everyday living are useful in preventing us from clinging even to impermanence! However, these kinds of experiences in facing death help us shed some of the fear of the journey. But really, it's the countless small deaths we encounter every day that are the real means to grow muscles. The continual letting go—of plans, people, dreams, and desires, of what *we* think is best—when life has another agenda. Do we keep clinging and screaming? Or can we let go with as much grace as we can muster, learning a little of what death is before dying?

A family trip to Greece some years later allowed me to continue my interest in death and rebirth stories of initiation, this time through the Greek myth of Demeter and Persephone. This myth was reenacted in the secret rites of Eleusis (which took place c. 1600 BCE until about 392 CE), providing a direct brink-of-death experience for participants and the uprising or rebirth that followed. The initiates were sworn to secrecy, so it is unknown what really happened on the sacred grounds of Eleusis, where once every autumn up to three thousand people would undergo the priestess-led rite, after preparing for it for over a year. But what is known is that those who participated were forever radically changed, no longer fearing death but knowing that life is eternal, that there is only change from one state to another.

All the great thinkers, writers, and sages of the age were initiates of Eleusis, from Socrates to Plato and Aristotle. To say that for eight hundred years this was the backbone of spiritual life for the ancient Greeks would be an understatement. And, as always, behind one teacher stands another, so it must also be acknowledged that prior to Eleusis, there is a trail that has all but been forgotten. Peter Kingsley, a scholar known for his groundbreaking work on the origins of Western spirituality, philosophy, and culture, traces this trail back to pre-Socratic philosophers like Parmenides and then further back to Pythagoras. Herein lies a much vaster, more mystical and fertile picture of the origins of Western civilization than the dry rationality that we have been left with. Our philosopher forebears were actually spiritual initiates—how can we not have known that?

Intrigued by this, when we arrived in Athens, I was eager to visit the town of Eleusis and the grounds upon which these ancient ceremonies took place. My Greek friend Vivian helped me get to this small town about fourteen kilometers away, traveling what was known as the Sacred Road. I'm not sure what I was expecting, maybe some rubbing off of the magic and mystery I had read about or a remembering of a past-life experience. On Monday morning, with great anticipation, I walked up to the entrance gate and read the sign: "Closed Mondays." *What!* I couldn't believe it! I had researched this archaeological site online and nowhere had it said this. I had to suppress the depressing feeling that I had somehow been deemed unworthy to enter these hallowed grounds.

Hanging around the periphery of the site, while my friend drank her strong Greek coffee in a nearby café, I marveled at how very ruinous the ruins were. Peering through the wrought iron gates, I could just make out the large courtyard and some steps, a few remnants of spiraling columns, and slabs of rock. I had to use a lot of imagination to picture this spiritual epicenter from antiquity.

Only much later did I learn that the mystery schools of this period, largely women-led, were dismantled in the third and fourth centuries CE by the Christian church. Initiates in the ancient mysteries were encouraged to trust their own thinking and feeling, and their diminished need and desire to obey external authorities, religious or otherwise, posed a threat to the emerging patriarchy of institutional Christianity. Eradicating these transformative rites helped to ensure conformity to the church.

In *The Immortality Key: The Secret History of the Religion with No Name* by Brian C. Muraresku, much more is told, like the supposition that the ritual drink given to participants was a mixture of barley and mint infused with the fungus ergot, a psychotropic agent, which may have contributed to the transformational visions and experiences. Only through the lens of the modern era would this be considered scandalous; however, that may be changing with new research that shows the universal prevalence of plant medicine teachers throughout time.

Indeed, today's growing acceptance of the role that psychoactive substances can play in treating depression, anxiety, and addictions is revolutionizing the future of the mental health profession. In medical trials treating people dying with cancer, just one dose of psilocybin has been shown to ameliorate fear and anxiety surrounding the dying process in some 80 percent of patients. The experience of being held in greater connectivity, meaning, and a love beyond our temporal bodies is indeed transformative, offering a glimpse into what is immortal, without requiring spiritual faith. Thoughtfulness as to how to use these medicines does seem paramount, so they aren't used without the proper preparation and support, and also so that they don't become just a chemical that is dispensed, separate from the earthy spiritual source from which they come. That would be going down the old road of medicine, where a single-minded "cure" is the goal, rather than transformation in relation to the whole.

Not having used drugs of this sort myself, I know there are many ways to have direct spiritual experiences without them. Indeed, perhaps we are meant to develop the capacities for insight into the greater dimensionalities of life without these plant aids. But I for one am happy to know that more people can potentially have access to and opportunity for such insight, healing, and relationship by using what was once regarded as a gift from the gods.

8

Becoming an Ancestor

Because of Peter's willingness to take on this task of carrying the dead, he has ensured that the corpse becomes not a ghost but an ancestor. . . . If we don't accept the heavy task, then we likely live haunted lives not ancestral ones.

MARTIN SHAW, *SMOKE HOLE: LOOKING TO THE WILD IN THE TIME OF THE SPYGLASS*

The voices of our ancestors and those yet to be born are a song within our hearts.

DHYANI YWAHOO, BEAUTYWAY WISDOM CLASS (2021)

The past has a cycle to it, and the cycle repeats until we become conscious of it. It's not a surprise that patterns of the past reappear—or that what happened to our forebears, culturally and historically, is also a part of us. Though this is not a new idea, there lately seems to be an increasing appetite for uncovering our particular inner warps and weavings—and understanding just how close we carry both the unfinished business of our ancestors and their blessing. Tracing back our roots is an instinctive urge, especially as questions about our identities get more complex. But how many generations do we count? Seven back? Seven forward? Ironically, it is my Indigenous friends who have challenged me, not just about the privilege that comes from my British Isle background, but also to get to know my *own* peoples' stories and *their* history of trauma. After I've done that, "maybe then we'll have something to talk about," they say.

One day, I'm sitting silently on a log in the woods with a Métis acquaintance, whose Anishinabe name is Mitig. He is singing his songs to the spirits of the land. The vibration of his chant sends a chill up my body, and I feel the air thicken around us. A breeze picks up as if in reply. Afterward, smoking a cigarette, he points his finger at me. "You," he says. "Who are *your* people?" I am startled and feel a rush of blood to my face, as stumbling I say that my fathers' people are from Scotland and my mothers' are from Wales. Mitig is looking for more than this. Some stories or songs, but I have none. He slowly rolls another cigarette, lights it, and inhales deeply, and then closes his eyes. "I see you way back, long, long ago, as one of the Picts." He emphasizes the word *Pict* and asks me if I know what he means. I say, "Hmmm, I've heard of them. Aren't they an ancient Celtic tribe?" He starts another song, this time a Celtic jig, looks pitifully at me, sorry that I can't say more or join in the song, and then laughs.

My Celtic heritage, though tinged with wistful longing, has often been a vague and abstract notion. Most of what I've read has felt too foreign, with strange myths, unfamiliar customs, and complicated names. With no family oral tradition left to help me find the breadcrumbs back, only a ghostlike shape remains and a tunneling hole where lies buried at the very bottom a small, tarnished key. Worst of it is, I don't even know what the key unlocks.

Why do I now sense a blackbird flying across my field of inner gaze with only one wing? It must be very hard to fly like that.

Maybe the thirst for knowing more of where one comes from grows over time or is serendipitously awakened by life events. Books, at the right time, can become keys.

A few months after my encounter with Mitig, *To Speak for the Trees* dropped in my lap. The author, Diana Beresford-Kroeger, is an Irish Canadian scientist with a unique understanding of ancient Celtic knowledge. When she described her early experiences as an orphan growing up in Ireland and the mentoring she received by wise women elders steeped in the Brehon tradition, I felt a jolt in my gut. I *recognized* these old Celtic teachings, the sense that all creation is sacred and interconnected. In the ancient lands of the Druids and Celts, trees were treasured for themselves and as sources of medicine, food, inspiration, and divination. (For most of history, trees have been revered, and forests have been filled with fairies and sprites and all manner of nature spirits.) In fact, the Brehon laws in antiquity, and well up into the seventeenth century, were so specific that the penalty for mistreating a tree was similar to that of mistreating a person.

Beresford-Kroeger speaks eloquently of the Celtic triad—the nurturing of body, mind, and soul—and the Celtic spiral of life, death, life. This Druidic understanding, dating back twenty-five centuries, is part of the universal lexicon on preexistence and rebirth. I take solace in knowing that *this* at least has been at the heart of my work for so many years. But it's been lonely work, braiding together a path, not recognizing the symptoms of uprootedness. (Only later will I learn that death rites and caring for the soul of the departed are key Celtic traditions.) I didn't know that a line runs through me, that a place of belonging was once mine, where kinship, nature, and wildness knit together with the seen and unseen worlds. To not know that the hollowness, the insubstantiality, the howling wind that leaves its drying mark within me is not my birthright but a *symptom* of the diaspora of our ancestors from a homeland and culture all but buried.

Buried, but obviously not completely forgotten, as I see how my body and soul have taken me on a journey of its own making. The rising up of an instinctual knowing happens at unexpected times.

I am on a camping trip in late July with some women friends, hiking through the pristine forest, and at one point we stop, awestruck at the beauty we have stumbled upon. Deep in the woods, we can almost imagine that no one has ever been here before. Our conversation turns to Indigenous peoples, who surely would have walked and hunted in these woods centuries earlier. We then imagine how it would have been to have white settlers arrive and state that they had been given the title to this land, the land that Indigenous peoples and their forebears had been on for as long as stories had been told. My friend, visiting from England, was quite overcome. Listening to her trying to grapple with this horror, I was struck that her forebears (and no doubt mine) would have experienced very similar displacements over centuries of invasions, gentry-enforced land grabs, and destruction of sacred groves of trees. She knew little about her distant past; nonetheless, her body seemed to vibrate with a sudden visceral knowing, waking up to a forgotten history, a fractured lineage.

Around the same time, I was struck by something a Scottish elderly friend said of her childhood, "My Irish and Scottish grandparents were steeped in the presence of their family members who had died and spoke of them as if they were in the next room." I could feel what this might be like, and tears poured out of me in recognition and longing. For so many years the very word *ancestor* felt borrowed; I felt something of an interloper in seemingly usurping its power and place from Indigenous peoples who use it freely and reverently. But now, rooting into my Celtic past, I am surprised by how embedded the notion is. The word has its hooks in me and wants to be known. In being led to this ancient door of my ancestral past, I seemed also to be awakening not just myself but those who reside there, in the "next room."

Wanting my own children to be aware of that doorway, one day I played the old tape recording of the interview I did with my grandmother to my daughter. Her face lit up at feeling her great-grandmother so vividly. "I like her," Elena said. "She spoke Gaelic! That's amazing! I'm so drawn to everything Celtic, the music, the moon, bonfires, wilderness, art . . . She must be part of the reason." From far off I imagine my grandmother's voice, 'S fhada bho nach fhaca mi sibh ban-ogha (Good to see you after a long while, granddaughter).

Growing up, I knew some stories of my deceased grandparents and a smattering of great aunts—Great Aunt Hannah, Marjorie, Maggie, Carrie. Strangely, there was a gap in people's recollections of the great uncles. Either they died early or were spoken of in a hushed way. Beyond their generation was even mistier territory. Gradually, a few more names were found, but it was not until a chance encounter of my sister's that a veil began to lift.

Carolyn was at a wedding in Stratford and began to talk with George, another guest. Through a strange coincidence, it was discovered that he was a long-lost cousin. We shared the same great-grandparents from the rural village of Finch, Ontario. Afterward, he sent a picture of the clan at a family picnic from 1948, and there is my then sixteen-year-old aunt Jean sitting in the front row while he, an infant, is being cradled in the back row. Through our newfound cousin, more branches of our family tree came alive. We next discovered that the first of our previously unknown forebears to cross the Atlantic Ocean in 1808 were named Nancy and Donald Hugh Cameron. I was delighted to find I shared the same name with my great-great-great-great-great-grandmother.

Time and distance shrink as I wave to these ancestors on the ship carrying them here. Looking for their names on the passenger lists, I am struck that all the men's names, under the heading "Reason for Emigration," are accompanied by the ominous words "farm taken from him," or "rent raised and could not live by it." They, too, had their crises, their leaky ships to board and perilous journeys to undertake. Such scenarios still resound around the world: people boarding ships, seeking refuge from trauma spanning generations, embarking on a new life in unknown territory.

In approaching the threshold to our ancestral past, the key to open the door may be in our manners. A beginning practice is simply to *say their names.* The very sound of such words has a particular kind of power; naming brings consciousness and is a direct way to connect with dead loved ones. Saying or singing the name, slowly and fully, and noticing the currents this sends forth, is a way to *remember* and *reconnect* to the person and to the greater worlds we inhabit.

Paying attention to this ancestral realm, naming my forebears, *saying their names* in my meditations, and imaginally following the long braid of relationships across an ocean seemed to awaken *us* to one another. The double helix of our genetic heritage, our physical as well as mystical inheritance, was coming alive in my hands. I had a series of dreams where one by one a deceased relative would appear, showing me that connections forged over lifetimes are never truly over, even when the relationship was not an easy one.

One dream is of my grandfather, Duncan McMillan.* My father's dad, or Papa, as everyone would have called him. He died two years before I was born and is known to me only in a black-and-white photo where he is sitting in an armchair, struck mute from a debilitating stroke years earlier. My sense of him was of a shadow at best, colored over by my very present and beloved and domineering grandmother. So how is it then that in my dream I am in a liminal space of forest and I feel someone with me—though nobody is visible? *An image forms, a sense coalesces, and the word* Grandfather! *awakens in the air*

---

*The surnames McMillan and MacMillan seemed to be interchangeable in the past, often leading to great confusion in sorting out family lines.

around me. As I peer about, I no longer see a dark shadow but rather a light in the distance, one that becomes a patch of a rainbow.

Once this interior bridge building and reconnecting got well underway, it became curiously mirrored in the outer world as well. Unbeknownst to me, my sister was digging deeper into the archives of our past and hit upon another gold mine of ancestral revelation. I didn't know what she was up to until a fat package arrived in the mail one day. It was a red binder she had put together of her detailed research, chronicling the MacMillan-Cameron lineage back past the ancestors who crossed the Atlantic Ocean, back through the time of the Highland Clearances, and even back through the time of the Battle of Culloden. At the top of the family tree is the name of my eldest known forebear: Ewen R. Cameron, Third Laird of Clunes, born 1655. Not only this, but details of some of these ancestors' lives showed up in John Prebble's evocative book about the famous battle in 1746—particularly that of my great-great-great-great-grand-mother Lady Mary Cameron and her mother, Mrs. Cameron. The dry bones of historical facts were reanimating. The Camerons, being solid Jacobites, were at the forefront of the battle. I learned that the infamous Commander Scott of the English army, in pursuit of any defeated rebels, tracked down what he thought to be their headquarters in Dun Dige so he could burn and sack it. The men scattered, while the Cameron women and their children of the household fled to a cave to take refuge. However, as the story goes,

> They burnt any cottage they saw, fired their muskets and hallooed the occupants into the heather. Five miles up the glen the road narrowed to a stony bridle-path. The mist was thicker and the birch and pine wept with it, but the detachment found Samuel's Cave and the women cowering there. All were stripped of their

clothes, although a petticoat was returned to Mrs. Cameron so that she might, as the soldiers said, hide her nakedness from them. . . . They struggled about . . . wounding the child [her son] in the neck. Mrs. Cameron lived in the cave for six months, well into the harsh winter.[1]

I have not read any of the novels in the *Outlander* series or watched the TV series; perhaps I should, as this might be a scene in it! I'm still enthralled with these new glimmerings of my Celtic past, my close ties with the hot-headed Bonny Prince Charlie—rough, tough, hurly-burly, passionate. I even recognize these characteristics from our boisterous, extended family gatherings. On the other hand, I also relate to a quip from a friend, "We Brits exchange jovial insults because we're too uptight and emotionally stunted to say how we really feel." Yes, also a long, long history of holding in the things that matter most. What is certain is that my own family shadow is braided into the complex reality of a culture steamrolled over, time and again. Yet, "if we carry intergenerational trauma (and we do) then we also carry intergenerational wisdom," writes Kazu Haga.[2]

Aha, the other wing of the blackbird coming into view.

And so it is in every family, hand over hand passed down, the good, the bad, the hard, the wise, becoming difficult to separate after a while. In the twisting and turning of these many strands, heat is generated, and it's in this crucible that an ancestor emerges, one very much present. As storyteller and mythologist Martin Shaw notes, awakening to our ancestors, letting them walk beside us, we open up to an "ancestral hot-line."[3]

How many ancestors to make a child? Southern Ontario playwright James Reaney counts back:

It takes

Two parents

Four Grandparents

Eight Great grandparents

Sixteen Great great grandparents

Thirty-two Great great great grandparents

Sixty-four Great great great great grandparents

One hundred and twenty-eight Great great great great great grandparents

Two hundred and fifty-six Great great great great great great grandparents

Five hundred and twelve Great great great great great great great grandparents

One thousand and twenty-four Great great great great great great great great grands[4]

Hello, all my relations!

My call to these Celtic Isles ancestors crosses the waters to a far shore, the land of *long time ago*—their return wave resonating back into the blood and the bone of my soul. An everyday aliveness with the natural world and the elements *is* my heritage. I'm landed, more grounded now, more formed, more found—less of an orphan with amnesia, as Stephen Jenkinson, writing in *Die Wise*, might say. Tracing a personal family line back into time isn't the only way to allow our ancestors room to speak. Perhaps a genealogical trail doesn't open for us or we reach a dead end (sorry), perhaps an adoption has happened—our biology is only one part of tuning into a past that lives in the present. The realm of ancestors includes *all* my relations, nonhuman life as well, as Indigenous people have always known. Tennyson reminds us of this, too, in the famous line from his poem "Ulysses": "I am a part of all that I have met."

I'm now struck by the dawning reality of becoming an ancestor myself. What will make me a *worthy* ancestor? My mind pivots, looking ahead, to my descendants. Trying to picture them and the landscape they inhabit. This requires a long vision and an empathetic picturing, not easy to do. Roman Krznaric writes of this in his book entitled *The Good Ancestor: A Radical Prescription for Long-Term Thinking*. He takes the perspective of deep time, posing the question: "How do we create a sense of shared identity with the unborn generations of tomorrow's world, the future people we can never meet but whom we must endeavor to embrace as our kith and kin?"[5] To do so is the making of a cultural revolution, one that will lead us out of a narrow preoccupation with short-termism and confer meaning by seeing ourselves as part of a much bigger picture—ancestors in the making.

Something is calling me to this shore, too. It's as if looking backward has loosened the confines of what constitutes time. I'm not the only one wondering about the legacy we are leaving future generations; suddenly, much of the world seems to be alarmingly aware of the perils. But the phrase *future generations*, while used a lot these days, feels abstract, making my mind go fuzzy and my attention go wandering. I need a way to focus, so I try to picture my grandchildren's faces, if there should be any. Fear enters.

I go for a long walk, babbling out loud, addressing my grandparents, great-grandparents, great-great-grandparents, asking them about these future ones waiting to be born. *Can* they be born? Grow up safe? Live with nature? Have clean water? Dark thoughts to be sure. An ancestor's voice speaks to my mind, *It's harder to be born.* Then, *It's not up to us.*

That night, I dream: *a child sits before me, looking into my eyes, absolutely still, present, with crystalline awareness.* The next night, another dream: *a small hand waving to me from far, far off in the starry night. With a bursting heart, I wave back, and we smile at each other.* Now, in the soft, early morning air, I listen. The unborn, our descendants, too, are more present than we imagine. And when their time comes to be here, how will they look back on us, their ancestors?

Me

Child

Grandchildren

Great grandchildren

Great great grandchildren

Great great great grandchildren

Great great great great grandchildren

Great great great great great grandchildren

Great great great great great great grandchildren

Great great great great great great great grandchildren

Great great great great great great great great grandchildren

Great great great great great great great great great grandchildren

Hello, descendants!

And now the memory of Baby June leaps forward. My friend Sue sent me a card with a bouquet of baby roses on it to acknowledge my great loss. We underestimate the depth of bereavement that miscarrying can bring, even an early one, hiding it, getting little communal support, thinking that it's a *no*-thing. When there is no ceremony, or mark, or moment to commemorate the nascent life we've sheltered, we don't know what to do with our heaving hearts and bodies. Such disenfranchised grief sends our sorrows underground, creating rivulets of malaise or anger that surface periodically or sink and make us leaden.

Baby June was due to be born on June 1, so many years ago, a surprise pregnancy, and with that some additional delight. But one morning, I woke startled, from a dream of bleeding, only to discover the reality upon getting up. Oh how I cried, and as I write this, I tear up again, recalling the grief of that day and those that followed, until that card of baby roses arrived from my friend. She, who had been through many miscarriages, knew. Quietly, I then began reaching out to this would-be child, letting my dreams of her go, while at the same time telling her we would always be together and that she wouldn't be forgotten. As I write I'm also now sensing and touching into a realm that is just here, there, all around and has this lovely presence within it. The rose card from my friend remains on my dresser, while Baby June remains within me, a star child, a gentle light just off on the periphery. Another message comes: I must walk slowly because so many presences surround me, making it hard to fit into some places.

I know women who've had an abortion who feel such a tangled mix of grief, guilt, and shame, along with relief, afterward. Like miscarriage, women who have gone through abortions know that the psychological burden is not insignificant. Most women try to move on and push these feelings away, but the important thing seems to be in conscious acknowledgment that a being has come close and that for a number of reasons it wasn't the time to welcome them. Having an inner dialogue with the unborn helps enormously. I suggested this to Nell, a sensitive, young Cree woman I met in my work at the hospital. In conversation, she admitted to still being troubled over the abortion she had two years earlier. I suggested she inwardly reach out and speak to this unborn child, letting him know he was a gift that couldn't be received at the time. Nell thought she wouldn't be able to feel the spirit of the child any longer, but I said not to worry; it's enough to speak from the heart. Nell wept in relief at just this thought. Later that night, she smudged and offered sacred tobacco and while focusing on the child spoke of the difficult circumstances that had led to the decision. She expressed her sorrow and regret and asked for forgiveness. What surprised her entirely was how much love surrounded her when she acknowledged and addressed the child directly. This seemed to liberate them both. Like a window opening, the conflict of her emotions cleared, and it felt like the child was telling her it was OK, he knew he might not stay, and now he could move on, freely.

The Māori concept of *whakapapa*, like other Indigenous world-views, gives us a sense of the deep well of connectivity that forms when we include lineage, ancestors, and place to our view of Earth and cosmos. As Krznaric notes of why we tend the dead, "It is the idea that we are all connected in a great chain of life that links the present back to the generations of the past and forward to all the generations going on into the future. . . . It allows us to recognize that the living, the dead, and the unborn are all here in the room with us. And we need to respect their interests as much as our own."[6] Although the words *lineage* and *ancestor* often only conjure up parental bloodlines, this is a narrow linear notion without this imaginative sense that our forebears are, indeed, present. *Here.* We are an integral part of a much bigger picture: What streams of knowledge and wisdom have I inherited? What is my spiritual lineage? Who and what has lent me life, including the mineral, plant, and animal world? And it begs the question, Am *I* carrying *this* inheritance responsibly?

It seems that tending the dead requires much greater imagination than we ever thought. In the corner of my eye, I see my Celtic great-great-great-great-great-grandparents nodding their heads.

The notion of intergenerational trauma is becoming a key for understanding our personal history. But it's also a key to understanding whole groups of peoples who have been affected by collective oppression and violence, the impact of which cycles through generations, like tumultuous waves rippling out.

Much is written about this. Simply put, from a psychological perspective, what was once violence and oppression from a perpetrator, or a political and social system, now becomes *internalized* oppression. The perpetrators of the past become the shadows and ghosts buried *within* ourselves, sabotaging and beating us up with self-recrimination, blame, and shame, attacking any sense of our own worthiness. Trauma is a wound that won't go away but persists, sometimes through generations. Without support for healing, a person may seek temporary relief in a number of ways, including numbing oneself in self-medicating addictions or externalizing inner rage and inadequacy through perpetuating violence against self and community, over and over. The repercussions on the collective psychology of a whole culture and people are barely acknowledged. Canadian Indigenous peoples have been pointing to this for a very long time.

For example, pretty much every time we're really upset with somebody, it's not about the present; it's about the past. We're remembering something, but not recalling it. In that sense, trauma has been called the tyranny of the past: the past is showing up and it's governing our present. The emotional upset, the pain and the hurt and the anger, have little to do with the present moment. It has to do with the memory of something that happened a long time before. Perhaps a *very* long time ago, as it seems we carry our ancestors, in part, by carrying their wounds; rejecting *our* troubled parts then becomes rejecting our ancestors, and vice versa.

For Nigerian writer Bayo Akomolafe, our ancestry is present and contemporary. *It is not a buried past.* The circular, "cybernetic" patterning keeps repeating. He tells us that listening diligently and humbly to the stories of ancestry is primary to finding ways through such trauma. Other researchers—like Thomas Hübl, Gabor Maté, and Peter Levine— agree, adding that it's not the hurt that causes trauma, it's being alone with the hurt, and that starting anywhere can change things. What is closest to you? Pain and physical and emotional symptoms, especially intractable ones that are hard to put a finger on, are our guides—they won't let us forget to pay attention.

Though the intergenerational trauma that impacts me is much more subtle and part of what constitutes "normal" in Western society (estrangement from nature, isolation, lack of meaning), and is nothing like the very close trauma of marginalized peoples, still a process of reclamation is necessary. Indeed, it seems critical for transformation of our collective culture. The noticing and making connections—the awareness that brings a first deep breath of understanding, self-compassion, and a trust in our inner knowing. It's a long journey, one where I find I'm bumping up against shadow parts of self, over and over, but then suddenly a hard edge will soften, dissolving into mercy for our human predicament, and understanding replaces judgment. In this world of trauma healing, the concept of quantum entanglement applies—that is, any shift affects everyone, modulating the tumultuous waves, letting them move on. Ongoing policies will intentionally break kinship ties and community mindedness, stoking divisions that promote agendas for control and power. But still, we must start somewhere to begin the unwinding of a perpetuating past, then trust in the intergenerational impact this will have on future generations.

Sally Berkovic, a writer and speaker on Jewish burial practices and a child of Holocaust survivors, poses a fresh and hopeful question to the theme of intergenerational trauma: "If our epigenetics change our DNA, like with trauma, can our DNA also be altered by great acts of kindness?—Like caring for the dead? Will future generations be molded by this?"[7]

9

Continuing Our Connection
beyond the Last Breath

Suffering occurs when you demand
reality be other than it is.

BUDDHIST TEACHING

Ar scáth a chéile a mhaireann na daoine.
(In the shadow of each other, we live.)

ANCIENT IRISH PROVERB

A stirring dream occurred a few weeks after Mum died. *It was Dad's birthday. In the dream, I've jumped into the cold lake at our family cottage and have become so cold there is no blood circulation in my hands. But Dad is there. He reaches out and takes my hands in his; and they are so warm, almost painfully warm. The heat rushes in, coursing through my body until I have to let go.* I awake from this intense dream still feeling the penetrating heat.

Shortly after Dad died, I had a distinct sensation and image that my arms were somehow longer—that I was seeing a picture of how Dad was going to be working through me, extending my grasp of things, enabling me to do and handle more than I could on my own. I'm wondering about this now, as I ponder this new language I'm learning, the language of the dead. I'm feeling a need to acknowledge and thank my father for this and to bring him more fully into this story. For I am seeing more clearly that it was his death, when I was thirty-seven years old, that became a primary teaching for my own ongoing apprenticeship with death. Certainly nothing that I could have predicted.

It's a vague impression I have of my dad as I grew up. Sometimes, vagueness covers difficult memories, things that don't want to be remembered. Other times, there is little to go on, a vacuum of sorts. I suddenly became aware of this lacuna when I encountered an elderly patient on the geriatric floor. Bernard, a warmly intelligent man in his eighties, had a red flannel shirt on and was sitting in his wheelchair when I approached. Sitting beside him, listening to his recall of his early family life, he suddenly stopped, and said to me, "You know, you listen to these kinds of stories all the time." He paused, awkwardly adjusting the tartan blanket covering his thin legs, and then went on, "I want to know about *you* and what *you're* thinking about. What is your take on the world?" A bit later, with soft eyes, he leaned forward and, relating to me as if I'm a daughter, tenderly asked, "And who takes care of you?"

I fell into complete countertransference at that moment. As psychotherapists, we learn about the pitfalls of identifying with clients to the degree that they become a stand-in for someone in our past. As I became his daughter, he became *my* father. Becoming aware of it is the main thing. Tears came to my eyes as I eagerly lapped up this fathering I was getting. And how I hungered for it. I tried to imagine what it would have been like to have a dad who saw me. Hmmm, father hunger, lots written on that. I was careful about how I related to Bernard after that; no one wins with transferences bouncing around, filling holes with the wrong person at the wrong time. But I had learned something very important about myself from him and about a father whom *I* couldn't see well.

My father, the oldest of five children, was born albino, with very white hair and very poor eyesight, though he had light blue eyes, not red. Was that remote cousin link between the grandparents closer than fabled? The next born, my aunt Irene, was also albino, then the gene skips over Uncle Hughie and lands on Uncle Gus. The youngest, Aunt Jean, was born with beautiful chestnut hair, and her high school voted her Miss KCVI in 1949. The word *albino* was *never* mentioned in our family. I didn't even know what it meant until much older and still didn't think it applied to *my* dad. Yet his poor eyesight, distinctive hair color, and small stature guaranteed he was the subject of bullying. He was considered stupid and illiterate in school because his first teachers didn't recognize he couldn't *see* the board or the printed page. But I thought of him as pretty smart, having grown up seeing my father voraciously reading history books and newspapers—albeit with a magnifying glass in one hand and his nose brushing up against the pages.

As an adolescent, I'm told, he became tougher, fighting back. A few days ago, I found his 1932 high school graduation yearbook online; I read the entry post and felt sad for him—as if he wasn't self-conscious enough: "Seyman MacMillan—Seyman works under the great handicap of poor eyesight. But they say you can't keep a good man down. So if that's true, a little bit of hard work, Seyman, and you'll make the rest of the class look pale. Best of luck."

Not passing the medical exam to enlist for war was a huge blow for both Dad and his brother, who also had poor eyesight. Enduring the shame of those momentous years, adding to what had already been placed upon him, continued to shape him. He learned to protect himself with a tough exterior and could be rough and rude at times. Yet he had a delightful mischievousness and a joviality that would endear him to others. This must have been what charmed Mum, along with his large family, who gave her what she was sorely missing. They got married in 1948, and he landed a job at the DuPont plant in Kingston,

Ontario, where he worked for thirty-five years, providing our family a modest working-class lifestyle.

The love of his life was our cottage on Rock Lake that he, his friend Tom, and brother Angus built. It became the love of my childhood life, too, anchoring me in the wild home of granite, pine, lake, and loon. Memories come back to me. Hiking to the pine point and jumping off the dock—cannonballs, stride jumps, back flips and front flips, over and over into the cold, deep lake. Gathering kindling, whittling the perfect green branch into a sharp point to roast wieners over the bonfire at night. Fire blazing, sparks soaring, marshmallows aflame! Oh, what perfection in the dusky, smoky night as a loon calls out and the mosquitoes bite my ankles. Later, crawling into the cozy double bed with my big sister. The smell of the fresh flannel sheets. The bug spray that Mum had duly administered moments earlier, pumped out of a pressurized spray gun, a cloud of insect poison, DDT, quickly exterminating any living little creature. (I shudder to think about this now.)

Nature was the gift he handed down to me.

Fast-forward to the end of his life. One night, as I was putting my kids to bed, I get an urgent call from my mother at the hospital. "Your father fell down the stairs and has probably broken his hip." She adds, grimacingly, "We've been here hours waiting to be seen, and he's in a lot of pain." And thus began a six-month odyssey of watching my dad, who had just turned eighty-one, steadily deteriorate in the hospital. A broken hip back in 1995 was a common death sentence for older people for whom immobility led to pneumonia. Surgery was not possible, physiotherapy was not enough, and there were no long-term-care options. It was a lonely, painful time for him.

I recall giving the eulogy at his funeral, no one else volunteering for the job. Afterward, my aunt said, "Nancy, that was moving, but I don't know how you could possibly have had the courage to stand up there and speak." A phrase slipped off my tongue, "You do one hard thing, and the next hard thing doesn't seem so hard anymore. Then you find you can do what you think you can't." I was referring to being with Dad while he was dying. While this was over twenty-five years ago now, it remains vivid. Something pivotal to my understanding of death happened that night, as I sat with him through the many long hours of his last breaths. It seems that being so close to him as he was trying to let go into death—too close it would seem—provoked an experience that is rather hard to talk about, but here's what happened.

Dad is laboring to breathe, and then at last, his breath just stops. For a long time. The sudden silence in the room is deafening. My father has died. But needing to be sure, I lean over to feel for a heartbeat, and then a voice speaks firmly from within: *Back away. This is not for you.* I'm leaning too far across a threshold and a force is pushing me back, as firm as if a person's hand is upon me. In my midnight liminal sensibility, I have the distinct sense that I'm encountering the Angel of Death. This is not a name I have even heard before. Dad takes a big inhale and resumes his staggered breathing.

I go back to the hospital cot and lie back down, rattled and more than a little awestruck. Somehow, I drift off to sleep, for how long I don't know. Then bang, unbelievably my cot collapses, and I'm on the floor. Jolted wide wake, I listen. I wait and wait, time suspended, and then at last, a faint breath heard.

Getting to his side, he takes one more soft breath, and this time it *is* his last. Looking at my watch, it is 2:10 a.m. I moan, "I don't want you to go." As I whisper prayers and fervent last messages, Dad's spirit rises up before me, and I hear the words, *"I'll still be with you and look over you, little girl."*

After phoning my mum and telling her, I spend the next hour being with him, not calling the staff—knowing that everything in the space will change once I do. I cry, I pray, I draw pictures, I move around the room in a kind of dance, weaving in and out with the currents of his releasing spirit. At last, totally spent, I go to the desk and tell the nurse manager. And yes, everything *does* change immediately. This helped underline that there is no rush after a loved one dies. This is *not* a crisis. This is a *sacred* time to be present to a profound liminal moment. While we may see death as a time of horror, Steiner tells us that from the other side, the moment of death stands out as the highest delight, the most beautiful reality in the period between death and a new birth, signifying the brightest beginning of spiritual life.

While Dad was in the hospital, I would visit him, bringing peanut butter cookies and coffee—it was our treat. So after he died, I decided to still honor this special time we had and continue our coffee-time chats. Sunday evenings, I took out Dad's picture, lit a candle, and then we "talked": I sang or hummed or read soulful texts to him. I found a poem by Albert Steffen, "I Have Made Ready a Room," and learned it by heart. It became a kind of mantra:

> *I have made ready a room*
> *Here in my heart*
> *With walls of warmth*
> *And windows of colour*
> *Towards every side of the cosmos.*
>
> *Oceans, mountains and clouds*
> *Are without;*
> *Within—loving and light;*
> *And here I invite you to come,*
> *Dear being I love.*
>
> *Lead me in what you have learned*
> *Now you have left your earthly*

> *Body with so long suffering*
> *And become a heavenly star:*
> *The up-rising in dying.*[1]

This time together brought comfort to me, at the very least. I didn't hear Dad speaking back in words, but my imagination allowed me to picture a bridge being built to him. This began my earnest consideration that there was more going on here than psychological comfort and that we really can connect with the dead. Moreover, I couldn't help thinking that those who didn't have a spiritual orientation in this life came to hunger for it when their personality dropped away.

A few years later, I came across a little book called *The Bridge over the River* that made quite an impression on me. Written by the sister of a man who died in the First World War, it is a series of communications that he gave from the spiritual world. The sister, in the quiet stillness of the night, would open her heart and mind to her brother, Sigwart, a highly gifted young musician. She gradually developed a conscious connection with him and, picking up her pen, would write what she heard as his words. I found my skin tingling while reading her account; there was something uncanny about what was written, which had a feeling of authenticity. One image offered by her brother is that after we die and shed our physical body, we have a gradual waking up. And those who are already in the spiritual worlds help those who have newly died know where they are, for it can take a while to comprehend this, especially in a sudden death. Another image given is how often after death there are profound realizations of how much more we could have done while on Earth, though our work continues, just on a much higher level. Moreover, those who've died want to be of help to the living and are ready and waiting for the invitation. They find it so deeply nourishing when we turn toward them, allowing the relationship to continue.

For me, there was a growing sense that this *felt* true. My body resonated with what I was reading. We, of course, must guard against delusions and wishful thinking and even spiritual trickery. Doubt is part of the terrain, as is becoming overzealous and self-interested, thinking that what speaks to us speaks likewise to everyone. But we must start somewhere with trusting inner experiences. Admittedly, many people have no inner sense of their deceased loved ones. Yet, even so, being able to grant this possibility is the beginning. In my work with people who are ill or bereaved, the conversation will often tilt to wondering what happens after death. Then the least likely people will suddenly remember unexplainable occurrences, odd synchronicities, perhaps the subtle presence of loved ones who have died. The question remains: How can we integrate these experiences and thoughts with the way we live and relate?

10

Grief, Communion,
and a New Conversation

There's love in there and love is all I got. Love and pain, and pain and love and it rolls around in this wild spiral, too quick to decipher with the logical mind so you let it all go and close your eyes and just feel it instead. I love my daughter and my love brings me agony. I have a broken heart and in amongst the rubble my steadfast love, imperfect and messy and whole.

TARA COUTURE, *SLOWDOWN FARMSTEAD*
(ON THE DEATH OF HER DAUGHTER)

Another world is not only possible, she's on her way. . . . On a quiet day, I can hear her breathing.

ARUNDHATI ROY, *WAR TALK*

Part of my endeavor in these writings is to help not only myself but also others find the courage to speak more intimately with loved ones in their dying days. I was shown the profound gift of this by a woman I met in the hospital named Estelle. A gifted artist in her mid-fifties, Estelle was stopped in her tracks one April day with a diagnosis of metastatic ovarian cancer. She was admitted when her blood count faltered after receiving several rounds of chemotherapy. The suddenness of this serious diagnosis meant that she was in shock. She was still trying to keep up with the fullness of her artistic commitments, not wanting to let anyone down, and optimistic that good news would surely come. Some days, however, she would be so angry that her mind wasn't clear even to do a few emails; other times, she would sleep all day, wrapped in misery.

Her husband, Matt, thought it was something *he* was doing that caused her mood swings. He would tiptoe around her, trying to appease, making embarrassed excuses to staff. I helped him understand that it had nothing to do with him, or anyone else. Estelle was accustomed to having so much vitality she didn't recognize herself without it, much less feel comfortable in becoming increasingly dependent upon others. Matt, in order to be more supportive, also needed to speak of his own needs and fears at a time when he thought he didn't have a right to. When he allowed himself to be vulnerable, they hugged and cried, neither having to protect the other. He became more consistent with his visiting times, knowing when to leave, go home, and take care of himself. Matt needed to do this self-managing to meet the long haul ahead. Estelle also needed the space to go through the many stages of reckoning with a shortened life. She reached out for more support to help deal with the emotional roller coaster and her spiritual emptiness, and in order to be more present when her family was there.

Similarly, the space between Estelle and myself was at first uncomfortable. She was focused on treatment plans and wanted answers and assurances that if she did such and such a treatment she would have longer to live. I didn't want to give her false hope, nor did I want to take away her sense of agency, so after reviewing the various pros and cons, I simply asked about her Plan B or Plan C. This gently led us into a hard "what if" conversation.

Over the seven weeks she was in hospital, I saw Estelle move through a range of emotions—not unlike Kübler-Ross's stages of grieving, healing, dying. Going through various versions of denial, bargaining, anger, depression, and acceptance is a process likely familiar to us when faced with dire situations. Estelle entered into all of these phases, albeit not in a straight line, gradually leading her to astounding clarity and acceptance. Healthy anger would still roll through, along with despair, but an inner quietness kept expanding. In the last two weeks, it was clear she was becoming less well, having trouble walking and sleeping more and more. Then swallowing became more difficult. Estelle was entering into the phase known as "active dying." I've seen this period be as short as a few days and other times extend up to three weeks. It's hard to predict, which can make it very stressful for families. But Estelle placed her attention on saying real goodbyes to friends and loved ones, one by one. I could see how she generously bestowed her remaining life forces on the many who surrounded her. Letting go and saying goodbye became a powerful *conscious* communion that left no one unchanged. What a privilege for all who knew her. And what an inspiration for how we can learn to die, tragically yet bountifully.

The reality for most of us, however, is that we feel we haven't had the chance to say what's most important, or haven't done enough for those we care for. Regret is a terrible thing to deal with. I wrote the following when I was surprised by my own feelings of guilt, weeks after Mum's death. Surprised because I believed I had done as much as possible to tend my mother's death *and yet* . . . a hole appeared.

> *Where are you, mother?*
> *After the festival of bringing you to the doorway of*
> *death,*
> *and blessing your way with flowers and prayers and*
> *tender holding,*
> *I am surprised by a hole,*

that seeks to be filled,
then I watch
as the hole starts filling in with remorse, inadequacy,
  guilt . . .

Better still to cry, filling hollow spaces
with tears that light the dark warmly.
Tears of praise and grief,
that softly sculpt an inner chamber,
—A cup, for my mother's essence to fill,
now a distilled stubborn spark of
love that carries on.

My work with the newly bereaved and now my own experience suggest that we seem hardwired to find a hole where what we did or did not do was *not good enough*. Then guilt and shame drive a wedge into that hole. Sometimes, this kind of soul suffering leads us to new understandings; other times, the shame and guilt of "not being good enough" is a whip that drives us down the well-worn neural pathway created in our childhood. Healing takes place when we don't push feelings of any kind away but let them live with us, with an acceptance, as raw as this may be. Fortunately, just as we may be hardwired to find holes to fall into when grieving, so do we have an innate part of us that seeks healing and transformation.

Bringing a discerning eye to the nature of our pain can be helpful. Mourning has a lot to do with our personal sense of loss and the undoing this means for us. Important and necessary as this is, in moments when we can let these emotions quiet, another dimension can possibly be felt—the very real dimension our beloved now inhabits. It's shaky ground, building this kind of new relationship, but over time we may get hints of their presence and the deep consolation they wish to bring.

Then, although grief may still be present, the *emotionality* of mourning can lift a bit.

A client of mine, Kay, speaks of being at her husband's side at the time of his death. Oh, how she misses him. She's been grieving for six months now, allowing her unraveling identity to coexist with her torn heart. She's a veteran, having gone through the pain of her first husband dying twelve years previous. What Kay has a lot of trouble with is other peoples' comments, varying from the earnest "How *are* you?" when she is on the elevator and has but a moment to respond to other people who uncomfortably avoid her or the topic entirely. "I'm becoming a recluse, wanting to hide away from social situations because it's so much work to help the other person feel at ease," she says, shaking her head. "But I know people are trying to be kind, and just don't know what to say. And there's nothing they can say that will help, really." I asked Kay what she thought would be good for people to know about being with a person who is in the deep end of grieving. She replied, "Well, when it's clearly a short interaction, something simple like, 'Thinking of you, Kay,' puts less pressure on me but is still acknowledging. Other times, I like when people say Roger's name, and bring up a nice remembrance of him. Something simple that makes me know he's not forgotten." Kay's voice grows quiet, "Sometimes, I'll get emotional and not want to talk further, but other times it'll make me smile, or even cry with someone. That's such a relief." The next session I asked Kay to bring in some photos. Holding them, asking for details and stories about their trips, the family gatherings, the family dog, brought us both to tears. A psychotherapist isn't necessary for this; we can do this for each other.

Kay has come to me for grief therapy, but I'm learning as much from her, as she has marvelously come to understand that grief is the natural order of things. Far from shrinking back from remembrances, she invites them in. Kay is recalling to me the details of Roger's long dying time, the arduous caregiving, the life stories, the backstories, the journeys, the guilt and the gratitude. She cries daily, her sleep is "the pits," but still she tells me, "I want to feel it all—I don't want to cover it up, numb it, or get stuck in it. No, I'm not happy. But I'm open, and curious. I wouldn't want it any other way."

Each Thursday evening, she tells me, on the day on which he died, she sits quietly, raises a glass to him, and tells him how she is doing. "I miss you, Roger." His response typically is "You'll be fine, Kay." One day as we are talking about this, a cardinal alights on the windowsill and peers into my office. Kay takes an astonished breath. Cardinals are her and her husband's favorite bird, and they are showing up regularly in her life these days. She takes delight in the synchronicity, telling me there is a folklore saying that "when a cardinal appears in your yard, it's a visitor from heaven."

It's not uncommon for the dead to make themselves known through nature. I've heard repeated incidents such as Kay's. Butterflies and honeybees especially seem to have a special affinity with the brevity of life and the presence of the dead, showing up out of nowhere at funerals and gravesites. In being open, and not overanalyzing, we can learn something about the language of the world our deceased are now a part of. Indeed, Chief Crowfoot, the leader of the Blackfoot Confederacy, in 1890 spoke to his people of his impending death with eloquence: "What is life? It is a flash of a firefly in the night. It is a breath of a buffalo in the winter time. It is as the little shadow that runs across the grass and loses itself in the sunset."[1]

Research is showing that rather than *seeking a final closure* at the time of death, there are ways we can build strands of continuity with our loved ones, and through this, grief may be more healthily integrated over time. Even Western psychologists, such as Robert Neimeyer, speak and write about cultivating a *continuing bond* with a deceased loved one. We are, after all, quite literally wired for attachment. And these attachments run deep, even with conflicting emotions that often come after a loved one has died. However, when there are abusive relationships, estrangement, and other unresolved issues, there can be even more to work through. Feeling anger, resentment, even hatred on one hand, and feelings of love and gratitude on the other, back and forth we go. Shame one minute, anguish the next, we can drive ourselves crazy, feeling something is wrong with us.

It takes time to sort through difficult memories that stand side by side positive ones. Sugarcoating problem areas, like we are tempted to do, is a way to hide from discomfort and stay in denial, while hanging on to anger and rejection undermines all concerned, both ways draining our energy and holding back the soul of the dead. Transformation and release happen with a loving and honest full picture. In difficult relationships it may take a lot of effort to find any redeeming memories. Sometimes, help is needed to find integration and acceptance, to bring both sides together—like two wings of a bird, or our two hands cupped and at rest upon our lap. A deep sigh follows. While living with the paradox of conflicting emotions and memories challenges our rational minds, it also lightens our burden by not having to make everything *fit* together and can ultimately make us laugh at life's many incongruities.

It was a client, Rhianna, who taught me this. She was in her late thirties and was desperately trying to crawl out of the dark tunnel of grief that she had been in since her husband died four months ago. On extended leave from work, she wasn't able to face her colleagues and clients. She didn't want to pretend to be OK, but that was what she had to do to get by. Her grief was mixed with the pain of the difficult last weeks of Jay's life, when he was angry and took it out on her, and her guilt at not being able to change anything for him.

As months went by, and she told and retold stories of this anguishing time, more came out. The relationship had been under stress for some time. Control issues, petty jealousies, and shouting matches had changed their blissful first years of marriage into a minefield, which compounded as he became sick and dependent. It was so hard for her to talk about this because of the guilt and shame she would feel at complaining, as if it meant she didn't love him and grieve him.

Her slumped shoulders, rapid respiration, speech, and avoidance of eye contact spoke the language of physiological stress. She complained of zero concentration and a choking feeling in her throat and a knot in her heart. This interplay of body, emotion, and the vagus nerve of our autonomic nervous system is becoming more understood, and with this the development of therapeutic somatic practices to help restore balance to our bodily selves. This is working from the bottom up, which then makes talking therapy more effective.

Important to this kind of work is first establishing a sense of safety and grounding. Then, depending upon the person and situation, eye movement and breathing techniques, sounding, and gentle movements can be gradually introduced. Rhianna and I did some of these simple exercises together so that she could then do them on her own. Over time, she gained more capacity to stay present and track troubling sensations, emotions, and images. Increasingly, she was releasing the stored-up nervous system tension that lay just under her swings of anger and sadness or her collapse into hopelessness. With her body more at ease, she found greater ability to face and accept the manner in which Jay died, and with her guilt lessening, she could bring more attention to the bigger picture of their relationship, one that held struggle as well as love.

As more months went by, she went back to work, went out with a few friends, and then hit another wall. There would be hours, and then days at a time when she would feel "normal"—and this was terrifying for her! "How could I be forgetting Jay already? What does that say about me?" Fear of forgetting one's loved one is normal—somewhere along the way you end up in what is sometimes called "the halfway house of grief," neither fully in it nor out. I encouraged Rhianna to pause and affirm this awkward new territory. She was becoming healthier and letting in life, like Jay would want for her. And I reminded her, she could find ways to keep a connection. What evolved was a way to honor and remember him daily that was satisfying for her. She placed their wedding picture, special mementos, and flowers on a shelf and developed an evening routine of lighting a candle and quietly reflecting—often crying, sometimes laughing at memories, and talking with him.

Rhianna would continue to be surprised at the waves of grief that could overtake her at unexpected times, but she was learning to ride them, knowing she would survive. She knew that sometimes she wouldn't get up off the couch, and other times she would. She realized she had not been entirely overcome by her grief, after all, and confidence was building. I read her a quotation from the poet David Whyte, and it resonated with what was now happening for her: "The death of anyone close to us is . . . a simultaneous goodbye to their physical presence and a deep hello to a more intimate imaginal relationship now beginning to form in their absence."[2] And, finally, Rhianna came to know that healing cannot take place in isolation and loneliness; she began to reconnect with friends and community. And then one day, she dared trust her heart to another again.

I for one haven't traveled the deepest realms of grief. Having a child die is surely the deepest loss to suffer. My heart still quakes when remembering, for example, the brutal pain of a friend whose teenage daughter was killed in a car accident. Such people can only be our teachers, showing us how to continue, daily, with no relief from having a heart that keeps breaking over and over. This is the high price of loving laid bare. But what of the child's experience?

Iris Paxino, a psychologist with unique spiritual abilities, writes in *Bridges between Life and Death* about her experience in connecting with children who have crossed the threshold, noting that "in contrast to the pain and despair felt by the grieving family, in the spiritual worlds the souls of children are welcomed with an exceptional amount of light and love."[3] She goes on to speak of the joyful atmosphere as they are greeted by angelic beings and deceased family members, and the help and comfort they want to send to their grieving loved ones. Also, she says that in most cases the early death had been planned before they had been born: "needing to only touch the earth like a drop" was how one child put it when asked why they left so young.[4]

When a dear one dies, we are first engulfed in the processing of what happened, its meaning in our lives, and the challenges to our identity. May we all have the help of a good listener for this! I was fortunate to be surrounded by friends, who heard the many tangled details of my mum's dying days and the aftermath, in the weeks and months that followed. (And still are!) Story is made through the telling. And this needs to happen over and over so we can build a big-enough story that can hold meaning and purpose, allowing some loose ends to stray and be lost in the mystery, while allowing other threads to organically transform through the telling. So if a friend sounds like they are repeating themselves with their story of loss, listen again, ask again. And if the pain of the story makes your heart quake, stay with it, don't flee. Our simple presence and willingness to enter the darkest void with another always allows something yet to stir.

In exploring a kind of integration that goes beyond the emotional and psychological, I'm finding it intriguing to imagine a *distilled essence* of a loved one who has died. Robert Sardello helps us understand that we can bridge the separation between those of us "here" and those in the "Greater Life" by noticing from within, where there is no separation between our "seeing" and "who is seen."[5] In our contemplations, in addition to saying their names from within our heart, he suggests, for example, that we call forth a characteristic gesture or a signatory quality of a loved one. In doing so we may catch a glimpse of a unique spirit that lives on unbounded by time, allowing an immediate resonant connection. Right now, I'm gazing at an old picture of Dad holding his new granddaughter, Elena, wrapped in a snuggly. He is awkward and tentative, holding her gingerly, a little away from his body, pride and delight in his mischievous eyes as he looks into the camera. It makes me smile. It seems to encapsulate his particular essence, kind of elfish, kind of rough, and kind of vulnerable in showing his tender side. The next instant, I am feeling him up close to me, smiling with me. Personal grief lifts a little in these moments.

I wanted to avoid talking about my dog. How can I speak about my dog's death in the same space as a human death? There is no comparison, yet my wrung-out heart knew I had undergone a deep passage, however short-lived. We can't deny how our hearts bleed when a beloved pet dies. Often, it is our first experience of death, an initiation into the pull and power of grief. After all, our pet can become a soulmate—how could we *not* feel such a loss? Our family has buried many cats, birds, a guinea pig, and now two dogs. Digging in the earth, placing the soft animal body gently in the hole, leaving offerings of food and flowers and kind words of blessing, all have accompanied these sojourns. Crying together as a family, while heaping praise on "the best dog ever," has helped our children taste death, be both moved and practical in its midst, and begin wondering about its mysteries.

Our old goldendoodle, Mali, was sick for a long time, though she appeared as happy and attentive as ever. When it finally seemed like she would hang on forever, just to make us not suffer over her death, I realized that it was time to let her go. An agonizing phone call was made to our vet, the appointment made. I would have loved for her to die naturally. I once heard the Dalai Lama speak of the gift we give our pets when we lovingly tend them at the end of their life, helping them cross over into death in a more liberated way. So I kept holding out for that: she seemed so close to death so often. Yet I've learned that it is very hard for dogs to die that way. She kept wanting to spend long times outdoors, even in the cold, and I realized she was instinctually looking to curl up on the earth, somewhere under a bush, in order to let go. She needed to be released from the tug of devotion that kept her here for us. I didn't let her, though; I was too protective, wanting her close by, thinking I could help her. I wasn't letting her be an animal in the wild. Our pet friends benefit greatly from becoming part of our families, but is there a hidden cost of domestication? *Sigh.* So it took a trip to the vet for Mali to be released.

Perhaps the more one experiences the keening wails that break open the walls of grief, the more readily accessible that pathway is. Driving home with Michael in the car, Mali's very still body in the back seat, I cried with abandon. There was just no choice. On and off for a day and a half I was gushing tears. Then, that night, I had a dream. *Mali was in the sky, and I was with her. My long hair caught in her fur. She was trying to tell me to cut the tangle, and at last I did, allowing her to keep going, and me to return to the ground.* When I awoke in the morning, I felt the joy that was released through my sweet companion moving on and joining in with life abundant. Though I felt like I'd been through the wringer, there was also a peculiar soul satisfaction in drinking from this unlikely brew of sadness and joy. I even found I enjoyed missing her. The void she created was like a real space that was ironically filled with her presence.

I don't know how animals pass through death's door, but it does seem with more ease than we do. Do we meet our animal friends again? Steiner mentions somewhere in his prolific lectures and writings that after we die, we are greeted joyfully at the threshold first by the animals that we have loved throughout our life. I'm not such a literalist to think that means I'll be petting Mali and throwing her a stick again but rather that the love that has bonded us remains and is experienced again.

Journal Entry: Mali Metamorphosis

Mali rolling in a dead snake: dream just before she became sick. Mali and I find a run-over, painfully dying snake on the road: two weeks before she dies. A baby snake slithers by in the sun: day of Mali dying.

Animal death is a topic that grips some of us, be it due to the threat of species extinction, through hunting, or through factory farms that deny animals their dignity as they are forced into becoming a commodity of consumption. These are matters that deserve thoughtfulness and entail seeing around more corners than I can muster. But a series of dreams has helped me to wonder, to invite in a bigger perspective. The word that kept coming to me was *sacrifice*, a word, admittedly, that carries a lot of baggage. A salmon, in my dream, told me to sit down beside him, to make a feast and partake of his flesh. Happy he was to be honored and fulfilled in this way. Likewise, the steer, who after a contented life of grazing grass, invited the knife to its neck, willingly surrendering himself to the purpose of providing nourishment for a community.

It seemed I was being shown what "joyful sacrifice" means. Oxymorons, like Zen koans, can take us out of either/or thinking and into a third possibility. What does joyful sacrifice mean to me as a human being? Giving up my ego need to always win? To be right? To be comfortable, happy? Sacrifice not out of a dour martyrdom but out of seeing the bigger picture where we are interrelated with everyone and everything. And where, surprisingly, something akin to joy breaks through. I sit with these paradoxical thoughts and add them to my growing wondering on how to be with the killing of animals that can be in sync with the greater cycles of life, as Indigenous peoples have always known.

True animal husbandry, the art of farming animals with care, is something to behold. Having a number of friends who farm in this manner has given me a picture of what this can look like. Not backing away from the cycle of life and death but being tutored by it, entering into it with practical awe, devotion, and gratitude. It gives me hope that a middle way is possible and necessary. How sad a rural landscape would be without seeing cattle grazing contentedly on real grass! The landscape, the soil and its numberless inhabitants visible and microscopic *need* the cow, the bison, the goat, the pig.

I've spoken about integrating opposites, living lightly with paradox, deepening into the present, and finding the essence within all things—ingredients for living, dying, and grieving. Today, though, we are challenged not just to consider our own endings but also those far greater. Holding the dying and grief arising from all directions in these rapidly changing times can seem personal, yet goes way beyond. It's about communal grief now, yet we're ever more isolated. Without a cultural container or ritual way for holding this grief, we're at the mercy of swirling collective emotions, where contagion-like fears, panic, and paralysis hold sway.

It's new terrain for us. We need to be awake to what's going on in the outer world, enough to unravel our old comfortable self, the one that wants everything to stay the same. At the same time, we must guard against losing ourselves in adrenaline rushes from the constant feed of information preying upon our fears. This is psychically demanding work. Not knowing what to do is a good place to start. After all, our usual moorings have come undone, and finding steady ground can be elusive. All I know is that there is no way around *feeling* grief, opening up bodily to sorrow, not for ourselves but for the sake of another or for the world. Then something is created. I think it is love. And love frees us from fear. In this time of grieving for Earth and the despair around world issues, we deepen. Clearing our minds, softening our hearts, engaging our courage, we find what matters most and aren't diverted. This will strengthen the communal, rather than weakening it. Ultimately, these times are not just about endings but about beginnings as well.

Allowing ourselves to grieve in relationship with others is now necessary, for the space between you and I is the medium where something new can enter. Though how we do this may seem baffling, I think small ways are good, allowing for immediacy and particularity. I remember being filled with sorrow when learning of Sudan, the last northern white male rhino, dying in Kenya. Reaching for a way to express this, I wrote the following poem:

White Rhino Remains

Ashes, portals and places
seeking to be lit with ceremony,
ancestors pushing through
and my body hurts.
A white rhinoceros crossed over
the other night,
she now lives here, in my heart.
—A grave freshly made
of piercing grief and tender holding.
Feelings stretch me taut, like the skin of a drum
That I don't know how to play.

Then I went online, trying to get a good picture of the northern white rhino. There I found an artist who had devoted himself to painting rhinos as his way of being with this latest extinction. I ordered a print of his beautiful watercolor painting, while sending him my poem. Our brief exchange was so tender, and somehow marking this death with someone else in this small way lit up my soul, so that now mixed into my grief over Sudan and white rhinos is this heartful moment.

Alas, we are not much good if we wring our hands and are paralyzed with gloom. So how are we to be with the woes of the world? I posed this question to a man in a dream one night. His kiss and the word *eros* written in red was the response, while in the background I'm shown honeybees ardently lighting upon blossoming trees. Love expressed through passion and desire within the natural world is a creative, fertile force indeed. Is this an antidote to deadening thoughts and forces? Surely, being struck in the heart by Eros's arrow of enchantment for Earth opens us to relationship. In the myth, when Eros and Psyche, which means "soul" in Greek, eventually marry, there is pure ecstasy, and *joy* arises. Though we're speaking imaginally, what happens here filters into our reality. Harnessing a drop of Dionysian energy, likewise, may serve to reanimate the world, enabling us to act as ardent co-creators. Then, our smallest heart attention has potency, bringing fertility and renewal to ourselves and all things. Maybe even a little joy, as both nature and our ancestors rejoice.

Indeed, all the climate action in the world will amount to little and be usurped by the same old power grabs until we come to know our Earth as the living presence she is. With the miraculous bounty that springs forth when we tend seeds in good soil, she reminds us there is enough. With clear eyes we see the beauty that is real and present and remember that Earth has the power of fecundity, self-repair, and evolution on her side. And yes, also death. Our planet is not immortal. Still, there are many versions of the future being shaped as we listen and shape ourselves. And then like the artist Estelle, whom we met at the beginning of this chapter, we too may find a new conversation happening: that standing beside our paralysis and grief is the heart intelligence and communion that will equip and buoy us for uncertain times ahead, even death. Like two wings of a bird, as Rumi would say, beautifully balanced, allowing for steady flight.

11

The Spiritual Road
to *Ars Moriendi*

You've got to learn to do everything lightly. Think lightly,
act lightly, feel lightly. Yes, feel lightly, even though you're
feeling deeply. . . . Lightly, my darling, lightly. Even when
it comes to dying. . . . So throw away all your baggage and
go forward. There are quicksands all about you, sucking at
your feet, trying to suck you down into fear and self-pity
and despair. That's why you must walk so lightly.

ALDOUS HUXLEY, *ISLAND*

Like the chess game that I couldn't win by cleverness, there have always
been other ways to perceive and know things.

Potential seems vast when we liberate ourselves from the fixedness
of either/or thinking that our language limits us to. Possibilities flour-
ish, and things like tending to our dead, the space between death and
rebirth, and the space between you and me become natural extensions
of living our human lives. This is the place of the heart, the place of
soul, interwoven with life and the world in all its forms and colors. *Soul*
may mean different things to different people. It's hard to pin down,
and that's OK. A word with many layers, like ourselves, it keeps evolving. In comparing it with the word *spirit*, James Hillman, the great
archetypal psychologist, expresses it this way: "Soul likes intimacy;

spirit is uplifting. Soul gets hairy; spirit is bald. Spirit sees; soul feels its way, step by step, or needs a dog. Spirit shoots arrows; soul takes them in the chest."[1]

I wonder if these spirit arrows, working their way through skin and bone, can reveal a different kind of light, the light that lives in the darkness. Exploring this liminal space through the words that we've inherited, I say the word *soul* slowly, savoring the long vowel sounds, drawing out the *l*, and feel a bodying, a relatedness, a roundedness with the sound, and then an ache in my heart. I now say the word *heart*, again slowly, and feel the fullness of the word as it shapes my lips and mouth, with the *t* providing a surprising, crisp alertness to the currents of warmth I'm sensing within and radiating outward. I linger in this embodying place, but it's hard to sustain. Maybe this is because I'm focusing inwardly. Now, turning myself inside out, moving particle to wave, as it were, I'm feeling heart and soul containing *me,* not the other way around. A warm cape is ensouling me in the many colors that connect me to everything. Is this what's called *anima mundi,* or "soul of the world"?

What about spirit? "As soon as Jesus was baptized, He went up out of the water. At that moment heaven was opened, and He saw the Spirit of God descending like a dove and alighting on Him" (Matthew 3:16, *New Living Translation*). Spirit has this sense of an infinite cosmos pouring down upon Earth and upon all us creatures. Perceiving this light from above, and relating with it, was the task of the great initiates, shamans, priestesses, and prophets over time.

Spirit light descending; Earth light arising. And where do they meet? Here. In the center. The human heart.

But it's an evolving, circuitous journey of hard labor to get to this mysterious simplicity of being. Religion grew out of meaning-making: the need to make sense and give expression to the awe, wonder, and mystery of nature, life, and death. But over millennia, once institutionalized, it can feel like there's but a trickle of living spirit remaining. Is that enough?

I'm pondering my own trickling spiritual journey now, my own life review underway, as a means to help me understand how I have come to relate to dying and death. Our own biographies tend to be full of teachings.

I have a memory of great religious confusion when I was seven years old. My Portuguese friends next door were celebrating their first communion—two little girls dressed up like brides at a wedding in white, frilly, crinoline dresses, surrounded by their big family, posing with flowers in their hands for the cameras. There was a palpable undercurrent that identified them as separate and different than us. Yet still, I say to my mother, "When will I get to wear that kind of dress for church?" She replies, "You're Protestant not Catholic. We don't do that." I was shocked. I knew myself as Catholic; I was sure I was Catholic. "They are the Protestants!" I argued, sure she was wrong.

Later, I discovered the strong Catholic line in our ancestry, one covered up because of religious shame and hostility. My Protestant grandmother married my Roman Catholic grandfather, proceeding to banish any reminders of his faith. As for his side of the family, I can only presume they thought this intermarriage sin would lead to hell. In a strange twist, looking at birth records, I only recently learned that my father was actually baptized Catholic but never knew it. (I suspect a deal was brokered and then reneged.) So I wasn't so crazy in my childhood insistence on being Catholic after all. Maybe this also explains my being drawn to the incense and the mysticism—but no creeds, doctrines of damnation, or papal obedience for me, please!

My grandmother's intolerance toward Catholicism, and vice versa, has to do with generations of divisive history, politics, battle lines, and clan warfare that still bleed forward in time. The riotous snowball fights that broke out on the street that separated my public school and the local Catholic school in the sixties had a serious, dangerous edge to them. I was totally perplexed, scared but also a little excited at the terrible cunning of some of the boys, who would climb to the school's rooftop. From this vantage point, they would pelt the St. Pat's boys, who were in turn hammering those of us trying to cross the street from the safety of their enemy outposts of snowbanks. Until the police were called. Intolerance seems to find a home anywhere, in any time period, if we let it in and pass it down.

Growing up in a minimally practicing Protestant family, I absorbed the simple fact that when you die you go to heaven (or hell, though that was soft-peddled). So yes, a continuity of spirit was assumed. My memory of Sunday school classes at Zion United Church is hazy; mostly I remember the sun shining through the stained-glass windows, the smell of polished wood, and a picture of Jesus, a tanned, handsome man with a beard, on the wall. I liked the stories, too, me sitting on a small wooden chair while the Sunday school teacher read from a picture book. I loved to feel immersed in something bigger than myself, to sense awe and reverence. I was told that Jesus was the gateway to everlasting life, that prayer was important and could influence things. I took this really seriously when I was nine years old, when my beloved black cat Whiskers was sick and dying. I intensely and devotedly sat by his side almost every waking moment of the day and slept beside him at night, murmuring encouragement and praying for him to live. Much to everyone's surprise, Whiskers rose from his deathbed, firmly attached himself to me, and lived for many more years. Something otherworldly had happened, that I was sure.

I yearned for church as a child. When my mother stopped wanting to go, I was at a loss. I would sit at the front window watching other families walking to church and feel such a pang that I was missing out on something essential. In grade seven, I had a friend, Lee Ann, who attended the Good Shepherd Anglican Church, and I wangled my way into going with her to Sunday school for confirmation class. Confirmation class was what you did when you were twelve, allowing you to become a full member of the Church of England. But in this white, clapboarded little church, Sunday school was a brouhaha, with a dozen or so high-spirited adolescents whom some well-meaning mother was trying to corral into memorizing the confessional creed—the criteria for "passing." I was able to recite the lengthy creed after a while, and I kind of liked the feeling of a church full of people mumbling together; it had a mysterious drone-like chant if you didn't focus too much on the actual words. But the words *were* there. And some would stick in my throat. Especially the sentence: "We believe in one, holy, catholic, and apostolic Church." For some reason, I couldn't get past that sentence. It felt wrong. Shortly before the final confirmation ceremony, I quit.

This quest for a place to belong in spiritual community then went underground but would occasionally get awakened. I *wanted* to like church, but my experience always fell short. I experienced the numinous within and around me in nature and expected this in church, rather than being preached to and made to feel bad or made to feel good, a play of emotions rather than a deepening into substance and meaning.

The need for something real and substantial took hold through my passion for social justice. This began in my teenage years after seeing the newspaper images of starving and dying children in sub-Saharan Africa. I can't help now recall, however, that as a child I was endlessly intrigued about the dramatic reporting of my father's cousin, Hector, a missionary in the African Congo. He was kidnapped as part of an international hostage crisis in 1964; later, he was shot, killed in front of his wife and children. I remember watching the grainy black-and-white television images, not really understanding but feeling the gravity and exoticness of this traumatic event. I now connect this to the additional memory of seeing myself, at age six or seven, running around the kitchen table, exclaiming, "I want to be a missionary in Africa when I grow up"—much to my parents' horror! The missionary ambition died out, but my interest in Africa and the world did not. It led me in high school to write editorials to our local newspaper, with headings such as "The Real Price of Our Steak," and ultimately to study international economics in order to support third world development.

The world opened up for me the day I got accepted into the World University Service of Canada's seminar program in Sri Lanka. A world of color, blasting horns, throngs of people, overcrowded buses, the lone boy pounding rock to make gravel. And tea plantations, Buddhas, and banyan trees. I was overwhelmed for weeks until one afternoon, drinking from a king coconut, I suddenly "landed." Clear as a bell, I woke up and could look around, taking in the dynamic Ceylonese culture, diving into it, meeting young Tamil Tigers in the forbidden north, sleeping on beaches, getting robbed, mobbed, and . . . I better stop. I'm looking over my shoulder right now, thinking of things I never told my mother, things you don't tell your mother. Though now I think she'd smile, envious at my opportunities for adventure. The friends I made in these travels were my first kindred companions—others who really thought about the world and struggled with philosophical ideas and religion. A few years later, I found a home within the aims of liberation theology and nonviolent resistance. This promised more than a trickle of spirit, at least in its passion to right the wrongs of the world. This was the 1980s when the peace movement was in full swing. I met with like-minded activists envisioning a better world who were willing to march at protests, be arrested for civil disobedience, travel to far-off countries, and find creative ways to awaken people to what was happening around us.

A memorable moment was dressing up as clowns and joining the Toronto Santa Claus Parade as a means to clandestinely hand out buttons and flyers that said "Don't Buy War Toys." We hadn't meant to but when the order was given to begin the parade, we edged our way to the front and ended up leading it! The children loved our antics, but our celebrity placement was quickly ended once organizers caught on to what else we were up to.

During this time, I spent Friday afternoons at the local drop-in shelter. I would make sandwiches and coffee and talk to the people who came around—often homeless men and women. My friend Rosemarie joined me, then Chris, and soon it became a place where we all hung out, playing cards, singing, listening to hard stories, joking, and making friends with a side of life beyond our known world. It seemed easy then, to just be part of community, in whatever way it showed up. My day job was teaching ESL (English as a second language) to women workers in the garment factories; my night job was attending meetings. The spiritual communities that anchored this involvement for many of us were important—they helped root our actions in reflection. Mostly in our twenties, we were the best of friends, living passionately, as one should at that time of life.

However, after an intense period of such passionate living—traveling as a group to aid Nicaragua during the Contra attacks; being arrested and jailed for a week for civil disobedience at Litton Factory (where they manufactured the guidance system for the cruise missile); being an organizer and keynote speaker at a large antiwar rally in Toronto—I reached my limit and crashed pretty hard. A long period of malaise and uncertainty followed.

Thinking back to these tumultuous times, I experience a mixture of thrill, embarrassment, and shock and horror. Our love affair with ourselves and the world buoyed us up, but our lofty ideals made us prone to self-righteousness, cynicism, and martyrdom, the dark twin of the impulse to do good. But there was more to it, for we had broached another kind of threshold, leaning into the dark underbelly of greed, power, and control. Being followed, having our phones tapped and apartments broken into and searched were all heavy things for young, idealistic, nonviolent activists. Feeling the tentacles of power that held sway, linking corporation, government, and law enforcement, became very disturbing. We weathered the consequences of challenging it for a while, but it wiped away our innocence and vulnerability, replacing it with a much greater soberness and wariness. I wasn't the only one to step back from this abyss once glimpsed.

Laughter can break forth when the opposites of life come together. So it was that, in an unlikely turn of events, I took a mask and clown course with legendary theater teacher Richard Pochinko. This, more than anything, brought me back to my inner self, cracking open creativity, intuition, sacredness, and fun—a clear living stream of what I craved as a child. What a paradox to find the deep end of soul work not in a church but in a downtown Toronto warehouse. Three times a week, we gathered and faced ourselves, standing counterclockwise in six directions: north, east, south, west, below, above. Integrating our many selves through mask work, plunging into oceans of sorrow, touching the sun with our fingertips, giggling like children, each of us was reborn a clown.

"If you don't know what to do next, put on your clown nose and follow it," summed up Richard's approach to finding one's direction. When I still struggled with where to go with my life, he saw into my ragged soul and offered the following sage advice: "Nancy, if you go looking for the bad in the world, your life will run flat, but when you look for the good, your life will soar." This advice reset my compass. Once, he took me aside after a rehearsal, saying, "I can tell by your mask work that you are a very old soul . . . and I dreamt last night that you were a spirit helper of mine." I was taken by surprise; I was far from the talent that many of the actors in the class had, so I indulged in this other kind of affirmative message.

Richard died a few years later. It was the era of AIDS, and once he contracted it, he quickly became very ill. When I received a phone call from a friend saying he had died, I was stunned. Looking out the window, into the woods behind my little country house, I remembered his words to me about being a spirit helper for him, and they seemed to echo into the present, into the immediacy of his death. I didn't really know what to do, or what help he might need. Feeling burdened with other life dilemmas at the time, I didn't even go to his funeral. I squirm now thinking about it.

As years went on, I kept sniffing out spiritual trails that eventually led me to both nature-based spirituality and to the more esoteric branches of Christianity and other religions. Out of this a deep and vast picture arose that featured more connections than contradictions, especially where dying and death were concerned. At the outset, my grasp on the history of Christianity was pretty vague, something that would make my eyes glaze over or would cause me to recoil against the dogma and the many repressive acts done in its name. However, I became eager to learn more when I found out that in the first centuries of Christianity there were far-ranging topics of debate. It was a time when what we now call Eastern and Western streams were not so differentiated. Many followers challenged the literalist interpretation of scripture, appreciating instead the different levels of understanding that come from metaphor and the timeless seeds of wisdom contained in the parables. In these early days, reincarnation was pondered. This really should come as no surprise given that such knowledge was embedded in the more mystical roots of Judaism and predates world religions as a whole. The earliest believers struggled to find consensus as different sects formed with the accompanying plays for power.

One such sect was the Gnostics (*gnosis* is a feminine Greek noun meaning "inner knowledge or awareness"). Generally speaking, Gnostics experienced Christ as an initiate who kindles the divine inner spark of light in each of us, enabling us through practice and inner training to know sacred truths for ourselves. They believed in repeated earthly lives, casting death and what happens afterward in a light more consistent with ancient wisdom traditions. According to the Gnostic teacher Theodotus (c. 140–160 CE), the Gnostic is one who has come to understand who we are, from what we are being released; what birth is, and what is rebirth.

However, in the highly political period of institutionalizing Christianity and determining what would constitute the canon of the New Testament, the practice of rewriting, redacting, and suppressing original manuscripts was pervasive. An example is the Gospel of Thomas, a text that was initially prized and then fell out of favor. Why? Perhaps because Jesus is shown to be more interested in illumination, love, and the kingdom of heaven found within than he is with sin and judgment. Not surprisingly, Gnosticism became heretical.

It would be centuries later, in 1054, when what had grown into the Roman Catholic Church split with its Eastern Orthodox counterpart, essentially over political differences. Then, there were the crusades and inquisitions—the series of religious wars that sought to conquer first Muslims and later nonconforming "heretical" Christian communities. The Cathars—a deeply spiritual and community-oriented people who believed in reincarnation and the equality of women and men and who cultivated inner knowing in a way reminiscent of the Gnostics—were systematically burned at the stake between the twelfth and fourteen centuries. Their crime? Not adhering to the hierarchical structure of the Roman Catholic Church. So complete was this genocide that we barely know anything about them. (Though there is a resurgence of interest in their beliefs and way of life.) What we do hear, through anecdotal stories written down at the time, is that when their defenses broke down after a lengthy period of resisting nonviolently, they uniquely showed no fear as they were led into massive bonfires. Rather, they held hands and sang as they surrendered themselves to the flames. During the siege of Montségur, in France, a community of Cathars surrendered to the forces of Louis IX, and over two hundred of them were burned in a bonfire. A monument commemorates their deaths, reading, *Als Catars, als martirs del pur amor Crestian. 16 de març 1244* (To the Cathars, to the martyrs of pure Christian love. 16 of March 1244).

Eventually, the Protestant Reformation in the sixteenth century forever changed the role of the Roman Catholic Church in the lives of every European. Protestant denominations are now almost count-less around the world, but with little trace of the esoterism of these early Christian communities. Instead, this understanding had to go underground, with the hope that a day would come when it could be known again. As for present-day Christianity with all its diversity, some basic tenets are held in common, like the ten commandments and the preeminence of love. And imagine how radical our society would be if we adhered to them! But so much else has got in the way—especially surrounding what death entails—bringing confusion and anxiety to words like *judgment, heaven*, and *hell*.

In my work as a registered spiritual care practitioner, when a patient identified as, say, Christian, Jewish, Muslim, or Sikh, I listened carefully to what this term meant to them, since it can vary so much. Interesting conversations transpired, and I got to know the person behind the word. When someone said they were agnostic or atheist or lapsed, I would likewise look behind these words to discover what it meant to *this* particular person. Ultimately, there would be similarities because we would be talking about values and feelings, about where meaning, strength, and acceptance could be found.

For most people, the early influence of even a nominally religious upbringing would work its way to the front, becoming something to look at again. Often, this could be reckoning with an image of God that has become outmoded. A God on high looking down upon us, instilling fear of judgment and a strict morality, is one that serves few. It seems that this voice is really our own merciless inner one. When we can let *this* voice soften, accepting our many-sided selves, a final surrendering to an all-compassionate loving Source may find us well at the end of our days. In seeking solace from something larger than ourselves, comforting images of God ingrained from childhood often regain focus. For those from a Christian background, this might be the Lord's Prayer or Psalm 23. Then, there can be times when someone, pressed over the edge of their usual sense of self, will have a felt experience of something greater or something deeper accompanying them through their dark night of the soul. This may come as a surprise, becoming a rudder in what might otherwise be a sea of fear and chaos. A deeply felt experience creates an inner knowing much sturdier than belief.

However, while the formative force of religion, or spirituality, on our collective psyche continues to shape our deepest values, it also, alas, shapes our deepest neuroses. Depth psychologists would say that the instinct to serve something bigger than ourselves, something evoking awe and gratitude, is so embedded in us that, if it is not filled, it is in danger of being usurped by a religious-like fervor for something else. That might be adherence to a narrow rationalism, a materialism now in service to unbridled technology, or perhaps the moralistic or dogmatic stance driving any "ism." In other words, we all pray to something.

I was literally on a mountaintop when I first began meditating. I was living in the Yukon, working out of the Native Friendship Centre with Vietnamese refugees who were relocated there, and reading an eye-opening book, *Zen and the Birds of Appetite* by the radical Catholic monk Thomas Merton. Merton upended the Catholic world in the 1950s and 1960s with his great interest in Eastern thought. This led many young people on a journey to rediscover and reclaim the mystical element present but long obscured in Christianity by learning from Buddhism. I was no exception, and his simple style of writing and impassioned call to inner silence had me closing my eyes on that majestic mountaintop, beginning my first clumsy attempt at meditation.

Buddhism is complex and diverse in form, and my limited experience of deepening into one aspect of it came several years later through studying and practicing *vipassana*, or insight meditation, over a seven-year period of my life. Going to silent retreats, getting up at four in the morning, sitting cross-legged for hours, and not speaking for seven- to ten-day stretches can't help but break down who you think you are! Even if it is only to come to the stark humility that you barely made it through the last sitting, given the knee or shoulder pain or circling thoughts that kept your mind in constant chatter nine-tenths of the time.

Buddhism has been influencing the Western world for over fifty years. We probably are all familiar with the secular term *mindfulness* that has found a foothold in psychotherapy practices, pain clinics, boardrooms, and even the military. Still, it's worth noting that the Buddha didn't come up with the idea of mindfulness or the cycles of life and rebirth—rather, these are timeless understandings from wisdom traditions worldwide that have either been lost, hidden, or less known. Yet it's where we can turn to today to find the most striking emphasis on the importance of the dying time and the state of consciousness at death. This is because one's consciousness is considered to directly influence the experience of navigating the afterlife states and the nature of rebirth. Buddhism considers that we all have an essential nature where good qualities reside and that we are reborn to perfect this nature until we no longer need or choose to.

The idea that we have many lifetimes of increasing completeness comes through most vividly in the *Bardo Thödol*, commonly known in the West as the Tibetan Book of the Dead. This classic Buddhist text for Tibetans is a map of consciousness on how to exit this level of reality and be in the interval between death and the next rebirth. Turns out there is a lot to know about this! And it becomes a map for the living as well, in teaching us to keep letting go, or "die" to what we want to cling to. The main instruction is for the dying to be as awake as possible to what is happening and as death approaches to stay focused on the *clear inner light that dawns like the sun*. In the immediacy of death, there is much to distract us: colors, shapes, forms, and sounds that are illusionary and diverting, enticing us away from this warm clear light. Accordingly, having a special friend at hand who will remind and recite these instructions is of highest value.

It's been a number of years now, yet I still vividly recall being with an old university friend as she lay in her hospice bed during her last days. I hadn't seen Cindy in a long time, and even though she was in pain from an aggressive cancer, her buoyant light-filled self would always be reaching beyond it to offer a joke or take interest in the lives of those around her. I knew she was eager for any spiritual guidance on dying and tentatively ventured to offer her a picture of how to navigate the moments after death, "Keep following a warm, clear light. There may be many lights but there will be one that beckons most lovingly and warmly." "And, Cindy," I went on, shyly adding, "I know you'll be in a good place, and we can stay connected, and maybe even help each other." Her eyes had been closed, but when I said this they sprung wide open. She died the next day, and though I don't know in what way this may have helped, I certainly have felt the glow of her loving light since.

Stephen Levine, a pioneering meditation teacher and acclaimed author of a number of books on meditation and dying, led the way for many people in the West to become intimate with some of these Eastern practices in the art of living in the here and now and "dying awake." Levine wrote that the best time to begin a mindfulness practice is the present, when one is well, before a crisis arises that requires heavy emotional lifting. We need to build up our spiritual muscles by bringing our awareness to life's smaller difficulties first. Then our capacity to meet greater suffering grows. So as much as I struggle with the practice of bringing awareness to my sore back or the pain in my shoulder, doing so invariably does allow a softening and a releasing, and sometimes insight comes, or just some gentle acceptance. At other times the practice allows awareness to settle around the ache in my heart from feeling rejected or shamed for something. This is what the practice of *letting go* really is—bringing loving, heart awareness to our anger, hurts, and terrors and by doing so transform them. But this is a practice that needs practice pretty much daily, I find. *This* kind of workout, I'm told, will help us to walk through death with more consciousness and less fear.

In many spiritual traditions, it is considered a great deed to accompany a dying person with loving awareness at the time of death, helping them navigate the demanding transition out of their aging or ailing bodies. As mentioned, a Tibetan Buddhist may have extensive rituals for this, while the motto at Zen Hospice Project is simply "Stay Close, Do Nothing." Practicing Roman Catholics may want a priest to offer what was once called last rites, now known as the sacrament of the sick. This includes an anointing of the body with holy oil along with hearing confession and offering forgiveness in order for the dying one to feel life's completion and release of the soul. But most of us will instinctively know the importance of being inwardly quiet and heart centered in the last precious hours of sitting with someone. A time of few words and minimal intrusion. Our own emotional turbulence may feel distracting and overwhelming, but we are stronger than we think, and struggling through it and putting it aside temporarily is possible. As is seeking help from others when we can't. Ultimately, it's above all a time when loving presence is what matters while allowing the deepest mysteries of the universe to unfold.

The experience being at the bedside of my friend Cindy happened before medical assistance in dying (MAID) was available in Canada and in a number of other countries. If this had happened today, Cindy would have been offered MAID. And perhaps she would have chosen to "take control" of her life in this way with a medical injection given by a doctor or nurse at a prescribed time. She may have been spared some suffering; it's also possible she would have missed out on some important conversations, some final experiences that cannot be planned or foretold, ones that bring completion in their own mysterious way. I'm convinced that much happens in our last days, hours, and minutes, as we take leave of our bodies, and worry and wonder that hastening this process through medical intervention in dying circumvents some vital natural processing. I also ask myself whether it might make it harder to orient ourselves after death. It's a complex issue, to be sure.

Was it my few steps into Buddhism that led me to my own convictions around dying and death? I know I was greatly influenced, but part of me wants to claim an earlier sense of such knowing—based on that thread of belonging to an ancient Celtic past, where I found a heritage intimately familiar with the interwoven cycles of life, invisible realms, dying, and becoming again. It's no wonder we seek out other traditions that resonate with a lost wisdom. Buddhism gave me a language and a map to borrow for a time, so I could find my own knowing way, closer to home.

My research finally took me to an obscure book written by European monks in the Middle Ages called *Ars moriendi,* or the "Art of Dying." In this text, and in another from the same time period called *The Book of the Craft of Dying,* I again found the universal thread directing us to the wisdom required to overcome our hurts, unhealthy attachments, and conflicts—all which builds our capacity for the ultimate letting go demanded of us at the end of our days: *Learn to die and you shall live, For there shall be none who learn to truly live, Who have not learned to die.*[2]

Having kids changes just about *everything,* and meditation and time for oneself is usually the first casualty. In my early thirties, I became a householder, as it is referred to in Buddhism and Hinduism. This is the path where spiritual development unfolds in our responsibilities within daily life—the way for all of us these days. And it was through parenting and the search for good education that I discovered the next big influence in my life: the work of Rudolf Steiner, especially his perspectives on caring for the dead.

Visiting friends in London, my husband and I were in awe at the schoolwork of their two children. How unexpectedly lovely the drawing, and the beautiful, hand-printed stories that made up their main lesson book! Rosemary, their mother, told me a bit about the Waldorf School they were in and how stories are at the core of the early curriculum. As a burgeoning storyteller myself, I was very intrigued. Learning more and then visiting a Waldorf school, I became enamored with the Waldorf ideals of truth, beauty, and goodness that permeated the teachings, and inspired by the motto of teaching for the head, heart, and hands. This spoke to me so much that in the mid-1990s I, along with a few other hearty souls, founded Mulberry Waldorf School in Kingston.

I was drawn to the philosophy that lay behind Waldorf education. I learned about Austrian-born Rudolf Steiner, the late nineteenth-century philosopher, scientist, artist, and clairvoyant, whose insights into child development and the social needs of the time brought forth the Waldorf School movement. Steiner's philosophy, known as *anthroposophy*, is concerned with all aspects of human life, spirit, and evolving consciousness; it is a path of wisdom, service, and personal growth. Steiner, a Goethe scholar, was influenced by the ancient Eastern mystery schools and the great pre-Socratic wisdom teachers. Both esoteric and deeply practical, his contributions also extend into other areas, including medicine, architecture, special education (the Camphill Movement), biodynamic farming, *and* work with those who have died.

The dead are always with us, Steiner tells us, and we have a responsibility to maintain a connection with them: "In earlier epochs the human soul was able to maintain a real connection with the dead, even though this was more in the subconscious life; such intercourse must now be rediscovered in full consciousness."[3] Steiner maintains that the dead seek to be helpers and guides for us, endeavoring to contribute meaningfully to our world through ideas, imagination, and inspiration, for they can see much better than we can what must be done in the social sphere for further development and transformation. To do this, they need their loved ones to remember them and make an inner connection. Poignantly, our prolonged tears of loss can be distressing for those who have crossed this threshold, becoming a gray curtain that can make it harder for them to connect with us.

A spiritual eclecticism is growing these days, along with a synthesis of many paths. This movement has growing depth as well as breadth—going deeper than parochial religion and deeper into Earth wisdom. This wisdom is obvious to Indigenous people the world over and has been fundamental to women's spirituality over time. Earth-centered spirituality, with roots in paganism, may be described as experiencing oneself as imbued with and a part of the ever-creating process of life itself and sensing this animating force pulsing through everything, from stone to tree to animal to human, from the oceans to the stars, and also including the cycles of birth, death, and rebirth.

Inspiring as this sense of universalism can be, it now seems, for many of us distrustful of a one-size-fits-all globalization, that something has been lost. There's a longing to reconnect to the particularities and peculiarities of place and culture. How fascinating to see so many people from different faiths picking up the tattered threads of their religion and wondering if they cannot yet make something from them. Something that is both old and new, both universal and specifically local and rooted. It's too early to tell if it's a naive throwback to what might seem simpler times, the danger being more divisiveness and intolerance. However, many cultural commentators, mystics, and astrologers are also pointing to a door that is opening, one of illuminating light pouring onto the earth, making available new frequencies of love. This is love greater than opinion, ideology, or creed, yet it has a home in each of our own small corners of the world. No doubt the difference will be found in the depth of self-transformation we are willing to undergo.

One person exploring this possibility is Paul Kingsnorth, Irish environmentalist and philosopher, who writes that we are living in what we might call a "desert time": a time of collapse and change and radical reinvention before renewal. "I feel like I am being firmly pointed, day after day, back toward the green desert that forms my Christian inheritance. . . . Back to the song that is sung quietly through the land. . . . Back to our roots, both literal and spiritual. . . . To seek out a wild Christianity, which will see us praying for hours in the sea as the otters play around us."[4]

One of the few contemporary Western teachings putting this together while at the same time bringing something new and original is integral spiritual psychology. This nuanced and evolving work of Robert Sardello calls our home Spiritual Earth and offers practices for dying awake as well as cultivating inner silence and heartful soul awareness—a region where the presence of our beloveds across the threshold can be felt, the deeper our receptivity. Moreover, it challenges us to develop new capacities as human beings, to be creators of love, not simply be carried by it, and to do so in relationship with the world. Its guiding inspiration is the maxim: "We are born not for ourselves alone, but for the sake of the world."

12

The Dying Time

Without an understanding of myth or religion, without
an understanding of the relationship between destruction
and creation, death and rebirth, the individual suffers the
mysteries of life as meaningless mayhem alone.

MARION WOODMAN, *THE PREGNANT VIRGIN:*
A PROCESS OF PSYCHOLOGICAL TRANSFORMATION

Leave nothing for death but a burned-out candle.

NIKOS KAZANTZAKIS, *ZORBA THE GREEK*

Flashback: My mother has been in bed for two months now. As I write, my stomach turns over remembering how this beginning of the dying time first started.

It is August 11, and I'm driving to the Toronto airport to pick up my son (whom I haven't seen in almost a year) and his girlfriend. Ahh, Casey's girlfriend—I'm finally getting to meet Danielle. Having had a stopover at a friend's in Port Hope, I feel I can manage the rest of the way, though I have a frozen shoulder, and it's been a painful and dreadfully limiting four months with no relief in sight. I am naively proud of my self-sufficiency in taking this trip.

Turning into the airport, I pull over to the side to text Casey to see if they have landed. Not hearing back, I wait for ten or fifteen minutes until a security car pulls behind me signaling me to move. I turn the key in the ignition, but the steering wheel is locked. It will *not* budge. No amount of yanking and coaxing does any good. The security man starts yelling out his car window at me. Finally, he comes over, too angry to hear me saying the car won't start. When it finally sinks in, his tone softens, and he now sees me as a woman in distress. I breathe out—I'm OK with the idea of being rescued at this point. He tries the car and finds it's true—the wheel will not unlock, and so the engine cannot turn over; furthermore, by now it is evident that the battery has died.

Meanwhile, I am getting text after text from Casey wondering where I am. *Damn it!* I'm frazzled, hurting, and so embarrassed to have ruined this special homecoming. Now the tow truck is coming. My car will be towed to the airport garage, and I'll have to figure things out from there. In the midst of this, standing along the speeding, looping airport roadways with an assortment of men and vehicles trying to help me, I get a phone call from home. Michael tells me that the long-term-care facility has called. Called about my mum. Something has happened; it is unclear what. I am to call them.

The next hours are so bizarre. Life can get complicated and intense when tending to key thresholds like dying, as if the stars are colliding in the universe. The security officer now is such a helpful person: while my car goes one way to the garage, he drives me the other way to the front entrance of arrivals. In the passenger seat I speak to the charge nurse, Jake, who tells me Mum has a high fever and is yelling my name over and over, begging me to come and help her. He suddenly needs to hang up and tells me to call back in ten minutes. My breaking point has been reached.

I go through the door and see my son and his girlfriend waiting there. I put on a good false face through the greetings and hugging and tell them first about the car, that we have no way back to Kingston, then about Nanny. As I do so, I burst into uncontrollable, hysterical sobbing—thirty seconds into my very first meeting with Danielle.

Hiding in the washroom to pull myself together, I get *another* call from Jake. They've concluded that Mum has had a stroke. She's delirious, calling out for me. "We may need to restrain her," he shouts. I blubber into the phone, saying over and over, "But I *never* go away. I'm always close by. How can this be happening *now*?"

By the time I'm out of the washroom, my dear twenty-eight-year-old son has taken control, doing what he can to iron out these complications. He's on the phone trying to find a rental car. After many such calls, he dismally reports that there doesn't seem to be anything available. Sold out! Two companies did not answer their phones, so off we go to hunt them down. The young man at the first rental company says they have cars left; however, they must be booked online. The trouble is, their online system is down, and Casey cannot get logged into it. No matter how we reason with this poor man, he will not release a car to us, even though we are right in front of him and the car only meters away! I'm still shaking my head. Casey goes down the road to the next rental place and finds one car left. They will only give it to us as a one-day rental; they insist that we return it the very next day. None of us can even imagine driving right back to Toronto after all this, but we keep quiet so we can just get the damned car.

On top of all this, I notice my phone, just like my car, has died. *Unbelievable!* And my recharging cord is in my car that's just been towed away! Now the guy behind the desk is trying to lessen my franticness by searching for a cord. He finds it, but the outlet is close to the floor behind his desk. As the paperwork is being drawn up, my phone rings *again*. I'm on the floor, straining to hear through the static of a bad connection and the noise in the car rental office. Jake is saying oops, sorry, there's been a mistake. It was a *different* Marion who was delirious and had to be restrained, not *my* Marion. Long pause, an *exhausted* pause. No room for anger, or indeed anything. It's all too much. Jake says there was some kind of incident with my mum earlier, but she seems OK now. Somehow, the ride home becomes hysterically funny after that.

That evening, going to see for myself how Mum is, I'm taken by surprise by how she looks. One side of her face is slack, her eyes very heavy. A languid dopiness prevails. She brightens up, though, in seeing me. She is sweet and dopey. I call my sister and give Mum the phone to let them talk; while doing so, Mum starts garbling her words, drifts off, and her breathing becomes very still. I can't believe it—like my car then my phone, she is dying right before me while my sister is on the other end of the line! I am holding my breath in absolute awe that it could be this easy, this peaceful, and her two daughters with her. Another part of me is screaming inside, *No, not now! I have not an ounce of strength to meet this moment and do the many things that happen after death!* Well, this prayer won out. Mum did revive after a minute of being *still as death*. But this second ministroke of the day set the stage for more.

The next two and a half months gave me the visceral experience of slow dying. It was a grueling time of being with Mum and her suffering. But this is a sticky point: Was she suffering? By my *image* of what suffering looks like, she indeed was—not able to move herself anymore, mind unhinged from time, and calling out "Can someone help me?" over and over again. My heart both cringes and softens with this memory of intimate caretaking. But with a frozen shoulder, it was often far too much for me. Funny, though, how we keep going. My sister kept suggesting I hire someone, but I couldn't imagine introducing her to someone she didn't know and wouldn't remember from one visit to the next. She had enough of that with the constantly varying long-term-care staff. And honestly, at this point, the effort to arrange and manage people felt too great.

Then an inspired thought came. Our daughter, Elena, had moved back home while studying and was looking for a part-time job. Knowing how Mum loved her granddaughter's company, I tentatively asked whether she would consider spending regular time with Mum in lieu of a getting a job. Both my kids had spent lots of time with their grandmother growing up. Mum would often pick Elena up from school and take her to her place where they would play cards, eat cookies, and watch TV programs—ones that were not allowed at home, of course. Perhaps with these fond memories, as well as concern with seeing her own mother floundering, Elena rose to the occasion and agreed. She began visiting her Nanny four or five days a week. It was another experience of grace. Elena later surprised me by saying, "I don't mind going. It's actually kind of peaceful just sitting with her and talking about the same things. You know, she is very different with me than with you."

After all these years of being an independent senior, who would scorn at and resist needing a walker, resist needing help washing or being taken care of in any way, Mum is now allowing and sinking into that vulnerable place of being entirely dependent. Nonetheless, a part of her mind always sought to understand what was going on, sometimes with a pleading desperation akin to a drowning person trying to reach a rescuing hand. "*Why* can't I walk? *Why* am I taking these pills? *Why* does my hip hurt? (She had fallen on her way to the bathroom, forgetting to take her walker.) *Why* is someone here again taking my temperature?" Each time, I would tell her the same thing: "Mum, you've had a small stroke. You're OK now, but you need to take it easy and be checked on." She would always express surprise, "A stroke!" Mum knew what this meant and seemed satisfied, almost relieved, that there was a concrete explanation that she understood. She'd want to know all about it, and for at least the fifth or sixth time that day, I would tell her all about it, sometimes embellishing details to offer her a satisfying story.

Journal Entry

As I sit with you, Mum, I am sensing something akin to relief, your relief that you no longer have to keep up your body, your mind, and personality. You are letting go, just as we are supposed to be doing as we age. I really took note of that when you finally stopped caring whether your hair was done in the style it had been for as long as I could remember. That was just a year prior to your dying! Until then, you held on sturdily to the mental image you had of yourself and resisted being "old."

Control was a favorite word of my mother's. "Are things under control?" was her way of saying, "How are things?" I often wanted to blurt out, "No, things are not under control! The kids are yelling, my body is hurting, and I don't know what to do with my life!" Instead, I would meekly agree that, yes, things are under control—subtext being I don't know how to talk to you about anything real because you will dive deep into worry and then advise how to shore up the ship, so to speak.

Journal Entry

As much as I resisted the word and message of "being in control," I know now that it infiltrated my very nerves and muscles. Perhaps that is why I breathed out, relaxing, as I watched your dismantling mind doing its own job of releasing you. And oh, how I loved your soft, gray, uncurled, undyed hair! Funny how I couldn't get enough of seeing you softened so and probably told you every time I visited, "You look beautiful today." How astonished and disbelieving you always were to hear this. For me, it was a surprise too—as I grow older, more and more people tell me that I look so much like you. Maybe I'm seeing through my own need to control by seeing myself in you and not minding it so much. (Well . . . I'm getting there.)

As I read this journal entry, another voice in my head pipes up: *But listen, there is more than just* control *at issue here.* I'm recalling a childhood glimpse of my mum dancing around on a Christmas night, playing a toy accordion and wearing a funny hat (while Dad is sleeping off a day of drinking with his brothers). This funny side comes out more and more as she builds her own life after Dad dies. Maybe this carefree spirit is more who she really is without the pressures of adult life covering it over. I see now that this is how we start building a relationship as she ages—I'm not only the dutiful and caretaking daughter; I'm also a playmate! I have a picture from four years ago of Mum with a banana up to her ear while she makes a call to Dad, asking how things are going *up there.* I could laugh a bellyful with her when both our controlling sides let up.

Journal Entry

There were times, Mum, when you were in such discomfort. I can't deny this. Like when you were given a drug for anxiety and depression because you called out for help so much and this was disturbing other residents and the staff, I presume. It immediately gave you an extremely dry mouth. It appeared that you were dying of thirst—nothing was able to satiate this crippling sensation in and around your mouth. It took many conversations with the staff to find solutions, but none of them worked. Finally, I implored the doctor, "Marion's quality of life is now terrible. Whatever benefits she may be getting from the meds just can't be worth it." The doctor found it hard to believe that you could be in so much discomfort from the small dose you were receiving, but in the end, he agreed to have them discontinued.

Mum, even after the medication was stopped, it took over a week for you to recover from it. This was such a harrowing time for me as most of my visit was spent giving you sips of water while you kept repeating, "My mouth is so dry. Why is my mouth so dry? Get me some water. My mouth is so dry." I would often visit you for a second time in the day or evening, finding you lying in the dark, calling out, "Help, I'm so thirsty." Crumpling inside, I would feel so helpless. And when was it you stopped eating? Food piled up beside you; staff bringing more, arguing and tricking you into eating a mouthful of something while you waved your arms for them to take it away. Couldn't they see your body was doing the natural thing in letting go? Digestion takes a lot of energy and made you uncomfortable. But even I got caught up in the illusion that you'd feel better if you took a spoonful of Jell-O, when it was really me that was trying to feel better, in this small act of normalcy.

Three months after Mum dies, I awake with a dream: *Mum, very old and withered. She is needing comforting. I guide her toward me, and she curls up like a baby in my arms.*

Significant dreams accompanied every step of the dying–death journey with my mother. It's strange, this thinning of margins, at great transitional times of our lives, especially during the night, when access to deeper realms occurs more readily. Dreams seem to be where many people may have an experience with a recently deceased loved one, symbolic, yes, but often with a sense of a real encounter.

As a child, I used to dream a lot. Outlandish vistas and encounters with the surreal would parade through my night. This stopped during adolescence, and I didn't think much about dreams anymore, busy as I was with the drama of being a teenager. Then I read in a *Reader's Digest* magazine, "You are always dreaming; you just don't remember them." Tips were given on how to remember. Like having pen and paper near your bed so you could record them whenever you wake. I did this, barely able to make out my writing scrawled across the page in the morning, but it didn't seem to matter. I had seemingly pressed the recall button, with one little picture fragment leading me to the next. It wasn't long before a steady stream of vignettes and images greeted me like old friends. An uncanny foretelling of events would occasionally appear in these nocturnal visitations, alerting me to the rich field of deeper knowing that is available, with some effort and inclination, to us all.

In my late twenties, it was Carl Jung, the great early twentieth-century Swiss psychiatrist, followed by Jungian and mythopoetic author Marion Woodman from southern Ontario, who opened the door for me to understand dreams as symbols of our unconscious. Not just for us individually but collectively as well. Other readings in myth, symbol, and shamanic practices revealed to me how dreamwork, since ancient times, has often been the gateway for initiation into more ways of knowing, just as any experience that takes one to a threshold and certainly encounters with death.

For those who want to explore symbolism and interpretation, there is a cascading amount of information available of varying quality. As tempting as it is to seek an immediate revelatory message, dreamwork is often subtler, an art in itself, requiring a soft eye and fluid, image-based thinking that attends to body, symbol, metaphor, resemblance, flow and mood, and the living context of our lives. The other way, of analyzing our dreams, trying to concretize the elusive, can lead to a mentalization of what is arising from the unconscious. As interesting as this may be, it is a blunt instrument, seldom leading to greater embodied understanding. (The exception could be in ongoing work with a depth psychotherapist.)

Some images simply speak for themselves. Like this dream: *On a snowy mountain hike with my dog. I am wondering if Mali can make the long journey still ahead; she looks tired and vulnerable. Looking down the slope, I see a train moving. I am seeing sandy beaches, stretches of sunny paths ahead.* Knowing that my instinctive body (my dog Mali) is so tired and vulnerable is disquieting. The frozen shoulder that I have nursed for months makes everything I do more difficult and painful. The dream is reminding me to acknowledge this, to give witness to and appreciate just how hard my body is working and let *her* know that easier times are promised.

However, in some dreams, it helps to go deeper. To embody the images and symbols that come to us from a deeper knowing is how we become more aware. Continuing the dream activity imaginatively—through poetry, painting, journaling, movement, or voice—not only develops greater consciousness but is also the pathway of art in relationship with the world. Integral spiritual psychology speaks of entering the dream itself, allowing an image to come into a distilled focus, and then with an act of will dissolving the image or content. By remaining inwardly poised in the stillness that remains, something often will arise as a soul response.

An example: *Several recent dreams have me singing onstage, a solo. My voice is strong, and my song is a good one. There is applause and recognition.* After the last such dream, I bring the central image to mind, give my full attention to it. Then with an act of will, I let it go, dissolving it. What then occurs is a subtle awareness at my throat, a loosening, an opening of a channel behind my throat extending through to the front, with a strong pulsing flow of energy expanding and contracting rhythmically. This sensation lingers with me for quite some time, and the words come: "Speaking forth becomes singing for the world." I write them down.

At yet another level, what happens when we drop our quest to discover meaning for ourselves and pay attention instead to the fluid, interweaving world of tone, mood, light, and movement? Is this field and source of all creativity? Behind the dream—or from within a place of inner stillness or at the center of a labyrinth—a space can open where clarity of perception deepens, presences can be felt, and sometimes whispers of words heard. For me, this invisible force feels immediate, intimate, rising up from within, yet ringing from a place of much greater dimension. I have been jolted awake with such phrases as *Love is a force,*

Life is generous, and *Love gets bigger with less*. The stern admonition *Leave your sister alone!* was once delivered so clearly in my father's voice that I felt knocked over with the sheer force of it. It was in reference to my angst and judgment over Carolyn not being comfortable with the nitty-gritty aspects of dying and death care. What an important message to untie *my* agenda from hers! Gradually, I've begun to take up my side of the conversation, conveying questions and offering help.

Today, neuroscience is also making great strides in understanding what happens in our brains during sleep, particularly our dream-filled REM (rapid eye movement) sleep. Bessel van der Kolk quotes this research from Robert Stickgold: "The sleeping brain can even make sense out of information whose relevance is unclear while we are awake and integrate it into the larger memory system."[1] Van der Kolk goes on to observe that the sleeping brain will underline emotionally relevant information, letting irrelevant information fade away. New and novel connections between recombined memories and experiences are forged, allowing for healing and insight over time. This also explains the emerging neurobiology therapies such as craniosacral work, EMDR (eye movement desensitization and reprocessing), neurofeedback, and other bilateral stimulation (tapping). They each use brain stimuli resembling the REM phase of sleep. The value of a rested brain for grounded creative activity is something inestimable.

So dreaming can be looked at through differing and overlapping lenses: that of the individual, transpersonal, and collective unconscious; that of the mysterious creating place behind these images; or that of our brain circuitry sorting, balancing, and integrating stimuli and experiences. On any night, we can experience all these processes. But will we remember?

Finding a rhythm in sleeping and waking is so hard these days.

Much is now written about how to nurture and protect sleep so that we can allow the brain to do its job. When we live closer to the natural rhythms built into us, the greater rhythms of Earth and world can be felt, allowing helpful *dreams* and *soft whisperings* to arise from the angels and ancestors of night. The Buddha calls sleep the "small death," and Homer refers to it as "death's little brother," so here we see the relationship—and the practice we get every night—of letting go.

13

Look, the Sun
Just Came Out

I'm tired of waiting for my mother to die.

ADMISSION FROM A FRIEND OF MINE

Crying out loud for help is Rumi's point. With that vulnerable breaking open in the psyche, the milk of grace starts to flow.

COLEMAN BARKS, TRANS., *THE ESSENTIAL RUMI*

October 21, a week before Mum dies, I'm dreaming that I'm visiting her. *It is early morning, still dark. I'm walking down the hallway to her room. It is totally dark—I can't see a thing. I'm thinking, Why the hell am I here? Have I crossed over too far into what might be the tunnel Mum is in as she exits from this life?*

I can't get back to sleep. Flashes of Mum behind my eyes, flashes of Mum in retrospect, as though I'm experiencing *her* life review. Indeed, *why am I here?* My old way of making boundaries is not working. So now instead, I allow Mum to permeate me consciously, meaning I am not fighting her presence or afraid of the merging. I find a firmer footing within my own self, one that is not so easily blown away yet permeable to presences. It is as if I have found a new way to be with her and am able to relax a bit.

Later in the day, I go to the backyard. I instinctively call upon our ancestors to accompany her. As soon as I say the word *ancestor*, a high-pitched, primal sound comes through me. This keeps up, reverberating among the trees. I allow myself to move, an animal urge takes over, an ancient ritual pattern that my body is remembering: writhing and wailing, the gush of tears, and a rhythmic rocking.

At the time, I was not familiar with this sensation. It is a force like that of giving birth, a power from a source well beyond the familiar. *Keening*: I'm aware of the word and know of it in the context of tribal customs in other cultures, so I am surprised to see it defined as coming from a Celtic past, my past as well. According to Wikipedia, keening is a traditional form of vocal lament for the dead. It comes from the Irish and Scottish Gaelic term *caoineadh* ("to cry, to weep") and references to it from the seventh, eighth, and twelfth centuries are extensive. Carried out by one or several women, a chorus of sorts may have been intoned, giving bodily form to anguish, along with rocking, kneeling, and clapping. Keening women were often employed to carry out this service on behalf of a family or the village. Providing permission to fall apart, the piercing call of genuine grief would strike a resonant chord in all present to remember all their ungrieved parts: the love and sorrows along life's path and the collective pouring forth of tears could become a community feast.

For along with grief comes its sister, praise—as wise elders tell us. Praise for all that is good and beautiful, in the deceased person as well as in the world. "Oh, what a good person he was, so generous to everyone." And "Oh my, what will we do without her beautiful spirit that always eased our day and cheered our hearts?" Then, "What a halo of light surrounds this autumn day." Grief and praise, both serving and helping the departed one to leave the land of the living and not get stuck in a limbo between the two realms. Also helping the bereaved to not get stuck either: in paralyzed sadness or in guilty thoughts, another limbo. This instinctual practice is found in many if not most cultures that have kept roots to their origins and to Earth. That a taste of it had risen so naturally in me was vivifying. In my journal, I wrote afterward: "I feel so alive—my body and soul merging with a deep river, unbounded, timeless, dark and familiar. In this place, I am meeting grief as sacred and as a gateway."

The rawness of grief, sharp and pure, pierced me at intervals over the course of Mum's dying and death. Being overwhelmed by these sensations and feelings, I could find myself suddenly falling apart. I entertain myself with the images the thought conjures: an arm on the floor, a leg in the corner, a head rolling out the door. Ancient Aleuts are said to have lashed hide bindings around the joints of the bereaved to prop them up so that in grief they wouldn't *fall apart* or *go to pieces,* just as the skeleton would once in the grave. I then think of other such phrases like *coming apart at the seams* or *cut to the bone.* It seems our metaphors say much about how our bodies register a *broken heart* and the intolerable notion of not being able to reach over and touch a loved one's hand ever again. Howling, from our deepest parts with others, may be the best response to coalesce anew.

Now, in my dreams, I am visited by a very old African teacher. *He is imparting a lesson. I am overwhelmed and begin to fall down, losing consciousness, but he helps me stay upright, and I am proud for having been able to stay alert—as if that in itself is the lesson. Yes, as hard as it is, I am trying to stay alert.*

October 22, 2019

MUM: *I am so proud of you, Nancy. Really, really proud. [I take her hand.]*
   Don't leave me, ever. I don't want to be apart . . . [She is clutching my
   hand hard now.] Why am I still here?

Me: *[Fumbling.]* *Well, timing is up to God or a greater mystery, isn't it?*

Mum: *Yes, I know. I really know that.*

Bent over her bed, inarticulate with the tears I'm trying to hold back, I'm startled by Mum's insights these days. I feel cut to my heart. I don't know this part of my mum, and suddenly I'm a little girl once again, wanting more of *this* mother and her wisdom. My grief is for this hungry part of me as much as for my dying mother. All my years of flying away from my mum—wanting to summit mountains, save the poor, save the whales, save souls, shine brighter—has come to this turning point, where I want to fly back to her. A gravitational pull not to be resisted.

She is now saying *Nicholas* over and over. Although my mother seems so inward and referencing only her immediate self and surroundings, she is now saying my nephew's name out of the blue. They have not really had contact since last Christmas, nine months ago. This alerts me to another subtle process underway: Mum looking around from a different level of awareness. Like a bird soaring above the fray, taking in her loved ones from this place. Who knows what gleanings she is receiving and giving? Even as I encourage her that it's OK to let go, I'm also aware that there may be things keeping her here that ask for her subtle attention. The question Why am I still here? is a good one. As tired as I may be of waiting for my mother to die, I marvel at the long unwinding some of us are given to finish our business.

Taking a break, I relax on a glorious late autumn day on a Lake Ontario beach. As I take some deep breaths and bury my feet in the warm sand, words come into my awareness: *She is ours now.* The grandmothers and grandfathers have spoken. I am being told I can recede now. I hadn't anticipated how active the ancestral world could be! My shoulders and neck let down with a deep sigh, as I realize how long I have been waiting for my mother to die. Responsibility has exacted its price, but now I'm being told: *It's not all on my shoulders!* A flutter of wings and a blue breeze soften the worry lines on my face. I'll need to remember this message many times yet.

At our next visit, Mum starts to sing "Happy Birthday"—over and over again. My mum *never* bursts into song. I begin to fill in the names: Happy birthday dear *Mum*, Happy birthday dear *Casey*, Happy birthday dear *Elena*, Happy birthday dear *Nicholas* . . . dear *Carolyn*, dear *Nancy*.

After I get home, I'm anxious. Crazy, kind of. All this ancestral involvement is cracking me open. A walk in the woods helps. Next morning, I'm still raw and on tilting ground. In my morning quiet time, time when I focus my attention inwardly before rushing into the day, I start talking to Dad, kind of demanding him to help. Soon, I start feeling a puffy cushioning around me. *Love.* Resting here for a while, I think of Mum's mum, Grandmother Etta. Underneath the sadness, a swell of anger rises up—at her for dying so young and leaving Mum so scared, at her absence for me as a child. Sweating starts. I hadn't realized how hot I was getting, and then the anger in my belly finds its target: *Why did I have to carry my mother's sadness all these years? It's not mine! It's not fair! Get off of me!* Stillness deepens. Some moments later, the sense of a butterfly arises. I enter into this feeling and let it be an antidote. Afterward, I'm standing taller and stronger.

Now, another memory comes back to me. My head is bowed over my mother's bed in exhaustion. An image comes, together with a feeling of being surrounded by great compassion. OK, I'll say it: it is the feeling and appearance of Mary, the mother of Jesus, or is it perhaps Mary Magdalene, the beloved companion of Jesus? In any case, our heads are bent toward each other; her warm, loving hand consoling me. Words arise: *The ancestral tree is holding.*

Why am I slightly embarrassed at mentioning an image of Mary?

Will it make me sound religious? Prone to fantasy and New Age notions? As a child, I would take blissful comfort from my bedtime prayer that began: "Jesus, tender shepherd hear me; bless this little child tonight." In the darkness of my little bedroom, I could feel a warm cloak wrap around me and tuck me in safely and lovingly. Perhaps this is what set the ground for an abiding sense of a spiritual *comforter* stored away, lying in wait for me when I needed it.

The next day, I am taken by surprise by my daughter serenading me with Paul McCartney's legendary song "Let It Be" on her ukulele: "*Speaking words of wisdom, let it be.*" Hum it to yourself. I bet you know the words—no denying something or someone gets evoked in the process. Since then, I discovered *The Way of the Rose* by Clark Strand and Perdita Finn. This beauty of a book tells the true story of Clark, a Zen monk, who hears the voice of Mary, and in following her lead, he and his feminist wife rediscover the healing, earthy heart path of praying the rosary. While not promoting Catholicism or institutional religion, the book reveals the old ways, known especially to women, of fingering beads, murmuring mantra-like prayers throughout the busy day, and beseeching help from the Mother of God, in our life and at the hour of our death. I love the feel of beads in my hands; they settle and calm me. It's as if I've done this before. Though the words of the rosary are not so familiar, the rhythm is, and I'm open to feeling into their ancient mythic strength that lies beyond the literal. It seems time to claim a heritage that can awaken the divine ancestral feminine simply and directly. Likewise, beginning to stir in our hearts and mind, is Mary Magdalene. Vulnerable, misconstrued, belied from day one, she has remained in silence for long centuries. But her presence is claiming the attention of many today. Jehanne de Quillan writes about her as the beloved companion of Yeshua, and as a spiritual initiate of the deepest order, in her book *The Gospel of the Beloved Companion: The Complete Gospel of Mary Magdalene*. When I inwardly utter the name *Mary Magdalene*, a tingling and gentleness fills me, a moment of illuminating clarity sweeps through my mind.

Over the years, I have learned that this face of "God" is not about perfectionism or conquering every mountain; it's about tender care, loving attention, and receptivity. It's leaving space unfilled. Pausing, waiting, and being part of the subtle movements of creating. It's falling and getting back up, falling and getting back up, and taking the hand that reaches out to help us do so. It's also about sovereignty and, like Ereshkigal, knowing when and how to be fierce, outraged, and unsentimental.

Like a clear spring bubbling up from a subterranean river, the divine feminine is reemerging everywhere: *Sophia, Gaia, Brigit, Shakti, White Buffalo Woman, Shekinah, Tara, Kwan Yin, Dark Madonna, Cerridwen, Kali, Our Lady of Guadalupe.* Her names and stories are honey and harbinger for our soul and the world, each guise of her offering a nuance resonant to a place, culture, and time. Sensing her is easier than we might think, especially in her role as creating force of nature. But also, from my experience, a very direct line occurs when in your hour of darkness you *ask for help*—loudly, silently, heartfully, and, preferably, on bended knees.

The ancestral tree is holding. The words that surfaced in the moment over my mother's bed give rise to a dream the following night, where I recognize the braiding of generations right here, right now: *In a small living room with family. There is a chair pulled forward with a younger Elena sitting cozy in her pajamas. I'm slightly behind on her right side, one arm extended upward reaching to an invisible hand, while the other reaches around to touch her womb. She reaches up to touch my long braid, and caressing my cheek says, "Nice Mumma." I touch her abdomen and say, "Nice girl." It is a very sweet feeling, this dawning awareness of the intertwining generations.*

October 24, 2019

Mum is curled up in a fetal position. I sit close by, stroking her hair.

MUM: *I'm so content. I feel good, I feel good. So warm.*

I am crying. She asks, *Why?* All I can say between held-back sobs is, "I'm thinking of you."

MUM: *Why? I'm all right. I really am. Look. The sun just came out.*

I look out the window. It is still cloudy.

MUM: *Simple.*
    Simple.
    Simple.
    I am simply.
    Touch my hair again.
    That feels so nice.
    So nice. So nice . . .
    I want to go home.

I really am undone, not just from grief but from amazement. She is radiating a sense of well-being, comfort at being touched, and contentment! Sinking back in my chair, Mum no longer aware of me, I'm wondering what *sun* she might be seeing that I can't? And is the home she is referring to the one we all ultimately return to?

That evening I'm puzzling over this latest revelation about my mother. My child-self says, "This is all I ever wanted—for Mum to be happy and contented." Yet really, this is something you would expect a mother to say about her troubled child, not the other way around! I can see that this was a role I had taken on for years. To make things run smoothly and to make both my parents feel better and be happy. I wonder how I learned that?

As children, we absorb the landscape of emotions around us. A vivid and sobering picture was once given by a Waldorf teacher mentor, "You may create a beautiful kindergarten environment, but when you carry your heavy emotional baggage into the classroom, you might as well be painting the walls black." Instead, she encouraged us to hang our backpack of burdens on an imaginary hook outside the classroom for the duration of the school day.

I grew up in a family where the walls were often painted gray, if not outright black, and I'm reflecting on what this did to my little child self. Young children see the world entirely as an extension of themselves; their boundaries are porous. When Mum or Dad is upset, children decide it must be something *they* did and so within their control to change. Children don't see that it's possible the outside world is to blame, including parents unable to regulate their emotions. It takes a good while to gradually develop a surer sense of self; though, of course, many of us still get stuck somewhere along the way. Being the "responsible one in the room" is a common lingering remnant.

Is this why I was so attuned to my mother's unhappiness and my father's shame my entire life? I see myself, age seven, at the top of the stairs leaning over the ventilation grate, listening to my parent's arguing, wondering if they are talking about *me*. Or bracing when my dad comes home after being out with "the boys." What's his mood like? How drunk is he? What's Mum's reaction? What can I do to help? And when it was all too much, hiding in my room.

Like so many people, especially women, being highly vigilant to the emotional tenor of my surroundings has stayed with me, like an antenna permanently up. It makes us the overly empathetic types. This scatters me and tires me out, especially as I'm attuned for signs of someone or something needing help (the classic rescuer!), but it also means I'm good at reading people and crowds and keeps me awake to opportunities. Of course, for those holding deeper trauma, this can turn into hypervigilance, making one on high alert for signs of danger, both real and imagined. Unfortunately, this in turn can create more havoc by making us prone to escalating fears, suspicions, and anxieties. (Witness our increasingly polarized society: the tendency is now to feel safe only if we can make other people's reality match our own.) There are a lot of new therapies, polyvagal theory among them, that give practical ways to temper this kind of hyperarousal or its inverse—shutdown.

To balance out the ingrained tendency to be ever on the alert for what we regard as danger, we can train ourselves to also look around for genuine signs of *safety*: smiling faces, voices that sooth, openness, good touch, relaxing vibes. Rhythmic motion and sound are surprisingly helpful: for example, remembering to take a breath in, count to four, and then exhale to a count of eight while sounding the tone *voo*. Or simply hum. I'm humming a lot these days. All this can relax our overly defended, revved-up nervous systems and bodies. And when we relax into our environment and relationships, our antennae come down.

Over the years, I have spent a good amount of time trying to figure myself out—becoming more conscious of patterns of reactivity, insecurity, and control. Nevertheless, I can still brood. While my sister recalls our childhood in vivid detail, I am vague and sometimes can scarcely believe that we were in the same family. I remember daydreaming a lot, swinging on our backyard swings for hours at a time, fantasizing having a best friend and going on elaborate, heroic adventures. The outer world would fade away. Imaginative play is vital for children, but this veered into a kind of early dissociation that helped me tolerate troubled times and sensory overload. I vibrated to the emotional cues in my home but not so much to the here and now.

Decades later, my clinical supervisor broke the spell of my usual vagueness when during one of our individual psychotherapy sessions, he asked, "Was it *all* tension? What *else* do you remember, Nancy?" I close my eyes and go back in time, lingering over the pictures that pop up. And ah, yes, a sense of *being held*. Hmmm. A warmth fills my body. I'm remembering my mother's arms; she's carrying me around the kitchen. Then, more warmth as I recall lying stretched out beside her on the couch, my body molded into hers, watching our favorite TV show together, *The Beverly Hillbillies*. I remember her being home with me when I was sick and buying me a toy to make me feel better. I remember regular meals, bedtimes, discipline, Saturday night treats . . . security . . . *home*. My understanding deepens as I revel in this body memory—absorbing the love and attachment that is stronger than the imperfection that lies between two people. This fuller story, remembered, is one that sustains. Thank goodness! The term the *good-enough mother* (or father) brings a welcome sigh of relief. Now, turning this phrase around, I see in a new light my attempts to be the good-enough daughter.

It's been a long road to learn how to carry my ancestors with reverence and gratitude while not carrying their wounds. It feels auspicious that after doing this work I came across a course entitled "Uncovering Hidden Trauma: Transgenerational Healing Approaches" offered by Peter Levine, Efu Nyaki, and Diane Poole Heller. I took this online training in September 2024. Here I found out about the insights of Bert Hellinger, who, through observing family life among the Zulus of South Africa, came to understand family systems and the importance of recognizing our rightful place of belonging in the constellation of our family. He used the term *the orders of love* to name the distinctions and laws that establish healthy boundaries between generations so that unresolved trauma does not get passed down. The emerging science of epigenetics is showing that trauma is, indeed, passed down, proving in effect the existence of hungry ghosts. So where do we begin to disentangle?

Efu Nyaki, one of our teachers, carries the ancestral wisdom of her tribal people of Tanzania and has integrated it with Family Constellations Therapy and Somatic Experiencing. She knows how often we as children take on adult roles in the family, merging with the unfinished business of our forebears, and has devised some simple ways to begin our untwining. She invites us to make a drawing of our family. "Very simple," she says. "You make an image of your father, your mother, and yourself. Just three of you, with your nondominant hand." I get out my paper and crayons, choosing a red for my father and green for my mother. Between them, I draw myself in blue. Efu then says, "Okay, so now look at your drawing. Look at the image as it is. Don't go into any story, don't judge it. You're just looking at it." She pauses for a moment. "Notice the sensations in your body. Do any emotions come up right away? Just look at it and see how you feel."

As I look at my crude stick figure picture, I'm struck with overwhelming sadness. Squeezed between my parents, my little head is downturned, and I have no feet. The feeling is one of being cramped. No air.

Efu's voice brings me out of this uneasiness: "I'm going to invite you to draw again, this time with the dominant hand. The dominant hand brings us into more of a conscious awareness." She tells us to draw ourselves on the lower half of a piece of paper. And above, to put our father on one side and our mother on the other. "Draw a horizontal line between them showing that they are on the same level, and then a vertical line dropping down to you, one step below. You and your siblings are another generation. Of course, you know this: your parents are a generation up and you are one down, but see what happens when you look at it. How do you feel in your body? How do your emotions change from before?"

I look at what I have drawn. I'm astounded at the difference. I'm more in focus, there's a smile upon my face, I have feet on the ground. I take a deep breath and feel such a sense of relief, spaciousness, separateness. This is too simple, I think.

But everyone in the class is experiencing awe and relief over recovering this boundary. Efu tells us that this generational organization is what Family Constellations Therapy calls the orders of love: (1) honoring those who came before you, (2) the right to belong, and (3) balance between giving and receiving. Efu reiterates that we must come to know our place of belonging and recognize that what lives in one generation doesn't need to get passed down. She wants us to know that we can give back what is not ours and just receive the good resources that our ancestors want to give us. She concludes with, "This is the basic image we start with. We can go deeper, and we will, but for now just take this in, and remember that giving pours downward, like a waterfall, from older generations to younger. All we need to give back is our thanks and reverence."

Someone raises their hand, asking about caring for an aging parent and how it can seem that we take on the parent role and they the child. Efu underscores that we will always be the child of our parent. Nothing changes that. We may serve our mother or father in their old age, but we do it in our role as a child. "Everything is attitude. If we start thinking 'I'm their parent,' I suffer and things becomes very heavy." She tells us to imagine sitting on the floor, like a child, looking up at our mother or father. "That way you will remember your place of belonging, and everyone relaxes, and there is no need to fight or save them from their fate." Then she adds, "If you think of your help as a little service for Mum or Dad, things are okay—and then maybe ask for their blessing."

Later we do a practice where we distill what the core wound may have been for a parent with whom we are having a related problem. Before beginning any family constellation work, Efu wants us to feel present in our body, and she first guides us in some somatic stabilization exercises. Then, moving into the role reversal exercise, we are asked what we feel the parent most needed, related to this core wound, and then imagine our parent receiving the support that would have helped. Efu reminds us that our parents didn't have the tools we now have, didn't have therapy, and didn't talk about these things like we are doing today. But because the family is an organism, we can picture a troubled ancestor being given what they needed to heal, from other competent *adults*—not from us as a child, who out of loyalty took on their burdens, unconsciously merging with them. In this way, we don't have to keep carrying their wound. They get a chance to heal, and the healing ripples out: backward, forward, and in all directions.

I think of my mother and her core wound of losing *her* mother and being alone with the hurt. I'm now imagining her surrounded by a beloved aunt, who is really taking the time to be with her, holding my mother's sobbing body, saying soothing words, and telling her she is there for her. I take a deep breath and can feel my mum's shoulders drop, feel her relax; she is not so alone in her grief. A smile. Comes to her, comes to me. This is easy to say, but doing the work—allowing body sense and feeling sense to engage in this way—takes effort. However, the relief and internal shifts are palpable.

I slip into thinking about my own adult children. Concern over this or that comes up, but then I visualize the generational picture and see them on a different line than me. Their lives, not mine. I'm eager to learn more about this nonlinear place where psychology meets a spirituality rooted in ancestral wisdom; it seems almost magical. Peter Levine, the other course teacher, describes healing these generational ruptures as moving from the circle of damage to the circle of grace. Later, in meditation, seemingly out of the blue, the words come: *Mother understands.* And that night I dream that Mum and I are renovating the living room, changing outdated wallpaper and painting the gray walls white.

14

A Ripe Completion

*I recall sensing she was well and truly lost—but only in
the wondrous way that is suggested when my people, the
Yoruba of West Africa, say "to find your way, you must
become lost. Generously so."*

BAYO AKOMOLAFE

Old age spiritualizes people naturally.

RAM DASS

In my sulkier, meaner, narcissistic moments, I have discounted my
mother's life as rather bland, vague, and unfulfilled. Perhaps, in these
same moments, I would have brought my own life under the same narrow lens, fussing about my purpose and wondering if there was such a
thing as a calling or having a destiny.

What strikes me is that much of Mum's unfolding and transform-
ing seemed to happen dramatically in later life and in *how* she did her
aging and dying. In her years as a widow, unencumbered by the weight
of marriage, she cherished her independence and started coming home
to herself—volunteering, traveling with friends, playing shuffleboard,
even having a male companion for a few years. (She refused to marry
him, however, saying, "I will never wash any man's socks again!") As she
entered her nineties, advancing dementia and the feeling of being out
of control unsettled her, making her demanding, crotchety, and *mean*.

But ultimately, her willingness to shed layers of her old stubborn self, to soften, to open, to be suffused in love showed more than anything else what a life coming to a ripe completeness can look like. It may take until the end of one's days, it may take another lifetime, but this kind of purpose beckons to us all. What a gift for her that I can now see her in this light and a gift for me, a daughter, who has wrestled with a lifetime of tensions, to fill in an incomplete picture of her mother.

In opening that narrow lens, I see the exercise of practiced hindsight required to perceive the hand of destiny at work in shaping our lives. Those who undertake intentional biography work discover much about "chance" encounters: the urges and promptings, veiled though they may be, that bring us to choice points. Do we respond out of past fears? Wrestle with the demons of our unconscious when served a difficult brew of life? Do we grab the hand reaching out to help us? Fortunately, it's not our place to judge the life of another, but our own lives may at some point beg to be revealed for more of the story that they contain, particularly as age draws us closer to death's door. My own biographical delving has me wondering if it is *how* we do something rather than *what* we do that truly gives rise to the meandering path of important connections and sense of fulfillment. Being willing *to change course, to get lost, to not know, to keep going* keeps us humble and open to life. I don't think I'm the only one who has wondered, far beyond an age where it was due, "What will I be when I grow up?" In my mid-twenties I posted a saying on my fridge door, "My calling is where my joy and the world's needs meet." That was enough to set my sails by for a while. It also meant that I was fairly footloose in pursing various paths of education and employment, for there was always a truer compass point I was aiming for.

Mythologist Martin Shaw helps orient young people today when he writes, "You are not here to be anything that you want, you are here to be something quite specific."[1] Shaw is turning us away from the current adage declaring that *you can do anything and be anything*. That glibly assures us that there are no limits and "the world is your oyster." Accepting limitations, the boundaries that are set when the world says no to the me that wants and expects more, or that wants to fit in and conform, is the measure of building character. When the world says "No!"—to a long, comfortable, painless life—it takes us to the underworld where sculpting forces make and take life, make and break relationships, and ultimately make and bring wisdom. In this way, we find that just about everything we encounter has the potential to take us closer to ourselves and others or further away. Out of this cauldron a moment may come when we recognize our specific self and know that this deed we choose to do, this self we are choosing to be, is coming from a deeper imperative. Maybe we can call it destiny—a gift given without seeking a payback, no balance sheet involved.

And so I know that my mother's dying time, the long, wrestling runway up to and over the edge of her death, has this feeling of destiny ultimately written on it. *A seed sown for itself and also for some future unfolding. How could it be otherwise?*

Journal Entry: October 26, 2019

A support nurse arrives and gives my mother water. Mum cannot clear the water down her throat, and it is stuck there. (She had been put on thickened fluids to prevent this.) She is now choking, unable to bring up the fluid or to swallow it. The choking coughing continues. Suctioning with their small tube does not work. (Deep suction is done only in hospitals.) I'm feeling helpless and stricken at the sight of my mum trying to rest but not being able to. Hours go by. We are both exhausted. Help is surely what is needed. My friend Sher comes to mind; she is a wise woman who has many healing skills. I call her and ask for some distance healing help with Mum. Again, belief systems aside, I'm finding an openness to all ways. Sher uses crystals and is "directing" the healing properties of aquamarine to my mum's throat area. Within the hour, Mum's throat has cleared, and she is sleeping deeply, relieved of the choking. The nursing staff are startled at the sudden clearing but also relieved. I murmur words of gratitude to Sher and the grace that follows us.

In the evening, from her semiconscious state, Mum is saying in a loud singsong voice:

Sorry, Sorry, Sorry

SORry

SORRY!

I'm baffled at this outpouring, but something stirs within me. Matching her singsong voice, I say:

All is forgiven, Mum.

All is forgiven.

Oh, how we all need those merciful words, now, and at the hour of our death. I feel she must be very near the end. I flash back to my father's last words before going unconscious: "Tell your mother I am sorry. Tell Carly [Carolyn] I am sorry. I love you." Remembering these last words is still surreal. They are too cliché-like, as if in a movie script. But there you have it. So this lesson is underlined with both Dad and Mum. There is so much happening for each of us right up to and over the edge of dying: growth, self-examination, life review, and the yearning to make reparations—to name a few. Who really knows what wrestling with devils, angels, the dead, and the living is happening at the outer margins of soul-spirit when a person is lying frail and uncommunicative in their dying days?

Renowned palliative care physician Ira Byock has been writing for over twenty years on themes related to dying well. In his book *The Four Things That Matter Most*, he speaks of the tasks that are part of bringing completion to relationships during dying and bereavement. Giving and receiving forgiveness are top of the list, followed by expressions of thanks and of love and saying goodbye. I must add a comment here. This is not easy, but when dying is involved, relational work speeds up and what was hard yesterday is urgent today.

Dr. Kathryn Mannix also writes about what she sees as the natural tendency of wanting to make amends and to say words of forgiveness (including self-forgiveness), love, and gratitude. She says this is typical for those in their second half of life who have moved from a "me" focus to an "everyone and everything" focus. She has seen the most unlikely candidates transform in ineffable ways into bigger, more generous versions of themselves as death nears.[2] Exquisite stories are heard at the bedside. Most are reflections on how good and beautiful life is—the importance of relationships and connections with nature. Seldom about bank accounts. It's as if a narrow sense of self starts crumbling, making room for much, much more.

My parents fit this picture. They were not inclined to sustained self-reflection, yet the dying process, the *long* dying process, seemed to naturally give rise to seeing life from ever-larger perspectives. And with it came a certain humility, even with the obstacles of dementia and delirium. There is the assumption that when an elderly person's cognition declines, their self is no longer present. But with my parents and with those I have worked with, I have repeatedly been startled by the veil lifting, revealing a piercing lucidity that comes seemingly out of nowhere, often with humor. Layers of self that rise and fall, endlessly mysterious.

The words of supplication for forgiveness made by my father, and then by my mother, were transformational. With my dad, it was the culmination of many months in the hospital after he broke his hip. What it gave us was a concentrated time to get to know one another. When else would I—a young mother with two small children at home—be visiting with my father three or more times a week? What began as dreaded time alone with him became something else when I decided to fill this time with conversation meaningful to me. I remember asking him, "Do you feel old?" He responded, "No, in my mind I feel the same as I did when I was in my twenties." (I've since asked myself that question. What is it that remains within us unchanging while also growing and evolving?)

As our visits gathered steam, I grew bolder. I had had several sessions of psychotherapy over the past year and was learning about childhood repression of memories and submerged feelings of anger and so on. So, not angrily but in a matter-of-fact way, I told him I wanted to get some things off my chest, to clear the air between us about some childhood experiences. I said, "Dad, you know how you used to exaggerate my good school marks so you could boast to the rest of the family? I'd hear you on the phone saying I got a 90 on a test when I just told you I got an 80. I really hated that. It made my good mark not good enough . . . And remember when you would hit the back of my head with your hand, in a scoffing, joking kind of way that was maybe *your* way of connecting? It really jarred me. It felt harsh and made me confused . . . And I felt so bad when you spoke meanly about immigrants or people of color that I would hide, covering my ears with a pillow . . . And I remember being scared of you when you were drinking." On and on this went. He didn't say much, but with his eyes fastened on me, he *was* listening.

One afternoon, relieved of some of these wounds, I remembered something else.

ME: *Dad, you know that time when I dropped out in the middle of my fourth year in economics at Queen's to do social justice work full-time? Being the first to go to university in our whole family, I was so afraid to tell you I was quitting, thinking you and Mum would consider me a failure.*

DAD: *Hmmm. What happened?*

ME: *Well, I told you it was hard, and its values I didn't share. I was accused of being a communist because I did a seminar on credit unions as an alternative to big banks. Economics had come to mean nothing to me and was not going to lead me anywhere I wanted to go. I remember I cried.*

DAD: *Oh yeah. [He's not remembering but has become more alert with the word* cried.*]*

ME: *Then you said the most important thing to me that you could ever say. You said, "Whatever makes you happy, Nancy, that's all that matters."*

DAD: *[Smiles.]*

ME: *I'll never forget that, Dad.*

Telling my dad what made me appreciate and be proud of him became as important as telling him of my criticisms and hurts. It brought us closer together and freed me from being only the hurt child with him. This time with Dad also reminded me that the elderly parent in front of me, who is dying, is not the same person who didn't provide what I needed as a child. I was freeing him, and myself, from those past roles. Maybe this enabled him to speak to me in a way he never did with anyone else, for when I go back to my journal writing from that time, I find a man who used his long and painful sojourn for some deep reckoning.

Journal Entry: January 1995

Here is the gruesome reality: Dad in hospital, sometimes crazy, sometimes more lucid than any time in his life. Mum scared out of her wits at maybe having to take him home, where she'll have to serve and care for him. He is calling her to recollect their past. Is wanting to bring it up and account for his stupidity, but then says a belligerent thing and everything blows up again. So it's me, and only me, who hears his regretful admissions, "I know the problems with your mother, and it started when I didn't do a damn thing around the house for ten years, and I didn't care. And then there was the damn cottage. And being too interested in drinking. I was so stupid. I don't know how I could have been so stupid. Now it's too late. It takes having an accident like this to make a person realize how important family is. Your mother is the cleverest person I know. I would have been a bum without her."

Reading these words, years later, I slip into the past, going down a rabbit hole of half memories and tangled emotions—in fact, a dream tells me clearly, in a dream image, that I'm sitting with snakes in the cellar of my old house. I thought I'd finished with this compost pile, as I squirm. But Dad is feeling close to me right now. It's my mother's birthday; maybe he is needing something too. I phone my sister, Carolyn, and read her his words. She says, "He said that! Wow, I never would have guessed he could." Then, continuing, says, "I don't know how many times I've wished that I'd known him better and could talk to him again." We're sad together for a moment, and then she tells a funny story about him and we are laughing. I guess life is like that. And the forward motion of life takes us onward. This little detour, however, has bought us a dose of realness and richness about what can happen at the end of life to the most unlikely people. Then along with the amazement comes the regret that Dad said the things that he did back then but to the wrong person.

By saying "I'm sorry," and meaning it, a lamp is lit on the past, allowing our minds, with their capacity for plasticity, to renegotiate what lights up. This is much different than forgetting. Forgiveness helps us move on, helps everyone move on, even if you don't get to hear the "I'm sorry" words. There's no one recipe on how to do this. All I know is that when the snakes come, just sit with them, compassionately. And when the waves of uncomfortable memories and emotions rise, ride them out. Is this what it means to die before you die? If so, resurrection forces are also at play because right now, miraculously, my memories are touched with a tinge of light.

Three days before Dad dies, I visit him. He's delirious, in some nightmarish world that I can only occasionally awaken him from. Then he calls out for my mum, saying "Marion, Marion, Marion . . . I love you so much. I'm sorry, sorry. Forgive me, Marion, Marion, Marion." Then, "Tell Nancy that I love her. And Carly, tell my little Carly." So when in turn I whisper back the awkward little words "I forgive you," they come naturally.

Shopping in an outdoor craft market one day, a woman vendor approaches me. I've been admiring her silk scarves. We start talking, and after a while she gets a faraway look in her eyes and leans into me, saying mysteriously, "There's someone with you." I looked around, wondering who she was talking about. She said, "It's a man. An older man. Someone who's died and who wants you to know something." Not taking this too seriously, I say in an offhand way, "Oh, my dad?" "Yes," she says, in a serious tone, "that's it. He is saying that he knows he wasn't always a good dad. He says he didn't know how to be. But he loved you and still does. He is saying that he is helping you now, to make up for what he didn't do before." Heaving a big sigh, I reply, "Yes, I know."

What *is* the purpose of living a very long life? When dependency and ailments come to dominate each day, this question will arise within the soul of the very old and those around them. (Here, I'm not talking about aggressive medical treatments that tend to prolong dying or other means of interfering with natural death.) Gone are the days when our Old Ones were revered for simply having lived a long unique life. Now we think in terms of *usefulness*, of being *burdened*, and the societal *costs* of caring for our elders.

But is it possible that in our aging bodies something else is happening that we don't understand, defying our usual ways of thinking that prioritize productivity? Could it be that in the long, slow demise of our physical bodies a spiritual process is simultaneously happening? While visiting Clara, a ninety-five-year-old patient one day, she commented, "I don't have anything to do most of the time, but I sit here and think good thoughts about my grandchildren and pray. You know, dear, I sit here praying for the world all the time." The very old do have a role, an important one, balancing out our frantic pace, maybe opening a door for us all to the spiritual realm that they are drawing closer to. This is a destiny, too, but will always remain veiled to our clever, busy selves.

Old-growth forests. No question of *their* worth. At the back of a farmer's field, I'm looking at a very old oak tree, bark peeling, limbs missing, and leaves yellowing and withering. I observe insects boring into the wood and birds eating the insects while squirrels busy themselves harvesting acorns. A little farther away there's another tree, one that has fallen. Decay has done its work: many seedlings are sprouting from the mossy, crumbling mass of humus. It seems that a tree lives half its life as a living tree and then a second life as a rotting trunk. In fact, it may be that when a tree's life has ended, its usefulness is about to peak, not diminish. Grandma or Grandpa in the nursing home is not an old tree. But nature always brings another way to ponder things.

15
A Good Death?

Striving to better, oft we mar what's well.

SHAKESPEARE, *KING LEAR*

Perfection is the enemy of the good.

VOLTAIRE, *DICTIONNAIRE PHILOSOPHIQUE*

Last March, my friend Allison called to tell me that her elderly father, Tommy, had been recently diagnosed with leukemia. He was dying, with just weeks to live. She and her dad had a contentious relationship that had not softened over the years, even with his advancing dementia. He was angry much of the time, medications only increasing his confusion. Allison was at a loss to know if she'd be able to have the kind of conversation with him that she felt was so necessary and whether she could address any of the very sore spots in their family history. Being at the very end stages of life is not the optimal time to expect great transformation if the ground has not in some way been prepared. This is true for both sides. A degree of emotional healing, or at least perspective, is required to not completely fall into a pit of still wanting the parent to fulfill an unmet need. (A good reason why it's never too early to start laying the groundwork for reconciling relationships.) But the courage to allow one's vulnerability may be the ingredient that loosens the brickwork. Being able to say something like, *Dad, we've had our ups and downs over the years, but I want you to know that I love you and thank you for what you have given me* is a huge gift to a dying man. And a lifetime gift to yourself.

As difficult as this was to say, it was even more difficult for Allison to find the right time to have this heart-to-heart with her dad. There is often a swirl of activity and bustle around the bed of a dying person when they are awake and increasingly long periods of quiet time when they are asleep. My friend had to be quite intentional to make a space open up to say what she wanted. Even then, she remarked after his death, "Words did not seem to penetrate. I *so* wanted this connection I longed for. But why would I expect it to be different? Don't we die as we have lived?" After a long pause, she said with resolution, "But it doesn't mean we failed." The biggest healing, she came to realize, was in the process of trying to articulate what it was she wanted to say to her dad in the first place. The soul searching, the tears, the words, the writing, all contributed to absorbing and meeting the situation as it was. What then was communicated, Allison believes, were gestures of care and love: a gentle touch here and there, noticing needs before he had to exert himself to ask, and her attempts to create a tranquil environment. This is a good reminder that communication is happening all the time, with or without words.

Still, my friend felt conflicted about whether she had been able to help her dad die a "good death." Allison had once been a hospice volunteer where she had witnessed what providing a loving presence for the dying could mean. Her training meant that she knew to be relaxed, to sit close by, to allow a quiet intimacy where compassion, loving awareness, and acceptance of death is made palpable, to trust that the person will do the rest, in their own way, on their terms. This role of being the warm but less attached witness, known throughout time and diverse cultures for its importance, is returning, as are opportunities for providing it now for others through hospice volunteering, death doula work, and community death networking. It's much, much harder to be detached with a loved one, as Allison found out. With her own father, her emotions and expectations, along with those of her siblings, kept surfacing. One sibling wanted to keep talking to her Dad while clasping his hand. Allison gently suggested to her sister that she could place her hand under her father's, so that he could move it if touch was becoming too much for him. Another sibling would sit in the room with the television on. It was awkward and stressful for Allison to try and protect the space around her father, knowing from experience that a quiet, peaceful atmosphere, where only a few soft words are occasionally needed, is most helpful.

Later, it struck us both that there is *no one way* of fulfilling the image of a good death. Life is about compromise, and somehow life adapts itself to meet us where we are. Every person has their own unique journey, and what is helpful for one may not be for another. Every situation has its own host of constraints. With Allison, this also included the COVID-19 outbreak. Her father could only go to the hospice facility with the agreement that just his wife could visit him, so he stayed home and had caregivers come and go. The care was uneven, but this did allow him to die in his own home. I said, "Maybe it's the willingness and courage to find openings in each situation, where a deepening presence can find its way, that is more the marker to aim for than an unattainable image of the ideal death." Nodding, Allison went on to describe the sense of completion and joy that came in the Zoom family gathering they held following her dad's death, with stories being shared and lots of laughter and crying. Then, a few days later, at the time of the cremation, with candles lit in their respective homes, family and friends from far and wide raised a glass to Tommy, honoring and blessing his way. These seemingly small markers fulfilled the most important needs—to grieve and support each other in a time of isolation and together to say goodbye to a loved one.

New York death educator, doula, and somatic therapist Jeanne Denney has written a small guide, available for free on her website, titled

Working with the Pain of Separation: A Guide for Caring and Mourning at a Distance. Under the heading "What Loved Ones Can Do," she gives practical advice on how to bridge the gap of not being physically present: "A memorial may have to happen in the distant future. This surely adds grief to grief. But it may help us to remember that time is especially malleable around the death. The same processes can expand into weeks or contract into moments. They are still the same processes, no less important."[1] Denney goes on to offer the following practical advice:

Inventory what you would want to say and do if you WERE at your loved one's bedside. Then set up a space in your home or outside to be your "sitting at a distance" place. Maybe you can place their picture there. Go there when you wish you could be with them. Sit. Imagine making a linkage between that place and their bedside. Try to center and bring them to mind with as much loving compassion as you can, just as a hospital visit. You may feel things or even see images of them in your "mind's eye." Some people do. Let yourself be open to that. . . .

When and if you feel that you might, just might, have a sense of them, say what you wish you could say out loud or in silence. Give encouragement. Shower them with affection.[2]

Denney emphasizes creating a loving, beautiful environment, perhaps by playing soothing music, bringing flowers, lighting a candle—tapping into both our heart and our imagination to do this. It's simultaneously a casual and a ritual space, one where, she suggests, you can complain about something as if you were in the kitchen together.

Sing them a song. If you have regrets, speak apologies. Hold your hands in your lap as if you could cradle them in it. Hold them in your heart. You get the idea. If you make this space for sacred communication, I am willing to bet that you will know what to do. . . .

Love powered by mindfulness at a distance can still be very much felt, especially by people who are ill, and who we are connected to. Behave as if this was so. Behave as if your heart was a cell phone calling theirs. It is something like that.[3]

Learning to give love and offer presence and touch from a distance became new territory for humanity during the pandemic days of physical distancing and restricted travel. I feel so fortunate that I was able to fulfill a daughter's role of caregiving and keeping vigil at the bedside of my dying mother, where unforgettable lessons about the preciousness of life, relationships, and death took place. When such a role is taken away, the anguish can be debilitating. It has become familiar practice to plan for funerals and celebrations of life at some point well after the immediate death to accommodate many circumstances. Though understandable in many cases, I wonder what gets lost. Let's not forget that when a death occurs, the skies open—for mourning, grieving, and some form of coming together with others. Let's not try to postpone everything. And yes, later down the road come together again for a memorial service. A memorial service offers a different kind of opportunity to gather, recollect, and honor the one who's died, time having eased some of its early shock and pain. The opportunity is less about fixing and freezing our recollecting into a memory of the past and more about allowing their presence to be uplifted, as well as our own, through our coming together.

Since time immemorial, creatures have huddled together during the dark and bleak nights—the season of the soul. Our deepest instinctual knowledge, let us remember, comes from observing animals and the cycles of nature. Tellingly, elephants have long been recognized for their uncanny instinct to come from afar to gather when one of their kin has died. Vigiling for several days, they take turns investigating, caressing, and standing guard over the body, appearing deeply moved while also reassuring each other. Tenderness and support beyond rationalization comes from just being together, no matter our species.

Just as death, dying, and grieving are pervasive themes around the planet right now, so is there a spotlight on injustices, present and long buried, that seek to meet the light of day. In the midst of the pandemic, the literalness of this struck me when I saw a newspaper headline: "Remains of Indigenous Children Found in Unmarked Graves." I read how hundreds of Indigenous children, having died while at residential schools from the late nineteenth century to the 1970s, were buried without their families knowing, without ceremony, without the prayers of their people to help them to the next world. I shuddered at the gravity of what this would mean for most of these children's families. Now, so many years later, it is important to pause, to give space to listen, and to tend the bones and lost dreams and ancestral lines of these many children, to help them to finally be seen. When tending the dead, time stands still for this all-important ritual. Years ago can be right now. I contemplate all of this as I offer prayers of my own. Many eyes look back.

During this same time in 2021, as some Roman Catholic churches in Canada were set ablaze and calls for a papal apology to Indigenous communities intensified, I came across some scraggly, loose notes taken from my time working with Roman Catholic sisters in their residence, the Motherhouse. It was a student work placement, and I found it difficult in that my conversations with these "nice" nuns left me feeling hollow inside. It just seemed so hard to penetrate the niceness, to get to what felt like *real* feeling, not just the overlay of what should be felt or expressed. Admittedly, I was a comparative youngster, and why should I, an outsider, be treated as someone to really open up to?

One afternoon, all the sisters in the area were invited to a workshop. It was eye-opening to listen to their ideas. Far from polite niceness, Sister Rene, standing at the podium, said fervently, "Don't be afraid to make a new image of God! Evolution means having a God big enough for us and our world today." Hands in the air, she continued, "Old images of God gave us the direction to push people out, or denigrate them for being bad or ignorant, because we were the true God-fearing people. We sure were God fearing! Afraid of everything!"

Sister Lillian shouted out from her seat, "*Slow down*, Sister. I'm an introvert. Give us some time to reflect." A ripple went through the group, and a silence became palpable. Sister Maureen then stood up. "I've been thinking of these things for a while. But I work with elderly sisters—they aren't able to work with these ideas. What they seem to need is a sense of worthiness at the end of life. For you see, there is regret that comes up. A lot of regret about how they were as teachers. They ask themselves, 'Was I too hard on the students?'"

Sister Rene replied, "We grew into the image of God we made for ourselves. We have to realize, humbly, our spiritual narcissism and self-sanctification. We created a distant and unemotional God from the Greek world and then thought we were all knowing about suffering and evil. Spiritual perfection is perfectly impossible. It has left us feeling guilty, sleazy, dead, empty, and wrong inside."

Sister Lillian spoke up loudly and clearly again. "But how do I practically do this?" Different voices answered out, "Catch yourself judging." "Deal lovingly without condemnation." "Struggle is a sign of new life emerging in us." "Stop terrifying the children!" Then from Sister Rene: "We really must go down into the womb and be born again."

There was fire in the room that afternoon. It came home with me, made me see that endings send us back to beginnings, especially these days, when the need personally and collectively is so great. What else is rising to meet the light of day? And can we meet it with mercy?

16

Building a Little Ship
for Your Dead

*Let children walk with Nature, let them see the beautiful
blendings and communions of death and life . . . and they
will learn that death is stingless indeed, and as beautiful
as life.*

JOHN MUIR, *A THOUSAND-MILE WALK TO THE GULF*
(WRITTEN WHILE CAMPING FOR A WEEK IN
BONAVENTURE CEMETERY, SAVANNAH, GEORGIA)

*The only remedy for the fear of death is to look at it
constantly in the face.*

ATTAR, SUFI SAINT

*Help thy brother's boat across, and lo! Thine own has
reached the shore.*

HINDU PROVERB

Some twenty years ago, I read an article in a magazine about something
called green burials. The writer was describing how a sensitive conservation area at risk of being redeveloped had been protected by local
green burial proponents who arranged to use it for natural burials. The
burial fees would go to maintaining the conservation area; the bodies
themselves would contribute to the replenishing of the soil by becoming

compost. I read, "Imagine your final resting place—a beautiful meadow full of butterflies, bees, and wildflowers. Your very presence restoring nature and protecting the land forever."

To me, it felt like a win-win combination of ideals and practical problem-solving. I was thrilled. I tucked the idea away—knowing that it was not yet the right timing for such an endeavor in my region. I kept my interest alive by subscribing to the magazine *Natural Transitions*, reading books, and talking to people about it.

The right time has arrived, and green burial sites and initiatives are emerging everywhere (natural burial has always been a part of Jewish and Muslim practices). Mum would have liked being buried in this kind of way, but she had chosen cremation many years ago when she did her funeral planning. My father had been the first of our extended family to be cremated, and Mum liked the simplicity of this approach. Cremation has become a popular option over the past thirty years or so, far surpassing conventional ground burial. Is it also because it is speedy, and we have become accustomed to fast everything? Burial slows things down, allowing the physical body to return to the earth slowly. Steiner says this could be of help to those who die suddenly, where the shock can mean not immediately realizing one is dead, or through suicide, where a longing for the body can remain. Today, many people are keen to consider green burial because of its lower carbon footprint and because the basic tenets are so appealing.

....

Five Principles of Green Burial

No Embalming

A loved one's body is well cared for with proper cooling and natural products before burial. The products are biodegradable, whereas embalming fluids are toxic for the earth.

Earth Burial

Using biodegradable caskets or shrouds, bodies are buried three feet down in the earth. This permits natural decomposition and nourishes the earth. Concrete vaults and liners are not used.

Ecological Restoration and Conservation

Green burials minimize environmental impact, have a very low carbon footprint, and aid in the restoration and protection of natural habitat.

Communal Memorials

Names are engraved on natural stone or wood and are placed centrally to identify those buried in the area. The green burial site as a whole becomes a living memorial to the persons interred there.

Land Use

Minimal infrastructure optimizes land use. The beauty and atmosphere encourage its use for rituals and celebrations, as well as for respectful enjoyment by the community.[1]

These are the basic principles, but what is it like to hear that our bodies can nourish the earth, much like good compost? I'm not against cremation, but I have found a longing to be buried, submerged into the belly of Earth herself, to give back my body to the root of all things, and in doing so to become a part of all things. It's worth looking at what causes us to shudder and gives rise to disgust. For many, it's often images of decomposition. But if we can get beyond squeamishness and enter into the rich alchemical underworlds of microorganisms and fermentation—processes of decay that transform and sustain all life (as our old preserving and pickling grandmothers knew well)—there is a wonder to behold. The writer Lia Purpura evocatively describes this terrain head-on:

Days after death, when the bloat comes on, scents rise and beckon very precisely to the (microbial) first responders—coffin flies, who find their way six feet down. Blowflies, carrion flies, and their young fill the dark, shallow spots next, probing the pouches and channels of us. . . . We reorder as gas, liquid, sugar, and salt. . . . The decades long stretching, darkening, and drying; time collecting as it does on wood, where it gets called by its forest names, lichen/moss/fungi.[2]

Reading this gave new meaning to noticing the earth beneath my feet and the understanding that our great-grandmothers and great-grandfathers are more than metaphorically alive in our midst. Whatever we may hold as a spiritual understanding of continuing after death, we cannot deny that we do live on in *becoming earth*. That molecules of our body are taken up by the roots of grass, flowers, and trees is not just poetry; it is something that really happens. Participation in this cycle of life-death-renewal cannot be avoided, only somewhat postponed with cement vaults, fortified coffins, and an array of environmentally *un*friendly chemicals. While the conventional depth of six feet under delays decomposition, three feet under safely allows our bodies to decompose rapidly and organically. Using shrouds and natural pine caskets and not embalming will do likewise. Green burial sites provide a place to visit and for community to participate in a memorial made sacred by the buried bones of our beloveds, in a natural locale of beauty, carefully tended. There is much solace in this.

. . . .

We Are Biodegradable!

Oxygen 65%

Carbon 18%

Hydrogen 10%

Nitrogen 3%

Other 4%

. . . .

It's a solace that animals, too, seem to feel. Koko the gorilla became famous for her gift with language, her compassion, and her remarkable friendship with the late actor and comedian Robin Williams. She communicated in sign language to an extraordinary degree, and when a trainer once signed the question, "Where do animals go when they die?" Koko replied, *To a comfortable hole in the ground.* So may it be.

It was in 2017 that the death guide Aileen Stewart and I organized a gathering of people to hold sustained conversations about death, in particular natural death care. Our Kingston community group of twelve women met monthly for over a year. We called the group Closing Time (influenced by that sultry Leonard Cohen song). Speaking about our own experiences with death—our fears, discomforts, and vulnerabilities—laid the groundwork for a deep engagement with a range of topics: preparing for death, what dying looks like, grief as a practice and way of life, advance care planning, home funerals, how to bring a body home from the hospital, and staying connected with our beloveds who have died. In the midst of this, we had a daylong workshop on how to wash and prepare a body after death, with one of our members volunteering to be the "dead" person.

She lay on a massage table while the rest of us took on caring for her body with reverence and with an awareness of an abiding consciousness still present. Gently washing her body with soap and water, doing hair care, and figuring out how to lift the dead weight of a body into a coffin, we moved slowly, hummed quietly, and spoke to our beloved dead friend to let her know what we were doing and to give assurance. Afterward, even though we were practicing on a living person, everyone spoke of how moved they were by this intimate and sacred act. We all pondered on the deep bodily knowing that caring for our dead is an ancient birthright. Several people spoke of how they did not see the body of their loved one when they died, let alone care for them, and how this still tugged at them. One woman said, "I was afraid that I would be haunted by the image of what my friend looked like, so I didn't go to her at the end or see her body. I really regret that; it would have helped me grieve and let go."

Perhaps it was how we began our first Closing Time gathering that set the tone for what followed. Aptly enough, our first meeting was on November 1, traditionally celebrated as the Day of the Dead. On this day, we are told, the line between the living and the dead is at its thinnest. These days, the focus is on Halloween, dispensing candy and dressing up, but its ancient origins lie in Celtic spiritual beliefs that the dead visited at that time of year when the harvest gave way to winter and that prayers were especially heard. This was a time that heralded a turning inward, to find the sun within us, to warm our souls through the cold and dark days ahead. However, as Roman Catholicism gained ascendency, this celebration of Samhain was instead converted into All Saint's Day. This was a common means by which the church appropriated customs to dislodge deeply held rituals that bound a people, a particular place, and their dead together.

Though the original impulse of the Day of the Dead has been diluted, it has not entirely disappeared. In Poland, for example, the occasion is celebrated by visiting and decorating gravesites with thousands of glowing candles. My Polish niece felt out of sorts by not having a graveyard to visit this past November 1, so she went to the closest cemetery she could find and lit candles at random tombstones, offering a prayer as she did so. Mexico is especially well known for its Día de los Muertos, dating back from Aztec times. In this community festival, home altars are adorned with pictures of dead loved ones, and there are vibrant celebrations of ancestors, even picnics, on their graves. My friend Gayle, who lives in Texas, recently wrote to me about her preparations: "I especially like that the Day of the Dead represents an acceptance of death, that it's part of a cycle of life that we can hold without grief, recognizing that those beloveds without bodies are always with us and our invitation to them to visit again is always open. Altars are a work of art and a work of the heart."

Many other cultures have similar tributes, such as in Japan with the equinox festivals of Ohigan (gathering on the other shore) and the summer Obon(a Buddhist festival and celebration of ancestors, whose spirits are believed to come back during this time to visit relatives). In China, there yet remain rituals for honoring the ancestors, one being the Festival of Hungry Ghosts. During this time empty chairs are left at the table for ancestors, and they are offered feasts of food to fill all their unsatisfied hungers.

The phrase *hungry ghosts* captures my imagination. Haven't I heard it elsewhere? Yes, Buddhism says this is what we can become if our insatiable desires follow us through the portal of death. I remember this term somewhere else, too. A friend who works in addiction counseling told me of the book *In the Realm of Hungry Ghosts: Close Encounters with Addiction* by Gabor Maté. Maté notes that at the core of all our addictions are hungry ghosts, emerging out of unmet basic needs for warmth and security in childhood. Hungry ghosts increasingly haunt us all. But there's another reference I'm looking for. I go to my bookshelf, run my fingers over the titles, and find it: *The Smell of Rain on Dust* by Martín Prechtel, shamanic explorer and teacher.

Prechtel speaks of the traditional way his Indigenous forebears considered the term. He says that a dead person's soul left ungrieved, unpraised, not communally lifted up, does not have the energy to move forward and to find its way. Without the will to move on, the dead person may hesitate, turn around, and want to return, but without a body the soul lingers around those who do have bodies—the closest family members. This unwanted, unmoored soul, far from being an ancestor, lives off the vitality of the living, usually the youngest or most vulnerable family member who may have holes in their auric field or an overly sympathetic resonance. A hungry ghost can wreak havoc down the family line, often expressed in the form of alcoholism and other addictions. This dire picture, Prechtel notes throughout his book, drives the understanding of why it is important to grieve, to praise, and to provide ritual for those who've died. And why, in many cultures, ceremonies to appease the dead who may still be hungry, who still remain close to the earth, are so important in helping them on their way, and, when necessary, *to send them on their way!*

Our current Western culture, alas, is notably threadbare when it comes to appreciating the significance of any of this, getting easily spooked, as it were, in such unfamiliar terrain that other societies have traversed for eons. Superstition and fear aren't the best motivators; rather, the felt connection, and the sense of settledness and peace that so often occur when our dead are honored, are the reward. We are increasingly being reminded of what has been let go of and lost sight of. The animated movie *Coco*, released in 2017, focuses on the significance of the Day of the Dead. As I watched, I wondered whether stories like this would help a new generation to restore and value our connections with the dead.

Imitating the old ways can, however, feel false, untrue to the present. Quiet reflection and inner sensing are the best starting places. And then join with others and bring out photos of deceased loved ones. Light candles, say their names, and offer nourishing thoughts and gratitude. I don't think we can underestimate the care and warm support this gives. This is especially true for those who have died a difficult death, such as suicide, and who especially need comfort and orientation, perhaps for a long while. In this way, we also subtly instruct the people who may be helping us when we die while rekindling a sense of responsibility and community with the *far shore.*

D. H. Lawrence wrote passionately and tenderly of this in the poem "All Souls' Day":

Be careful, then, and be gentle about death.
For it is hard to die,
it is difficult to go through the door,
even when it opens.

. . .

Be kind, Oh be kind to your dead
and give them a little encouragement

. . .

Each needs a little ship, a little ship
and the proper store of meal for the longest journey.
Oh, from out of your heart
provide your dead once more, equip them
like departing mariners, lovingly.[3]

After we recited this beseeching poem on our first Closing Time gathering, we posed the following question to one another: Who brought you here tonight? In the stillness that followed, taking turns, we each named and spoke of a dear one who had died and who provided inspiration for us to come to the group. I spoke first of my dad. Others named their departed ones, and in the deepening quiet, the room felt very full. We continued this practice, lighting a candle each time we met and naming the Old Ones who gathered along with us. It was a remarkably gracious time.

As it turned out, in addition to being drawn to death talk, most of us in Closing Time also had a love of singing. "What a great combination," reflected Aileen one day. "Why don't we propose developing bedside singing for the dying?" I was familiar with music thanatology—a discipline used to comfort and support the dying person using prescriptive music for harp and vocals. Practiced in some palliative care units, it has its historical roots in medieval monastic times—the ethereal sounds evoking other realms to be sure. Though we didn't have a harpist, nor the in-depth training of a music thanatologist, we wondered if some carefully chosen vocal arrangements could be a welcome offering for some people.

We formed the group Encircle and gathered monthly to practice chanting, sounding tones, improvising, and singing rounds, lullabies, and hymns. We were always contemplating what a dying person might find comforting versus jarring or overstimulating and how to recognize this. Sometimes, one of us would sit or lie while the rest of the group gathered around them, singing, humming, or chanting. This gave us important feedback. We learned what it felt like, bodily, to receive and be immersed in these sounds. We then had to imagine the extra sensitivity that a dying person would have and keep adjusting. We enjoyed the friendship and beauty of our fledgling group, but trying this out in real time, with real dying people, was tricky. How to start?

Mum's slow dying time meant that I didn't have a sense of her imminent dying until, suddenly, she was. And then I couldn't quite think of her being open to having strangers come in to sing for her. What did happen was that Sher, a dear friend and herself a singer, came with me to visit Mum just three days before she died.

Journal Entry: October 27, 2019

Mum is in a semiconscious state, curled up on her side like a small child—her knees drawn up and her hands tucked under the thin flannel sheet. I ask Sher, "Will you sing something for her? Something old and familiar?" We think for a few moments, and "Away in a Manger" comes to mind. In a beautiful soprano voice, Sher quietly and slowly starts singing Mum's favorite Christmas carol. Mum turns her head, trying to hear better. When Sher finishes, Mum whispers, "More, more." Sher sings it again and pauses. Mum looks rapturous, and so she goes on to sing "Silent Night." At the end, Mum reaches

her arms out, crying, "Mummy!" It was the sweetest moment, for all
of us. That sweetness now becomes a pool of water in front of me.
I feel myself lean over, stirring it with my own aged hand, while the
currents of time swirl achingly together.

The next day, I dare repeating this sublime moment. I invite four
people from Encircle to come to Mum's bedside. What begins as sheer
beauty becomes a mixed experience. Is Mum in a different place now?
Are there too many of us in the room? Is she in discomfort? She calls
out in a plaintive voice, interrupting the singing, repeatedly. Sometimes,
it's as if she wants more, and then as if she wants it all to stop. Maybe,
I'm wondering, she can't hear because her good ear is facing down. I
carefully help adjust her head on the pillow. Now she settles and is taking in the harmonies, like gentle waves upon the shore. But less is often
more. So after a short time, my friends leave, glad for this invaluable
experience that shows there is much to know and be mindful of at the
bedside of a dying person.

17

Bringing Mum Home

Houses need births and deaths to become homes.
ISABEL ALLENDE, *PAULA: A MEMOIR*

As committed as I was to the idea of bringing my mother home after her death and knowing I had good support through Aileen and our community of friends from Closing Time, the closer the reality got, the more nervous I got. I became full of doubts about my ability to handle everything. I was seeing all the complications that could happen, scared at my dwindling energy and the impact that bringing Mum home would have on my family.

Michael knew of my interests and inclinations over our many years of marriage, and he shared them. Of course, interested as he was in cultivating a new approach to dying and death, doing so is a different manner. A lot of people are squeamish around bodily functions and excretions, blood and the like. Although Michael starts to swoon at any graphic mention of medical procedures, he was game for the adventure of bringing Mum home. Still, it was *me* being worried about *him* that added to my nerves. Then there was twenty-six-year-old Elena. She had heard me talking about this interest of mine for some time now, but again the practical details of what might be asked of her was another thing. I didn't want to impose or freak her out, so this, too, added to my nerves. Casey, twenty-nine, lived in Edmonton. I spoke with him by phone a number of times about bringing his grandmother's body home so he wouldn't be taken by surprise. He accepted this rather matter-of-factly. It seems that young people these days have not grown up with just one set way of doing things. Contemporary traditions are weak enough that new ways can inch in without arousing established defenses.

Carolyn did not want to be part of this stage of the journey: the literally hands-on caring for Mum's body. This kind of unfamiliar intimacy made her, not unlike many people in North America certainly, uneasy and uncomfortable. What seemed a natural inclination to me was something that she found difficult, even to talk about. Her response to the nitty-gritty physical aspect of dying and death is neither unusual in our society nor in our family: Mum was like this, too, not wanting to be close up to Dad as he lay dying. It takes intentionality, exposure, and willingness to go beyond what's become an ingrained conditioning. (Remarkable, really, given that it's only a few generations since the duty of caring for the bodies of the dead has been taken over by business models and interests.) However, peering over unknown edges has always served me in taking roads less traveled, and circumstances themselves have pushed me out of the comfort of my hobbit hole often enough.

The best of relationships allows for differences, and this is what Carolyn and I were attempting, knowing that maintaining our sisterhood was more important than either of us "being right." I admit I was frustrated and perplexed. I was afraid of offending her, overstepping my bounds, overpowering her with my experience and determination, eclipsing her needs and her own sense of how things should go. For Carolyn's part, I'm sure she was alarmed, worried about me, and uncertain about her role at this pivotal time.

Outside my family, everyone I spoke with about bringing Mum home was more *intrigued* than anything else. We were breaking ground in more ways than one. Yet my nervousness persisted—until the day, three days before Mum died, when an inner voice commanded, *Get the casket.* It was like a switch turned on, and I knew the timing was now to make the vigil room ready. I needed to see things in place to imagine the steps that would come afterward. The long inward preparation was moving into the next phase of action. Soon Jeff, a family friend, was on his way to help Michael pick up the pine box coffin from the funeral home. Shortly thereafter, Aileen came to go over the supplies and room setup. We had been warned that in home death care, the casket had to be maneuvered both in *and* out of a room. I considered this a small detail that would not be an issue; after all, we lived in a regular-sized bungalow, not an apartment building. It soon became evident, however, that the casket went into the room *only* by standing it *upright* and jostling it through the doorway. This would not do.

A few good minds go a long way: I let Michael and the others figure out the mechanics that would eventually mean we would be *lifting* Mum's body out of the casket using her sheets as a sling, then upending the coffin to get it out the doorway and through the narrow hallway to the front door. Mum would then be placed back in the casket, where she would wait for the van to pick her up. But I'm jumping ahead.

Picking up the storyline where I left off back in the long-term-care home: My mother having just died, the nurses and the doctor having finished their parts, the death certificate made out, and Michael and Elena having just left . . . I collapse in Mum's big blue armchair. A moment later, the door opens: it's Chris, Mum's most regular personal care worker and her favorite. I hadn't seen Chris in the past week and had been really missing her presence. I felt she knew Mum and had an important relationship with her—she could cajole her into taking a shower or a spoon of soup when no one else could. Not knowing that I was still in the room, Chris had come to say goodbye. "I have to tell you," she admitted, "that I asked to *not* take care of Marion this week. It's so hard to always lose them, especially ones like your mum. She was tough, but underneath we understood each other, and we had our fun."

She leaned over Mum and whispered, "I love you Marion, goodbye," and departed tearfully. I had to marvel at the bonds of relationships that can happen right up to our final days, becoming so significant at the end of life. Our devoted health care workers are often the stand-in for that son or daughter not there in the final hours, offering the warm touch of companionship and compassion as death arrives.

After Chris departed, I was finally alone in the room with Mum. In a daze, I tried to rest, but couldn't—too much adrenaline, too much shock. In my hospital work, I often saw family members in this state after experiencing a death. Shock is a buffer zone that provides a helpful cushion for body and nerves and hormones to adjust to a radical event. So I allowed myself to be in this awkward place, knowing my internal rhythms would align if I just let myself be and try not to force anything. It was difficult for me not to rush into the many phone calls that should be made, but after the first few essential ones I knew the others could come a little later.

If this transition was a struggle for me, then I knew it must be so for Mum. Letting her body rest while she was going through the initial transitions seemed a courtesy. Among the most important lessons I have learned, and have offered to others, is to *slow everything down*. As I emphasized earlier, death is *not* an emergency. It is helpful to be in conversation with caregivers and staff or management to find ways that *slow* can prevail, so that tending the moments around death is not a hurried affair. Being hurried and getting distracted is a common symptom of our discomfort. And, with adrenaline coursing through our bodies, it's hard to just sit; it's easier *to do something*. Just make sure there is still time to slow down; make sure you don't miss the important moment because stress hormones have taken over. Having someone remind us of this is something we all will need at such intense times.

In most circumstances, I have found a great willingness to meet a family's request for time. In our case, the staff at the long-term-care home bent over backward to be accommodating. They showed us into a family room where we could gather and rest, providing refreshments and snacks. And they let Mum stay in her room after death for as long as we thought necessary. This lingering time felt very important, and it was only after many hours that I could feel the next step had come. The tending to the feeling of *right timing* prevailed over every juncture of this death journey. It was as if I had acquired a new sense: not knowing in advance what to do but discovering it.

The funeral home directors would be arriving soon. Both in my capacity as a member of Closing Time and on behalf of my mum's needs, I had developed a good relationship with this local family-owned-and-run company—one that has roots in and a commitment to the community, not part of the corporate funeral industry that can be driven by profit. About five months before Mum died, thinking it time to get organized, Aileen and I went to speak with Sarah, the assistant manager, and to Heather, head of preplanning and a funeral director herself. We were surprised at their openness and willingness to consider how to work with families who wanted to bring their loved one's body home. Although our interests were unusual, we were not made to feel strange, looked upon suspiciously, or considered to be taking business away from them. Indeed, we were *all* greatly heartened by this chance to work collaboratively in this emerging societal movement.

In our initial meetings, we talked about transporting the body home, the most environmentally friendly casket and shroud for cremation, and options for a family to remain with their loved one's body if choosing to make use of the funeral home's services. I like to plan. That's how I envision things to know what lies ahead, and my need for planning particularly shows up when I'm anxious. I began to make a list of needs based on the different scenarios Mum's death could take.

I'd thought of every detail. But two weeks before Mum died,

accompanied by my sister at this next-to-last meeting with Heather and Sarah, I was shaking.

ME: *I'm getting cold feet, Heather. I'm so tired now, and when I think of the days ahead until Mum dies and then the work and details of bringing her body home . . . I'm starting to feel so overwhelmed.*

HEATHER: *Remember all the support you have around you, Nancy.*

ME: *Yes, but it still falls on me ultimately. Maybe I should give myself a break. It's good to know when something is too daunting, isn't it? You have some nice rooms here. It would be so much easier to just be here, and you said it could be arranged that I can be here a lot of the time.*

HEATHER: *[Turns and leans toward me] Yes, we could make something nice work in one of our viewing rooms . . . but it won't be the same, Nancy. At home, you will have all your family around and your beautiful things. I know you'll be able to do it, and it will be amazing!*

I am startled by Heather's confidence and conviction, jolted into remembering what I really want. Yes, there are some unknowns, but what is trust about, anyway? *I am not alone* and *It's not all up to me* are the measures of my learning. I'm struck at the irony that it was a funeral director who helped me get back on track to having a home funeral! That Carolyn was there to see my vulnerability and witness the cheering support behind me undoubtedly allayed some of her own fears as well.

It was 7 p.m. when the funeral directors came to pick up Mum's body. My death care team, already gathering at my home, was preparing the room. I couldn't believe how fortunate I was—not having to face the harsh reality of immediately saying goodbye to my mum's body. I had days ahead still.

Driving home behind the funeral van, I thought back to a concern that my sister had expressed about bringing Mum home: What would the neighbors think of seeing an obviously dead body being brought into our home? I responded that my neighbors are all very open, that I have talked about this interest of mine openly over the years. Still, I was glad it was dark. I did not want to make anyone uncomfortable. As it turned out, over the days that followed, the abiding community sense was one of interest and curiosity, if not incredulity, that this could actually be done.

Natasha, the lead funeral director in attendance, came into the house first to see what our arrangements were. She was assessing how the stretcher would maneuver around the hallway and doorways to the small room on the main floor that we had chosen as the vigil space. And, frankly, I sensed she was checking out how prepared we were for this undertaking (no pun intended). In her gentle and experienced professional role, she greatly encouraged the use of a big plastic body bag that they had brought with them. It could be put in the bottom of the casket, then when being transported back for cremation the body could be zipped up, ensuring there would be no leaking through of bodily fluids.

A quick glance across the room at my friends Aileen and Janeta and I knew that we were of like mind to question this assumption that there could be extensive leaking. After some discussion, during which we assured Natasha that we had supplies on hand for possible leakage and that we were confident in the means we were using to keep the body cold, Natasha agreed that they could let go of this usual policy but reviewed the risks with us again. In a funeral home, a body does not need constant monitoring because the home uses body bags and has freezer storage in its morgue; on the other hand, with a home funeral, family members pay continual attention to the body of the loved one. So we felt confident that we could take care in a timely way should there be any unforeseen bodily needs. I mention this to underline how each step of a new process may need assessment, creativity, collaboration, common sense, and the freedom to ask why or why not along the way.

Once Mum's body was in the room, on the massage table, and the funeral directors were gone, Michael and I looked at each other in surprise, even delight, that we were here and in the midst of this great thing. *We did it!* Taking a deep breath, ready to set into the task before us, it was Janeta who reminded us that *there was no rush*, to slow down and have a cup of tea and eat something first. Going to the kitchen, I could smell something delicious—my daughter, Elena, had baked a pumpkin pie for us. Now with tea mugs in hand and hungrily eating a late supper and pie, a sense of giddiness overtook us. Elena said, "This feels like a party. This is the way it should be." It certainly did. We ended up lingering in this comforting, womanly space, called together as we were to renew the ancient and timeless practice of caring for our dead.

Less than a year before, Janeta had accompanied her mother through dying with a home death and home funeral. Janeta along with her four sisters performed all the body care for their mum, and their large extended family gathered at the family home for the three days of vigil. The story Janeta told of those sad, difficult, and beautiful days was filled with so much love, family reconciliation, and growth—it was mesmerizing. I felt so glad she was able to be present and share her first-hand knowledge. Barbra Rose, a skilled body worker and wise woman friend, was also very instrumental in bringing warm and practical intelligence to our small group.

As the four of us gathered around my mum, a deepening silence entered. We were in sacred time now. With lights low and candles and incense lit—the pungent, sweet smell of burning sage and cedar wafting through the room—we were opening and deepening. What happened is hard to describe, but the words that flowed from our mouths addressed this mystery—the mystery of death and what carries on. I gave thanks to Mum for giving us permission to be with her in this way and asked her forgiveness should our inexperience and clumsiness feel harsh. I then named the names of her family tree, her ancestors and the land from which they came. We all felt slightly altered and duly humbled by this presence we had landed in. Then, turning on the lights to get to work, we became immediately both very practical and lighthearted.

Aileen began by pressing on Mum's abdomen to allow for gas to be expelled and any possible discharge. Janeta then reminded us that washing the body was not only a nice thing to do but also was an important step in minimizing bacterial growth that could cause odor and skin breakdown. With facecloths and warm soapy water, we began to wash Mum's face, arms, legs, feet, front, and back. Of particular importance was cleaning orifices. This was taken on stalwartly, some of us more comfortable than others. Mouth care had been difficult for Mum to handle leading up to her death. This is not unusual for the old. So here extra attention was given with wipes, Q-tips, and mouthwash spray.

Mum's hair needed a wash, that was certain. It had been a long time since her personal care workers had been able to do this. But were we taking on too much? Everyone thought why not give it a go—we had seen it done in a film after all. Carefully, we shampooed her hair, and using a pitcher filled with warm water gently rinsed it clean. We were using a washbasin on a stool to catch the water that was funneling down the open-ended garbage bag from under her head. This might be hard to picture, but it worked well. With a little blow-drying, Mum's silvery white hair was soft and glowing once more.

It was time to dress my mum in her vigil clothes. My sister, Carolyn, had bought Mum a beautiful outfit on the occasion of her son Nicholas's wedding to Barb. The bright floral top and blue dress pants made her look elegant, even with her bare feet sticking out. "Even a dead person should not have cold feet," Barbra Rose said, hastening to put socks on her, as the rest of us laughed.

We had been speaking to Mum all the way through these late evening hours, letting her know what we were doing. Even if this talking was not literally being heard by her, it meant that *we* were always aware that this body was that of a loved one, *not* an object, and that she was gradually releasing from this form.

18

Practicalities and Mysteries

A deep silence revives the listening
And the speaking of those two
who meet on the riverbank.
RUMI, FROM "BIRDSONG FROM INSIDE
THE EGG," *THE BOOK OF LOVE:*
POEMS OF ECSTASY AND LONGING,
COLEMAN BARKS, TRANS.

maybe death
isn't darkness, after all,
but so much light
wrapping itself around us—
MARY OLIVER, FROM
"WHITE OWL FLIES INTO AND
OUT OF THE FIELD"

Excarnating, just as we incarnate, is a process. That is why a vigil lasts three days. Some people may leave their body more quickly; some may take a little longer. How do I know this? Well, I've read about it, and didn't Jesus lay buried three days before rising? All cultures have rituals to honor the dead, and so, too, do they have customs about the optimum time for burial. In Judaism, for example, there is a special ceremony called taharah, where the body is ritually washed and cared for and never left alone until burial, usually within twenty-four hours. And certainly in customs that arise in hotter climates, a body is buried or cremated within twenty-four hours so that decomposing is not an issue.

Living as I do in a northern climate, the need for a quick burial is not paramount. I'm also influenced by notions that stem back to ancient texts like the Tibetan Book of the Dead and explored in the teachings of Rudolf Steiner, which indicate there is good reason to slow things down and allow a gradual release of our life forces over the first three days.

Author Nancy Jewel Poer in her book *Living into Dying* employs some of Steiner's insights to inform practical death care. She writes about how our life forces stream out of our body in the first days after death, uniting Earth and cosmic forces. The result is our memory being freed and surrounding us. A life review begins, deepening into more complex levels where the intent is to view the life just lived in a non-judgmental way. In this review, we experience the consequences of our thoughts and actions on others, as well as the deeds we have left undone. We may find that we need to make reparation or complete a task and with helpful spirits begin the long preparation for a future incarnation.

A friend said, "How strange. Why would you begin a life review after death?" Yes, it does sound strange if you think of death as a final stopping place. But we get a curious parallel of this idea from those who have had a near-death experience. For such people, a life review, a reliving or a rewinding of one's life in segments, is one of the most commonly reported aspects. Moreover, people speak predominantly of feeling loved and accompanied and of a sun-like radiance eclipsing any fear of death.

Of course, there is nothing like firsthand experience. Twenty-five years ago, when my father-in-law died, he was placed in the cemetery morgue to await cremation. My husband and I agreed even back then that there was no need to rush Will's cremation and asked the cemetery morgue caretaker to allow some time to pass. On the third day, Michael went to the crematorium. The caretaker said in a straightforward manner, "Will is ready today. He wasn't the past two days. He seemed a little disoriented, but today I can see the change in him. It was good you waited." Michael and I were astonished. We assumed our request was odd, but the cremation operator corroborated, from firsthand experience in tending many dead bodies, what was obvious—leaving this Earth is a process.

The evening was late now, and with all our ministrations, Mum was looking good. It was time to get her into the coffin lying on the floor next to the table. Trying to ensure an environmentally friendly exit, we had chosen one that was made from locally sourced wood with no adhesives or metal. It was actually quite elegant in its simplicity. I bought it without the liner because I felt our bedding would be fine, and this would save yet another cost, something my frugal mum would approve of.

I had hoped for other options to avoid consuming wood resources. My preference was a cloth shroud. This is becoming an option, especially with green burials, but it had not yet been done for cremation. After asking why and pressing the issue with our local funeral home, they went away and came back with, "We can work with this, but the shrouded body would need to be placed upon a wooden platform to enter the cremation oven." And then, with further thought, our funeral advisers said that the body would also need to have a rigid cover. There were reasonable explanations given, such as oven temperatures, combustion rates, and safety issues for the operators. But it was getting complex.

My next inquiry was using a less-resource-intense cardboard container. A cheaper, mixed material casket was available to purchase at the funeral home, but it was put together with glues. Online, I found some cardboard containers that seemed pretty nontoxic, and I put this proposal to our funeral advisers. At first, the answer was no, this would not work. Once again, we pleasantly enquired, "Why not?" Eventually, after they did more research and wondered among themselves, they came back with "OK, we can do this." It was always so heartening to work with this funeral home and their team. Indeed, we were becoming friends, even having fun via these unusual back-and-forth conversations to chart more options for sustainable and mindful death care.

In the end, due to the pressure of timing and my escalating fatigue with all the decision-making, we ended up purchasing the wooden casket in the funeral showroom. It sat on the floor before us. Really, quite a lovely piece of "furniture." The trick now was to lift Mum off the table, place her in the casket, and lift the casket, with her in it, back onto the table. It was all hands on deck. The room was small to maneuver in, but with Michael's and Elena's help, and allowing for some inelegancy, we handled it like pros. It seemed like all our squeamishness was gone by this point, replaced with a lightheartedness and a felt sense of competency.

More practical details: Techni Ice has made home funerals so much easier. Dry ice still will suffice, but it is more complicated to handle. Techni Ice is a polymer-based refrigerant made from nontoxic materials that you can purchase online. The packs are used for putting in coolers and picnic hampers, for sports injuries, and so on. For our purposes, I had ordered a package of sixteen. You soak the packs, they expand, and you freeze them. Once frozen, they stay that way for a long time and don't drip as they thaw. A package of eight to sixteen (depending on the situation) is ample to keep a body cold (primarily the organs) while also rotating the packs over the course of the vigil time. I had put mine in the freezer a few weeks before to be ready. "How big a freezer do you need?" an interested friend asked me. "They easily fit in our small basement freezer, but if you really cleared out your fridge freezer, it would probably do," I replied with new confidence in such matters.

Keeping Mum cold was not a problem. We placed two packs of Techni Ice beneath her torso, two on her abdomen, a smaller one behind her neck, and one behind her head. It was also the end of October, and we left a window partially open. We ended up replacing the Techni Ice approximately every twelve hours with ones out of the freezer. What at first seemed like a big deal swiftly became almost routine for Michael, Elena, and me. Each of us had our own roles and techniques for rolling Mum to one side, pulling out the old packages and putting in the frozen ones. A rhythm developed that was satisfying. More than that, the combination of being practical and matter-of-fact but also so intimate with Mum's body, together with the by now magical quality of the room, became for each of us a soul tonic.

Later that first night, after my death care team left, I fell into bed, exhausted. I slept well. It felt so good to me to close my eyes knowing that Mum was just across the hall. She looked so happy, so at peace. Everyone commented on it. Her happiness was palpable—we could feel it.

The next days were full, as they are in the aftermath of every death. Still, I couldn't go into rush mode or look too far ahead. Things mostly got decided by finding out what was needed in the moment, and then things would surprisingly come together. Carolyn and my brother-in-law, Braden, had arrived, staying in a hotel not far away. It was difficult not having them at the house, for my sister not to feel able to visit and even briefly take in the extraordinary scene of our mother, so beautiful and cared for and at such repose. But my father's words—*Leave your sister alone!*—still rang in my ears, guiding me wisely.

We met in the hotel restaurant for coffee. I was nervous about the gulf in our realities right then. I described as best as I could what was transpiring, foisting some pictures on her of the coffin and the room, taking care not to show anything more graphic without her consent. This enabled us to move on to other important topics, ones that I couldn't grasp undertaking at that time. Fortunately, she was. She reminded me about all the practical details that needed taking care of to get Mum's things moved out of her room, along with the paperwork. She and Braden took over these pressing tasks, including eventually settling the estate. We then spoke about the service and agreed upon it being a small home funeral on the day of cremation. Not being a large family, and my mother having outlived most of her peers, this proved easier than it may be for some.

We had talked about it before, but for all my planning on other matters, the service part had remained more nebulous. When I got home, I phoned Don, a retired minister and former teacher of mine who had also become a family friend, and asked if he could officiate. I could say by "luck" he was available, but in this liminal zone, I gratefully realized more was at play, as yet another important piece of the story came together. Don had met Mum before, which added the touch of genuine familiarity that is often missing these days. With Don's participation, the home funeral could take shape, greatly relieving Carolyn, for whom the service would be the most important event in honoring Mum's death.

Though traditions break down, the underlying intent behind them still yearns to be honored. We have a psychic need to do something for the newly dead; that's why there are ceremonies, rich in symbols—the language of the unconscious and spirit. But these are becoming rationalized out of existence. Coming together in community at the time of death is a given across time and culture. These customs have arisen to support the bereaved but also, importantly, *to help the deceased on their way.* We didn't have a rollicking Irish Scottish wake—though there is something very compelling, if not a bit romanticized, about ensuring *wake*fulness for the full three days of vigiling, with music and storytelling to accompany the newly dead. We didn't have a Catholic mass. Nor did we sit shiva for seven days as a Jewish family might do, offer *pinda* (rice balls) as a Hindu might do, read from the Tibetan Book of the Dead, or keep a sacred fire burning and offer tobacco, food, and tools as an Anishinabe might do. But we did hold Mum in our hearts with love, keeping watch.

For myself, however, I couldn't resist the instinct to draw together my closest friends and our Closing Time group in some way at this extraordinary time. So, without any advanced planning, we decided to hold a visitation for two hours on the second day. I have musical friends, so it was easy to sing together, and everyone took turns offering poems and prayers as we sat in a circle in our living room. During this time, people would get up one by one, go into Mum's room, sit with her for a few minutes, and then come back. Without planning or trying, it *became* a ritual, and the last hymn, my mum's favorite, "Amazing Grace," surely reached the place of heaven on Earth, surrounding her on whatever journey she was on.

Things, though crazy, were going well, yet I kept wondering if I was going to crash. That evening it happened. Perhaps the visitation went on too long, by the end becoming more socially oriented than I was prepared for. I ended up having to retreat to my room, and when Michael noticed, he went out and said, rather bluntly but effectively to the growing group, "It's time to go. Nancy needs to rest now." Having a person who can act as a guardian or boundary keeper at times like this is helpful, indeed.

Still, my unraveling continued. My body and soul felt torn up, and I was confused, irritated, and restless. As my husband held me, I let go into a new round of tears. A new realization hit me: I was becoming used to having Mum here in this beautiful way! I had finally come to an authentic way to be with my mum, and she was here and so welcome in my home. An easy guest! I wanted to hold onto this version of Mum. I was a child again—one who had ironically found a more secure attachment with her mother and was grieving that this would be lost when her body was gone. As this realization emerged, I was able to cry for this particular loss, consciously and fully.

Regressing into childhood when confronted with a reality that evokes something emotionally charged from the past is not uncommon. Francis Weller reminded me of this in his book *The Wild Edge of Sorrow*: "I have often witnessed . . . individuals regressing into a childlike state when feelings of grief emerge. They suddenly feel panicked, overwhelmed, hopeless, alone, and ashamed."[1] Having someone whom I loved and trusted witness me, hold me, and reassure me when I became overwhelmed provided the container I needed to regain my adult self. This is what is known as *attunement* in grief-trauma work. An adult *attuned* to both physical *and* emotional needs is what we *all* need in childhood and is very often lacking. If these needs are not met, then they will revisit us later. As adults, when we meet these knots of bound-up energy, we still have the potential to create a new story for ourselves, to create a new narrative that meets our present life. A mindful and loving family member or friend, perhaps a good therapist, can provide the presence we need.

I am always amazed how this tending to feelings and allowing emotions to flow in a safe space, with a trusted one nearby, is such a relief and how quickly acceptance settles in and the moment moves on of its own accord. After my tears had eased, I went to sit with Mum, just to *be* in this ragged moment together, with all the layers that made us mother and daughter, with all our ancestral and spiritual presences, letting the page turn over.

I should have known, from my years working with the dying in long-term care and the hospital, how complicated it can be to have a parent die, even when they are old and ready to go. Our hearts yearn to make amends, to change the script that may have haunted us. It is important to realize that the person who is dying is not the *same* person as the one who fed you and washed you and disciplined you and tucked you into bed—or neglected you. That parent or caregiver is more often a memory that has been internalized into our own psyches, sometimes hardwired into our neurons, and it often takes a lifetime of work to sort that out. (Note: So-called large T trauma, from serious injury, sexual violence, or life-threatening experiences, has many levels and must be sensitively addressed, deserving more attention than I'm giving it here.) Taking on the complex work of mending ways at our parents' dying time is not always possible, but cracks do invariably open up, and the smallest gestures—a caress of a hand, an utterance of love—can become the healing balm that changes everything. Walking the grief path *consciously* requires careful tending, along with stamina, courage, and support, as our past inevitably erupts and calls for attention and healing.

That same night, after the vigil with friends, around midnight, Casey returned home. Although he knew what we were up to, I was still apprehensive, though I needn't have been. Shortly after arriving, he went into the room to visit his Nanny. I left him alone. Though he didn't linger, he had taken in what death looks like—or can look like, at home with his family.

Nowadays, it seems easier to question the impulse to return home for a death. Should the grandchildren come all that way? There is work and school, the time and the expense. Casey had traveled all the way from Fort McMurray in Alberta, where he had been working as a welder since finishing university, and he had only just been home a few months earlier. No one size fits all, but I have come to wonder what it is that makes a family if it is not to come together at pivotal times such as a death, even when it takes a great effort to do so. And how do our young people learn about death otherwise? In today's mode of thinking, a young person might be counseled to "take care of themselves," to be free of such expectations and burdens. But as Casey came out of the vigil room, I couldn't help notice a subtle shift in my son: sober, reflective, his shoulders broader, *and* a little buoyed.

The third day, the day of the service and cremation, was upon us. Timing was everything to keep the flow going. That morning when touching my mum's body, I could feel how cold she still was, even though the Techni Ice was not. I decided we could skip that step today. Going to her head, I held my hands above her for a moment and was shocked at a pulsing heat that seemed to be pouring from her in waves. My daughter, Elena, a registered massage therapist, came in, and when she put her hands above the body, she actually jumped back.

19

To Carry Our Dead

The Tao-way we cannot perceive; we can only see its tracks and traces in nature—in patterns of flowing water, in swirls of wood, lines of stone, curling smoke, the veins of leaves and clouds.

RALPH METZNER, *THE UNFOLDING SELF: VARIETIES OF TRANSFORMATIVE EXPERIENCE*

Ritual is important to me. A language older than words, it shifts levels, orients focus, and invites a sacred presence. We all have our rituals. Something we do over and over again until a rhythm is established, and it just becomes part of who we are. Unlike habit, ritual requires aware-ness and an opening to the aliveness all around us—like greeting the sun in the morning and the stars at night.

When done with others, ritual creates a coherent field and a potent portal. Ritual doesn't have to be big or formulaic and certainly not heavy or moralistic. Just recently, my friend Sandy has gotten sick, very sick, with incurable liver cancer. He wrote about the small ritual that he is doing each day:

> My oncology doc came to tell me the tumor is growing and the therapy is not working. So I'm doing some building! A hermitage in the center of my being, in my heart. I wish you could see it: cedar scented air, fresh, clear, and golden with rosy/silver light streaming

in one window. There is a table and chair, with space for precious
things on the table—but for now just a notepad and a list of my own
beloveds. In front of me, stuck on the cedar walls, are my mantras,
my evening prayer, and some Post-it notes with inspiring words. This
is my hermitage. I drop in daily, several times. It has space for a
cot: one day I may lay me down there to soar, flying upward and
outward, embracing all.

In the meantime, our community is currently grappling with what
to do. Sandy told me, "People keep asking me how they can help. Really,
I'd just like to ask them to pray for me, but that feels old and awkward."
I said, "*Prayer* is one word, but there are others. We need to reimagine
the power of our heart forces, especially when together with others."
After speaking for a while, we decided to invite some close friends to be
part of a circle of care group. The idea was that every Thursday evening
at 7:45 p.m., each of us in our own homes would light a candle and quietly hold Sandy in our heart, with loving attention. We would do this
for ten minutes. Prior to this, we would send an email message saying
hi, that we were present, and then go offline. Sandy was deeply touched
to be the center of such care; he was also wise enough to understand
that it would be something that would help us all. He said, "If I have a
year to live, I have a space to do something. I wasn't sure what it could
be, but it would be fine if it's just this, to be the catalyst for a bit of community forming." And so this is what will happen, week after week: a
simple, humble but potent group ritual. It's already becoming infinitely
enriching for us all as well as for our ancestors and spiritual beings who,
because of it, are able to lean in a little closer.

In our family, we are used to marking moments with a combination
of gravitas and levity: small rituals like blessing our food at dinner-
time and expressing words of gratitude for each other and the world at

Christmas, birthdays, long partings, and the launch of new endeavors. I have been the main initiator, and I guess that is a role I have taken on, even when groans and rolled eyes have dampened the mood. But it is all worth it.

When my son was twenty, I once asked him what he most remembered and liked about his childhood Christmastimes. He said, without hesitation, "The part at the top of the stairs in the morning, when we stood in a circle and Nanny was with us. You made us all be quiet, and we lit candles and gave thanks for what was more important than the presents under the tree." Recalling that validation, I knew we could gather around Mum's casket and make a meaningful transition for her out of our house. With minimal preparation, we each read a small poem, verse, or saying, and then placed rose petals on her body. Standing together in this rich silence giving thanks, the room was beautiful; Mum was beautiful. It was complete.

Fifteen minutes later, there was a knock on the door. Two friends had arrived to get Mum safely through the narrow hallway so she would be ready at the door for the funeral staff to transport to the crematorium. We had agreed to have her ready in this manner because time was tight between transport and cremation. And besides, we still wanted to do as much as we could ourselves. Casey, Elena, and our friends Linda and Jeff lifted Mum up while others slid the casket out and turned it on its end to get it down the hall and into the entrance way. To then see my son and daughter tenderly carrying their grandmother's shrouded dead body is a picture that will stay with me forever. And conceivably it may be a gesture imprinted on them as to what it means to *carry our dead*.

It was now time to bring our entire family together. In opting for a small service in my home, we all felt relieved at the simplicity and informality this would bring. Reverend Don was happy to lead the ten of us: my family, my sister's family, plus Aunt Jean in a small gathering in the living room. We each spoke about Mum and her life in our own personal way, interspersed with hymns my sister and nephew had arranged. And we included a few scripture passages and prayers that Mum would have appreciated. There was lots of laughter, as there always is when we gather. Later, we would have a big Indian food feast, along with pizza, in our home. It all felt perfectly tailored for how Mum would have wanted it, a friendly time.

Before everyone left, Carolyn and I had a few minutes alone in my room. It was in that moment, looking at her and realizing what we had all just gone through, that I realized I had overlooked something big. In the intensity of my own involvement, I had overlooked truly recognizing all that she had been holding in her own way. I managed to say, "Thank you, Carolyn. You've done so much, the less visible things, that were so important. And thank you for just being open and letting me take over in other ways. I know this made it hard for you to be involved, and I just hope that you didn't feel too excluded because of it." This was a meeting of truth for us both. Carolyn quietly admitted, "Well, I admit I had those feelings." Then added, "But the service, our time afterward, and our meal together really has made up for it all." I felt the warmth and sincerity of her words, and we hugged. I couldn't have scripted a better sisterly moment.

Cremation took place at 2 p.m. We had time to wait, to do the final vigiling in the more conventional setting of a stately funeral home. A funeral service was taking place next door to our sitting room, and we could hear the singing of hymns. Mum had voiced her preference of hymns she would most like at her funeral service, and here she was getting them all! We laughed to think how all the details were being taken care of without our doing.

The last goodbye was not hard. From this side of the threshold, all felt *complete*. Marion Ruth MacMillan indeed was ready to go—her spirit facing forward, eager to flame up with the fire, and to show the way for loved ones who will one day follow.

> *I want my funeral to be a friendly time, not a*
> *   horrifying one.*
> *Not with tears running down the face.*
> *You better tell your sister, she has to know this too.*
>
> MUM, A MONTH BEFORE SHE DIED

There's Always Grace

Now I'm standing underneath the cottonwood tree in our backyard that shelters your clay flowerpot of bones and ash. I'm liking this graveside visiting and the tending of the ground around you—sweeping away the snow, the twigs, and an assortment of fallen acorns while the chipmunks natter at me. Chipmunks are always nattering at me. In this small refuge, a breeze picks up, and I give thanks for you, Mum, and also for the trees, the wind, Earth, the birds, and all my ancestors.

Sitting at the keyboard, putting finishing touches on this writing, and continuing to talk to my mother. But she wants less frequent cups of tea now, shorter visits, pointing me back to the fullness of my life. And she says, "I have my own work to do." Our contact comes through little prompts, owl sightings, a smile in the air, *the love between.*

And then a dream: *Mum leaves a phone message that I'm to call her. She is worried, not having heard from me in a while, and I feel bad that I have neglected this.* Later that day I recall the dream and inwardly and imaginatively phone my mother. "What can I help you with, Mum?" The sense arises of her wanting a hug. I embrace her and feel love pouring through. A few minutes later, I'm riffling through books on a shelf and come across one read long ago, the *Tibetan Book of Living and Dying*. Mesmerized by the clarity of the content, I read about how we help the dead by sustaining a *warm spiritual hug*.[1] I close my eyes in surrender. Simple, simple, simple.

Connection with my mother comes in new ways, too. Daily flashes. Looking in the mirror, I see her in the set of my mouth. Walking around in my sloppy pajamas, I feel the same gait, same shrug of the shoulders, same disdain for orderly conventions of dress. In photos, I am often shocked at our resemblance. And then there are her death pictures. I know what I'm going to look like when I die. My mother's face, my face, easily blur into one. Death stares back. Do I run from Death? Or can I linger and press a little past the dissolution of my body?

Getting older, letting go of what primes our personalities and plumps our cheeks, do we always merge into the lingering shapes and gestures, the bones and flesh of our parents, their parents, and so on who knows how far back? It's a funny thought. In tending the dead, awakening to our ancestors, and waving to the far shore, I do hope we each add something unique to the parade of our departed,

> *A silver thread*
> *for the next generations,*
> *—A hearty laugh,*
> *a mischievous wrinkle around the eyes,*
> *the careful*
> > *placement*
> > > *of a foot*
> > > > *upon the earth . . .*

'Til the circle turns, a door opens, and we meet ourselves anew.

In fact there's always *grace. When you search, when you call, there's* always *a hand helping you. And looking back, you realize how marvelous it was: there's such a caring, sweet, kind hand that watches over and . . . reaches out when you no longer know or can do anything on your own. Especially when you no longer can do anything yourself. That's when the grace comes.*

SATPREM, *MY BURNING HEART*

Acknowledgments

Deep thanks to the many dear ones who have helped shepherd this book into form. First among them being my husband, Michael Hurley, who painstakingly read and re-read many versions of this manuscript, helping my wandering prose and irregular grammatical style become more coherent and offering wise counsel at every turn. This is his work too, and as life partner and ardent supporter, his soul is embedded in these pages.

An enormous debt of gratitude goes to Robert Sardello, founder of integral spiritual psychology. Much of my perspective and experience evolves out of this emerging field of heart consciousness. And also to the late Cheryl Sanders-Sardello, who showed me the ways of the living dead, and continues to do so.

I am grateful as well for the excellent clinical training offered through the Canadian Association for Spiritual Care and in particular for my supervisors, Don and Bonnie Misener and Neil Elford.

To dear friends who read or listened to early drafts and provided helpful insights while cheering me on: Andrea Mathieson, Julie Salverson, Linda Nagel, Aileen Stewart, Linda O'Neill, and Sher Peters. To members of the Closing Time death group, for your support and for being game to enter unknown territory together. And to Sandy Sellers, for the countless legacies he has generously established over decades, and for showing us how to face our dying time with grief, wisdom, wit, and community-mindedness.

To my first editor, Ellie Barton, for really understanding what I was trying to write about and offering clear and precise help on how to say it better, time and again. To Inner Traditions acquisitions editor Richard Grossinger, who responded to and accepted my manuscript enthusiastically. And to senior editor Jamaica Burns Griffin and all the staff at Inner Traditions, who have been supportive and kind at every step.

Stephen Jenkinson continues to make us reckon with our living and dying and has opened up new ways of seeing for me. I came across Phyllida Anam-Áire's book *A Celtic Book of Dying: The Path of Love in the Time of Transition* as I was finishing this manuscript. I am very grateful for the Celtic orientation she brings in rekindling the sacred pathway to be with the dying and dead. Perdita Finn is leading us all into new ways of reimagining our ancestors—thank you, kindred one. Special thanks also to Diana Beresford-Kroeger and her husband, Chris, for an enchanted afternoon by their woodstove, drinking tea and sharing stories of the old Celtic ways, and for their deep and wise encouragement.

Warm thanks to my immediate family members, who are part of the lifeblood of this book: Marion, Seyman, and Carolyn. And to my children: Casey, for your strength of will, humor, and capacity for doing what's right. And Elena, for never tiring of hearing these stories, your natural radiance and timeless knowing, and for the child you are now carrying to this side of the shore.

When all is said and done, the true authors of this book are many, and I have been but a compiler. Nothing that I say is new: it has all been expressed before and much better by wiser ones than I . . . but the light of *wisdom* weaves on and on, showing up in ever-changing garments. My best hope is that *this* garment honors her well, serving to carry on the prayers and teachings of the ancients dedicated to the sacred art of dying and death and our connection with those of the far shore.

Notes

Chapter 2.
Scenes from Frontline Health Care

1. Mannix, *With the End in Mind*, 152.
2. Mannix, "'It's Not What You See in the Movies.'"
3. Mannix, *With the End in Mind*, 7.

Chapter 7. A Different Kind of Medicine

1. Bonheim, *Goddess*, 131–33.

Chapter 8. Becoming an Ancestor

1. Prebble, *Culloden*, 219–22.
2. Haga, *Healing Resistance*.
3. Shaw, *Smoke Hole*, 71.
4. Reaney, *Colours in the Dark*, 32.
5. Krznaric, *The Good Ancestor*, 230.
6. Krznaric, *The Good Ancestor*, 65.
7. Berkovic, "Jewish Burial Practices."

Chapter 9.
Continuing Our Connection beyond the Last Breath

1. Barnes and Hutchinson, *The Up-Rising in Dying*, 5.

Chapter 10.
Grief, Communion, and a New Conversation

1. Ratcliffe, *Oxford Essential Quotations*, s.v. "Crowfoot."
2. Whyte, *Crossing the Unknown Sea*, 35.

3. Paxino, *Bridges between Life and Death*, 99.

4. Paxino, *Bridges between Life and Death*, 101.

5. Sardello, *The Collected Notes of Integral Spiritual Psychology*, 331–32.

Chapter 11.
The Spiritual Road to *Ars Moriendi*

1. Hillman, quoted in Nisker, "The Soul of the Matter."

2. Comper, *The Book of the Craft of Dying*.

3. Steiner, *Links between the Living and the Dead*, 5

4. Kingsnorth, "A Wild Christianity."

Chapter 12. The Dying Time

1. Stickgold, quoted in van der Kolk, *The Body Keeps the Score*, 262–63.

Chapter 14. A Ripe Completion

1. Shaw, *Courting the Wild Twin*, 100.

2. Mannix, *With the End in Mind*, 319.

Chapter 15. A Good Death?

1. Denney, *Working with the Pain of Separation*.

2. Denney, *Working with the Pain of Separation*.

3. Denney, *Working with the Pain of Separation*.

Chapter 16.
Building a Little Ship for Your Dead

1. Green Burial Kingston: "Principles."

2. Purpura, "Imagining Burial."

3. Lawrence, "All Soul's Day," *The Complete Poems of D. H. Lawrence*.

Chapter 18.
Practicalities and Mysteries

1. Weller, *The Wild Edge of Sorrow*, 5.

Postscript. There's Always Grace

1. Sogyal Rinpoche, *Tibetan Book of Living and Dying*, 32.

Bibliography

Akomolafe, Bayo. Foreword to *Life After Progress: Technology, Community, and the New Economy* by Helena Norberg-Hodge et al. East Hardwick, VT: Local Futures, 2022.

Anam-Áire, Phyllida. *A Celtic Book of Dying: The Path of Love in the Time of Transition*. Rochester, VT: Findhorn Press, 2022.

———. *The Last Ecstasy of Life: Celtic Mysteries of Death and Dying*. Rochester, VT: Findhorn Press, 2021.

Barnes, Christy Mackaye, and Janet Hutchinson, eds. *The Up-Rising in Dying: Words and Verses*. Hillsdale, NY: Adonis Press, 1990.

Beresford-Kroeger, Diana. *To Speak for the Trees: My Life's Journey from Ancient Celtic Wisdom to a Healing Vision of the Forest*. Toronto, ON: Random House Canada, 2019.

Berkovic, Sally. "Jewish Burial Practices." Presentation, Lifting the Lid: An International Festival on Death and Dying, November 18–20, 2022.

Bishop, Orland. *The Seventh Shrine: Meditations on the African Spiritual Journey*. Great Barrington, MA: Lindisfarne Books, 2017.

Bonheim, Jalaja, ed. *Goddess: A Celebration in Art and Literature*. New York: Stewart, Tabori & Chang, 1997.

Bringhurst, Robert, and Jan Zwicky. *Learning to Die: Wisdom in the Age of Climate Crisis*. Regina, SK: University of Regina Press, 2018.

Byock, Ira. *The Four Things That Matter Most: A Book about Living*. New York: Atria Books, 2004.

Chochinov, Harvey Max. *Dignity Therapy: Final Words for Final Days*. Oxford, UK: Oxford University Press, 2011.

Comper, Frances M. M., ed. *The Book of the Craft of Dying*. Charleston, SC: BiblioBazaar, 2009. First published 1917 from manuscripts from the Middle Ages.

Couterre, Tara. "In My Kitchen, Around the Farm, and Then Some." *Slowdown Farmstead* (blog). August 19, 2023.

Dass, Ram, and Mirabai Bush. *Walking Each Other Home: Conversations on Loving and Dying.* Louisville, CO: Sounds True, 2018.

Davis, Wade. *The Wayfinders: Why Ancient Wisdom Matters in the Modern World.* CBC Massey Lectures. Toronto, ON: House of Anansi, 2009.

Denney, Jeanne. *Working with the Pain of Separation: A Guide for Caring and Mourning at a Distance.* SOULL (School of Unusual Life Learning), April 16, 2020.

de Quillan, Jehanne, trans. *The Gospel of the Beloved Companion: The Complete Gospel of Mary Magdalene.* Ariège, France: Éditions Athara, 2010.

Dickson, Elinor. *Dancing at the Stillpoint: Marion Woodman, SOPHIA, and Me: A Friendship Remembered.* Asheville, NC: Chiron, 2019.

Duncan Rogers, Jane. *Before I Go: The Essential Guide to Creating a Good End of Life Plan.* Rochester, VT: Findhorn Press, 2018.

Evans-Wentz, W. Y. *The Tibetan Book of the Dead.* Oxford, UK: Oxford University Press, 1960.

Gawande, Atul. *Being Mortal: Medicine and What Matters in the End.* New York: Metropolitan Books, 2014.

Green Burial Kingston: Advocating for Sustainable Burials. "Principles" (website).

Haga, Kazu. *Healing Resistance: A Radically Different Response to Harm.* Berkeley, CA: Parallax Press, 2020.

Hickman, Martha W. *Healing After Loss: Daily Meditations for Working Through Grief.* New York: HarperCollins, 1994.

Holecek, Andrew. *Preparing to Die: Practical Advice and Spiritual Wisdom from the Tibetan Buddhist Tradition.* Boston: Snow Lion, 2013.

Jenkinson, Stephen. *Die Wise: A Manifesto for Sanity and Soul.* Berkeley, CA: North Atlantic Books, 2015.

Johnson, Kimberly Ann. *Call of the Wild: How We Heal Trauma, Awaken Our Own Power, and Use It for Good.* New York: Harper Wave, 2021.

Jung, Carl G. *Man and His Symbols.* New York: Doubleday, 1964.

Kimmerer, Robin Wall. *Braiding Sweetgrass.* Minneapolis, MN: Milkweed Editions, 2013.

Kingsley, Peter. *A Book Of Life.* London: Catafalque Press, 2021.

———. *In the Dark Places of Wisdom.* Port Reyes Station, CA: The Golden Sufi Center, 1999.

Kingsnorth, Paul. "A Wild Christianity." *First Things* (March 2023).

Krznaric, Roman. *The Good Ancestor: A Radical Prescription for Long-Term Thinking*. New York: The Experiment, 2020.

Kübler-Ross, Elisabeth. *Living With Death and Dying*. New York: McMillan Publishing, 1981.

———. *On Death and Dying: What the Dying Have to Teach Us*. New York: Scribner, 2014. First published 1969.

———. *The Wheel of Life, A Memoir of Living and Dying*. New York: Scribner, 1997.

Kübler-Ross, Elisabeth, and David Kessler. *Life Lessons: Two Experts on Death and Dying Teach about the Mysteries of Life and Living*. New York: Scribner, 2000.

Lawrence, D. H. *The Complete Poems of D. H. Lawrence*. Hertfordshire, UK: Wordsworth Editions, 1994.

Levine, Peter A. *In an Unspoken Voice: How the Body Releases Trauma and Restores Goodness*. Berkeley, CA: North Atlantic Books, 2010.

———. *Waking the Tiger: Healing Trauma*. Berkeley, CA: North Atlantic Books, 1997.

Levine, Stephen. *Healing into Life and Death*. New York: Anchor Books, 1987.

———. *Who Dies? An Investigation of Conscious Living and Conscious Dying*. New York: Anchor Press/Doubleday, 1982.

Lofland, Lyn H. *The Craft of Dying: The Modern Face of Death*. 40th anniversary edition. Cambridge, MA: MIT Press, 2019.

Lyons, Jerrigrace, and Janelle MacRae. *Final Passages: A Complete Home Funeral Guide*. Sebastopol, CA: Final Passages, 1997. Revised edition published in 2022.

Mannix, Kathryn. "'It's Not What You See in the Movies': Doctor Demystifies Dying." Interview by Brian Goldman. *White Coat Black Art*, March 13, 2020. CBC Radio.

———. *With the End in Mind: Dying, Death, and Wisdom in an Age of Denial*. Boston: Little, Brown Spark, 2018.

Maté, Gabor. *In the Realm of Hungry Ghosts: Close Encounters with Addiction*. Berkeley, CA: North Atlantic Books, 2009.

Mockett, Marie Mutsuki. *Where the Dead Pause and the Japanese Say Goodbye*. New York: W. W. Norton, 2015.

Muraresku, Brian C. *The Immortality Key: The Secret History of the Religion with No Name*. New York: St. Martin's Press, 2020.

Neimeyer, Robert A., ed. *Techniques of Grief Therapy: Assessment and Intervention*. New York: Routledge, 2016.

Nisker, Wes. "The Soul of the Matter: James Hillman in Conversation with Wes Nisker." *Inquiring Mind* 11, no. 2 (Spring 1995).

Paxino, Iris. *Bridges between Life and Death*. Translated by Cynthia Hindes. Edinburgh, Scotland: Floris Books, 2021.

Pearson, Patricia. *Opening Heaven's Door: What the Dying May Be Trying to Tell Us about Where They're Going*. Toronto, ON: Random House Canada, 2014.

Poer, Nancy Jewel. *Living into Dying: A Journal of Spiritual and Practical Deathcare for Family and Community*. Placerville, CA: White Feather Publishing, 2002.

Pollan, Michael. *Second Nature: A Gardener's Education*. New York: Grove Press, 1991.

Prebble, John. *Culloden*. London: Pimlico, 1961.

Prechtel, Martín. *The Smell of Rain on Dust: Grief and Praise*. Berkeley, CA: North Atlantic Books, 2015.

Purpura, Lia. "Imagining Burial." *Emergence Magazine*, February 1, 2019.

Ratcliffe, Susan, ed. *Oxford Essential Quotations*. 6th ed. Oxford, UK: Oxford University Press, 2018.

Reaney, James. *Colours in the Dark*. Vancouver, BC: Talonplays with Macmillan of Canada, 1969.

Sardello, Robert. *The Collected Notes of Integral Spiritual Psychology: Foundations for a Spirituality of the Future*. Vol. 111. Benson, NC: Goldenstone Press, 2020.

———. *Freeing the Soul from Fear*. New York: Riverhead Books, 1999.

———. *Heartfulness*. Benson, NC: Goldenstone Press, 2015.

———. *Love and the Soul: Creating a Future for Earth*. Benson, NC: Goldenstone Press, 2008.

———. *Silence: The Mystery of Wholeness*. Benson, NC: Goldenstone Press, 2006.

Shaw, Martin. *Courting the Wild Twin*. White River Junction, VT: Chelsea Green, 2020.

———. *Smoke Hole: Looking to the Wild in the Time of the Spyglass*. White River Junction, VT: Chelsea Green, 2020.

Sogyal Rinpoche. *The Tibetan Book of Living and Dying*. New York: HarperOne, 2020.

Steiner, Rudolf. "The Forming of Destiny and Life after Death." GA 157a, November 20, 1915. The Rudolf Steiner Archive.

———. *How to Know Higher Worlds: A Modern Path of Initiation*. Translated by Christopher Bamford and Sabine H. Seller. Hudson, NY: Anthroposophic Press, 1994. First published 1904.

———. *Links between the Living and the Dead: Transformation of Earthly Forces into Clairvoyance*. London: Rudolf Steiner Press, 1973.

———. *Staying Connected: How to Continue Your Relationships with Those Who Have Died*. Edited by Christopher Bamford. Great Barrington, MA: Anthroposophic Press, 1999.

Strand, Clark, and Perdita Finn. *The Way of the Rose: The Radical Path of the Divine Feminine Hidden in the Rosary*. New York: Spiegel & Grau, 2019.

Troyer, John. *Technologies of the Human Corpse*. Cambridge, MA: MIT Press, 2020.

Van der Kolk, Bessel A. *The Body Keeps the Score: Brain, Mind, and Body in the Healing of Trauma*. New York: Penguin Books, 2014.

Von Schilling, Karin. *Where Are You? Coming to Terms with the Death of My Child*. Hudson, NY: Anthroposophic Press, 1988.

Weller, Francis. *Entering the Healing Ground: Grief, Ritual and the Soul of the World*. Santa Rosa, CA: Wisdom Bridge Press, 2011.

———. *The Wild Edge of Sorrow*. Berkeley, CA: North Atlantic Books, 2015.

Wetzl, Joseph, trans. *The Bridge over the River: After Death Communication of a Young Artist Who Died in World War I*. New York: SteinerBooks, 1974.

Whyte, David. *Crossing the Unknown Sea: Work as a Pilgrimage of Identity*. New York: Riverhead Books, 2002.

Wijinberg, Nicholas, and Philip Martyn. *Crossing the Threshold: Practical and Spiritual Guidance on Death and Dying Based on the Work of Rudolf Steiner*. Forest Row, UK: Temple Lodge, 2003.

Wohlleben, Peter. *The Inner Life of Animals*. Vancouver, BC: Greystone Books, 2016.

Woodman, Marion. *Addiction to Perfection: The Still Unravished Bride*. Toronto, ON: Inner City Books, 1982.

———. *The Pregnant Virgin: A Process of Psychological Transformation*. Toronto, ON: Inner City Books, 1985.

Resources

Bereaved Parents of the USA (bereavedparentsusa.org)

The Compassionate Friends: Supporting Family After a Child Dies (compassionatefriends.org)

Crossings: Caring for Our Own at Death (crossings.net)

Death Cafés (deathcafe.com)

Death Over Dinner (deathoverdinner.org)

End Well (endwellproject.org)

Final Passages: Institute of Conscious Dying, Home Funeral & Green Burial Education (finalpassages.org)

Five Wishes: Advance Care Planning Program (fivewishes.org)

Green Burial Council (greenburialcouncil.org)

The Grief Recovery Method programs and books (griefrecoverymethod .com)

Heath Care Chaplaincy Network (HCCN): Caring for the Human Spirit (healthcarechaplaincy.org)

The Inspired Funeral: Support, Ceremonies, and Inspiration for Modern Families (theinspiredfuneral.com)

Jeanne Denney, death educator, doula, and founder of the School of Unusual Life Learning (SoULL) (jeannedenney.com)

The Living Dying Project: Imagine Living Life without Fear (livingdying. org)

National End-of-Life Doula Alliance (NEDA) (nedalliance.org)

National Home Funeral Alliance (homefuneralalliance.org)

Natural Transitions: A Resource for Green and Holistic Approaches to End of Life (naturaltransitions.org)

The Order of the Good Death (orderofthegooddeath.com)

The Orphan Wisdom School / Stephen Jenkinson (orphanwisdom.com)
The School of Integral Spiritual Psychology (robertsardello.com)
Take Back the Magic / Perdita Finn (takebackthemagic.com)

CANADIAN CHAPTERS AND ASSOCIATIONS

Bereaved Parents of Canada: look online for local or provincial chapters
Canadian Association of Spiritual Care (CASC) (spiritualcare.ca)
Compassionate Friends of Canada (chpca.ca/listing/the-compassionate-friends-of-canada)
End of Life Doula Association Canada (endoflifedoulaassociation.org)
Green Burial Society of Canada (greenburialcanada.ca)
My Voice Advance Care Planning Guide (available digitally in multiple languages on the official website of the Government of British Columbia, gov.bc.ca)

BOOKS

In addition to those listed in the bibliography, I recommend the following books:

An Autobiography of Trauma: A Healing Journey by Peter Levine
The Fall of Freddie the Leaf: A Story of Life for All Ages by Leo Buscaglia
From Here to Eternity: Traveling the World to Find the Good Death by Caitlyn Doughty
The Green Burial Guidebook: Everything You Need to Plan an Affordable, Environmentally Friendly Burial by Elizabeth Fournier
The Grief Recovery Handbook: The Action Program for Moving Beyond Death, Divorce, and Other Losses by John W. James and Russell Friedman
Healing Collective Trauma: A Process for Integrating Our Intergenerational and Cultural Wounds by Thomas Hübl
Healing the Soul Wound: Counseling with American Indians and Other Native Peoples by Eduardo Duran
Healing Trauma through Family Constellations and Somatic Experiencing: Ancestral Wisdom from the Snail Clan of Tanzania by Efu Nyaki
Home Funeral Ceremonies: A Primer to Honor the Dying and the Dead with Reverence, Light-heartedness and Grace by Donna Belk and Kateyanne Unullisi

My Father's Wake: How the Irish Teach Us to Live, Love, and Die by Kevin
　Toolis
Passed On: African American Mourning Stories by Karla FC Holloway
Take Back the Magic: Conversations with the Unseen World by Perdita Finn
*Undertaken with Love: A Home Funeral Guide for Families and Community
　Care Groups* by Holly Stevens

FILMS

The Art of Natural Death Care (2017). This film by Katelyn LaGrega is just
　under half an hour and is available to view online at Vimeo. Looking at
　the growing movement of home funeral and green burial care, it shows
　how families can care for their loved ones at the time of death, bringing
　individuality, sacredness, love, and reverence.

Coco (2017). In this animated Disney/Pixar film a boy who dreams of
　becoming a great musician embarks on a journey to uncover the myster-
　ies behind his ancestor's stories and traditions of the Day of the Dead.

Departures (2008). This Academy Award Winner for Best Foreign
　Language Film is a poignant story set in Japan of a young unemployed
　musician whose life is changed when he takes a job preparing the dead
　for their funerals.

Dying at Grace (2003). Documentary by Allan King on the final months of
　five terminally ill cancer patients at the Toronto Grace Health Centre.

Dying Wish (2008). Documentary about Dr. Michael Miller, an eighty-
　nine-year old retired surgeon with end-stage terminal cancer who
　chooses to stop eating and drinking in order not to prolong the dying
　process.

In the Parlor: The Final Goodbye (2015). In this documentary by Heidi
　Boucher families in search of a more personal and fulfilling way to say
　goodbye take an active role in caring for relatives who have died.

A Will for the Woods (2013). A Documentary by Amy Browne, Jeremy
　Kaplan, Tony Hale, and Brian Wilson: Determined that his last act
　will be a gift to the planet, musician and psychiatrist Clark Wang pre-
　pares for his own green burial.